Human Well-Being Research and Policy Making

Series Editors

Richard J. Estes, School of Social Policy & Practice, University of Pennsylvania, Philadelphia, PA, USA

M. Joseph Sirgy⦿, Department of Marketing, Virginia Polytechnic Institute & State University, Blacksburg, VA, USA

This series includes policy-focused books on the role of the public and private sectors in advancing quality of life and well-being. It creates a dialogue between well-being scholars and public policy makers. Well-being theory, research and practice are essentially interdisciplinary in nature and embrace contributions from all disciplines within the social sciences. With the exception of leading economists, the policy relevant contributions of social scientists are widely scattered and lack the coherence and integration needed to more effectively inform the actions of policy makers. Contributions in the series focus on one more of the following four aspects of well-being and public policy:

- Discussions of the public policy and well-being focused on particular nations and worldwide regions
- Discussions of the public policy and well-being in specialized sectors of policy making such as health, education, work, social welfare, housing, transportation, use of leisure time
- Discussions of public policy and well-being associated with particular population groups such as women, children and youth, the aged, persons with disabilities and vulnerable populations
- Special topics in well-being and public policy such as technology and well-being, terrorism and well-being, infrastructure and well-being.

This series was initiated, in part, through funds provided by the Halloran Philanthropies of West Conshohocken, Pennsylvania, USA. The commitment of the Halloran Philanthropies is to "inspire, innovate and accelerate sustainable social interventions that promote human well-being." The series editors and Springer acknowledge Harry Halloran, Tony Carr and Audrey Selian for their contributions in helping to make the series a reality.

More information about this series at http://www.springer.com/series/15692

Valerie Møller · Benjamin J. Roberts

Quality of Life and Human Well-Being in Sub-Saharan Africa

Prospects for Future Happiness

Springer

Valerie Møller🆔
Institute of Social and Economic Research
Rhodes University
Grahamstown (Makhanda), Eastern Cape
South Africa

Benjamin J. Roberts🆔
Developmental, Capable and Ethical State
(DCES) Research Division
Human Sciences Research Council
Durban, KwaZulu-Natal, South Africa

ISSN 2522-5367   ISSN 2522-5375   (electronic)
Human Well-Being Research and Policy Making
ISBN 978-3-030-65787-1   ISBN 978-3-030-65788-8   (eBook)
https://doi.org/10.1007/978-3-030-65788-8

This Springer imprint is published by the registered company Springer Nature Switzerland AG
The registered company address is: Gewerbestrasse 11, 6330 Cham, Switzerland

Preface

Our volume on the prospects for future happiness in sub-Saharan Africa has taken a long journey in the making. Until recently, our research efforts had focused on documenting life quality on the southern tip of the continent. Here, we widen our lens to include a much broader landscape. In the past few years, we were invited to participate in a number of ambitious global projects on human well-being. Our assignment was to provide an African perspective to these undertakings. Thus, we set about looking at Africa's past history in order to gain an idea of how the lived experience of African people over time may have shaped contemporary well-being on the continent.

This book is informed by our contributions on African quality of life to these global projects. In this volume, we build on the knowledge and insights we have gained, but we also move on to explore new themes and to add fresh voices to our discussion of African well-being. In rewriting, we have distilled and updated our earlier work, by drawing on case studies and examples to illustrate both the obstacles and rewards experienced by African people seeking to better their life chances. We have deliberately avoided Afropessimism but do not gloss over the many challenges facing the region in the twenty-first century. We have made liberal use of *The Conversation Africa*, launched five years ago, that report evidenced-based news and analysis articles authored by expert scholars from universities and research institutions across Africa. Perhaps, most gratifying for us in compiling our report on sub-Saharan Africa has been to discover the many emerging young African scholars who are keen to share their knowledge and insights on how to optimise African prosperity in future. We are delighted to have this opportunity to showcase their work.

Our book is divided into three parts. In Part I, we retrace the largely undocumented untold history of well-being on the oldest continent populated by humans. We speculate on the key values and virtues that have promoted both the survival and well-being of African society over time.

In Part II, we turn to the success story of our age. Never in history have humans experienced greater progress in meeting their basic needs, which are essential for human happiness. Progress made in Africa is no exception.

Since ancient times, there has always been something new coming out of Africa. In Part III, we look to the future of well-being of sub-Saharan Africa. We take a longer-term perspective and report on the many positive stories that might possibly foretell a new African century. We examine how Africa's novel experience with democracy is supporting citizen's life goals; we look at options for turning the continent's youthfulness into an asset; and we list steps taken to enhance life chances for minorities in African societies. We also portray Africa's practical sense of innovation for enhancing everyday well-being as well as innovations that inspire a sense of awe in us humans. In our concluding chapters, we review our discussion of the importance of Africa's time-honoured virtues and the region's exceptional optimism as drivers and harbingers of a brighter future for sub-Saharan Africa.

Grahamstown (Makhanda), South Africa   Valerie Møller
Durban, South Africa   Benjamin J. Roberts

Acknowledgements

To Richard Estes and Joe Sirgy for their boundless patience, support and encouragement during the production of this volume, as well the preceding chapter, we prepared for their edited volume *The Pursuit of Human Well-Being* (Springer, 2017).

To Halloran Philanthropies in recognition of its foresight and dedication to telling the untold histories of well-being both globally and across various world regions. In particular, we are grateful to Harry Halloran and Tony Carr for their support.

John Helliwell kindly invited us to contribute a regional chapter on Africa for the World Happiness Report 2017, and we are further indebted to him for granting us permission to draw freely on this material for this expanded publication.

Jay Loschky, Regional Director for Africa at Gallup, provided invaluable assistance with accessing the latest available well-being data for the region.

We are also grateful to Lynette Paterson for bringing a Shakespearean eye to the proofreading of the manuscript and to Bronwyn Tweedie for her assistance with the production of the maps used in the volume.

For much-needed administrative assistance at Rhodes University, our gratitude also goes to Bulelani Mothlabane and Gail Bint.

Springer Press was, as always, professional, efficient and ever-helpful during the production process, and we are especially grateful to Prashanth Ravichandran and Ameena Jaafar in this respect.

This volume is based on research supported by the National Research Foundation (NRF) of South Africa through the Algeria/South Africa Research Cooperation Programme on Quality of Life in South Africa and Algeria: A Multi-Method Approach 2011–2013 (grant UID 77926 and additional NRF research grants 85343 and 119399). Views expressed are those of the authors and should not be attributed to the NRF or others.

Finally, to our long-suffering partners, Per and Pranitha, a heartfelt vote of thanks for allowing us to take precious family time over the years to focus on our research on quality of life in sub-Saharan Africa.

Contents

About the Authors

Valerie Møller Rhodes University, Grahamstown (Makhanda), South Africa.

Valerie Møller is Professor Emeritus of Quality of Life Studies at Rhodes University, South Africa. She studied sociology, earning her Licentiate and Doctor of Philosophy from the University of Zürich, Switzerland. She has lived and worked in sub-Saharan Africa since 1972. In 1971, she arrived in North Africa from southern Europe in a Volkswagen Kombi. She and her husband, an architect, had converted the Kombi into a camper for their African adventure. Their intended destination was Dakar, Senegal, where they planned to undertake a joint urban studies project. When their vehicle proved to be no match for the sand pistes of the Algerian Sahara, they rerouted back to Europe, shipped themselves and their VW on a Portuguese immigrant boat to Angola, and travelled along the southern coast of Africa to present-day Zimbabwe.

Since that time, Valerie has held positions in social research institutes at the now University of Zimbabwe (1972–5), the University of KwaZulu-Natal (1996–1997), and as Director of Rhodes University's Institute of Social and Economic Research (1998–2006). Valerie pioneered the first quality-of-life and social indicators studies that have tracked South African life satisfaction and happiness from apartheid to the country's transition to democracy. Her original research has employed both conventional and less conventional measures and approaches to study a wide range of life domains and issues that impact on quality of life. She has published numerous journal articles and chapters in books,

including two articles awarded the *Social Indicators Research* annual best-paper reward. She has edited a number of Springer volumes devoted to the South African and international experience of quality of life. She is a lifetime member of the International Society for Quality of Life Studies (ISQOLS), hosted its 7th conference at Rhodes University in 2006—the only one to be held in Africa to date and served as its president from 2007 to 2008. Her endowed ISQOLS track for the Advancement of Quality of Life and Well-being in sub-Saharan Africa aims to showcase local scholars' contributions to well-being research in the region. In 2016, she received the society's lifetime award for her contribution to a better understanding of quality-of-life issues. e-mail: v.moller@ru.ac.za
https://www.ru.ac.za/iser/people/staff/profvaleriemoller/

Benjamin J. Roberts Developmental, Capable and Ethical State (DCES) Research Division, Human Sciences Research Council, Durban, South Africa.

Benjamin J. Roberts is Chief Research Specialist in the Developmental, Capable and Ethical State (DCES) research division at the Human Sciences Research Council (HSRC), South Africa, and coordinator of the South African Social Attitudes Survey (SASAS). He helped develop the SASAS series in 2002 with the assistance of the late Prof. Roger Jowell and has coordinated each annual round of surveying since its inception in 2003. He received his Ph.D. in social policy and labour studies from Rhodes University, South Africa, based on a thesis on the topic on inequality beliefs and preferences for government-led redistribution.

His research interests and areas of expertise include attitudinal measurement and social change, subjective well-being and quality of life, poverty and inequality, and social cohesion. Select recent publications include: "Family Matters: Family cohesion, values and well-being" (2019, co-edited with Mokomane, Struwig and Gordon, Cape Town: HSRC Press); "Waiting for Happiness in Africa" (2017, with Møller) (in Helliwell et al. (Eds.) World Happiness Report 2017); "New Beginnings in an Ancient Region: Well-being in Sub-Saharan Africa" (2017, with Møller) (in Estes and Sirgy (Eds.) The Pursuit of Global Well-Being,

Dordrecht, NL: Springer); "Shadow of the Sun: The Distribution of Well-being in Sub-Saharan Africa" (2015, with Gordon, Møller, and Struwig) (in Glatzer et al. (Eds.), The Global Handbook of Quality of Life, Dordrecht, NL: Springer); and "Beliefs About Inequality and Redress Preferences in South Africa" (2014) (*Social Indicators Research*, 118, 1167–1190).

While pursuing postgraduate studies in the mid-1990s, Ben came across Valerie's research on quality of life in South Africa and was struck by the critical relevance of this field of study for the young democracy —and indeed the continent. In establishing the SASAS series, quality of life was deemed a core thematic priority, with an emphasis on continuing the South African Quality of Life (SAQoL) series that Valerie established in the early 1980s. As South Africa draws close to its milestone of four decades of quality-of-life research, Ben wishes to express his heartfelt thanks to Valerie for her generosity, enthusiasm, committed mentorship and abiding support. Through her pioneering efforts, research in this field of study is flourishing in the country. e-mail: broberts@hsrc.ac.za

http://www.hsrc.ac.za/en/staff/view/?i=BJ&f=Benjamin &l=Roberts

Part I
Introduction

Mambila protective statue, artist unknown, c. 19th to 20th century, Donga Valley, Nigeria/Cameroon. Musée du quai Branly, Paris. Inventory no.: 73-1986-1-88 (*Photo by* Siren-Com; https://commons. wikimedia.org/wiki/File:Statuette_Mambia_Nig%C3%A9ria.jpg)

Chapter 1
Locating Sub-Saharan Africa
on the Globe

Abstract In this chapter we introduce our readers to the sub-Saharan region of Africa and to the people living there. We present an overview of the region's geographic boundaries on the continent, as well as Africa's range of climatic conditions, its riches in minerals, and its biodiversity of flora and fauna. Africa's cultural heritage is unique: the continent is the cradle of humankind and features the world's richest diversity of languages and customs. The length of time that African people have walked on this continent, and the geographic and cultural landscapes they have traversed over centuries, will have shaped their historical experience of well-being. Outsiders have viewed the quality of life of sub-Saharan people from different perspectives. In this book we shall attempt to present Africans' own appreciation of their life circumstances.

Keywords Sub-Saharan Africa · Well-being · Life satisfaction · Happiness · Socio-cultural diversity · Cradle of humankind

1.1 Introduction to the Sub-Saharan Region of Africa

Sub-Saharan Africa is unique in that it is the cradle of humankind and we all have ancestors from this continent. In geological time, it was the central continent from which Asia and the Americas split off. Some 3 million years ago, the first hominids appeared and around 100,000 years ago, the first anatomically modern humans left the continent to populate the globe. Their descendants were to return to Africa countless generations later, as strangers in the 1400s (Oppenheimer 2003).

Meanwhile, the people who remained in sub-Saharan Africa experienced a turbulent history. They survived times of climate change, feast and famine, internecine wars, slavery, colonialism, and exploitation, all of which will have shaped myths of origin, self-esteem, and values and aspirations that will influence evaluations of present-day well-being.

The region is bounded by the Sahara desert in the north, the Atlantic Ocean on the west, and the Indian Ocean and Red Sea on the east. Many of the rivers that flow from the centre of the region are either difficult or impossible to navigate. Many states are

V. Møller and B. J. Roberts, *Quality of Life and Human Well-Being in Sub-Saharan Africa*,
Human Well-Being Research and Policy Making,
https://doi.org/10.1007/978-3-030-65788-8_1

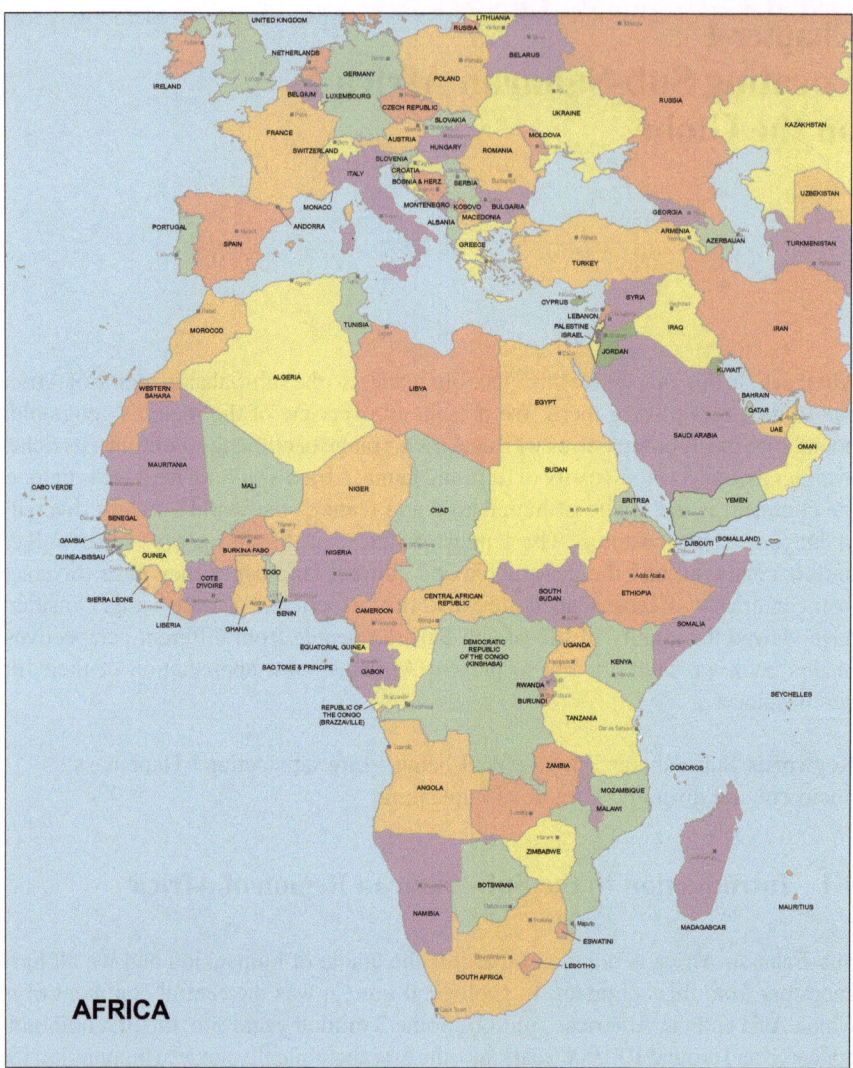

Map 1.1 Regional map of Africa (public domain)

landlocked. This isolation meant that many earlier technologies did not reach Africa until later (Map 1.1).

Today, sub-Saharan Africa is home to just over a billion[1] people living in 49 countries. Given the length of time that humans have lived on the continent, it has the world's greatest language and genetic diversity. An estimated 3000 languages—300 in Nigeria alone—are spoken. Many Africans speak several languages, an indigenous

---

[1]http://worldpopulationreview.com/continents/sub-saharan-africa-population/ (Accessed 29 April 2019).

local language as well as the national lingua Franca, which is often a colonial-era language adopted as their country's official language after independence.

Most sub-Saharan states are home to a number of ethnic groups, often distinguished by their unique languages and customs. For example, Cameroon, an erstwhile German colony that was divided between France and Britain after World War I, has a population of some 23 million and includes over 200 ethnic groups within its geographical boundaries.

The sub-Saharan region features a wide range of climatic conditions. The tropical belt in Central Africa gives way on both sides to more temperate bush- and savannah grasslands, as well as desert landscapes. Habitable regions are limited and rainfall is erratic. There is a high burden of disease, mainly in the tropical belt. Sub-Saharan Africa is rich in many different minerals. It boasts great plant and animal biodiversity and even a unique plant kingdom on the southern tip of the continent. The African continent may become the last refuge in the world for non-domesticated animals that still roam freely (Anthony and Spence 2012).

1.2 Africa Is Not a Country

In this first part of our book, we seek to better understand how people in Africa have experienced their personal and collective well-being over time. A perspective on the past is important if we are to make any credible extrapolation of Africa's prospects for future happiness. In a chapter to follow, we briefly trace the history of well-being on the continent.

At the outset, it will be important to remember that much of Africa's history predates written documents, and its history has produced an extremely diverse cultural and linguistic landscape.

The expansion of the Arabian Islamic Caliphate into North Africa in the seventh century (Tiliouine 2015; Tiliouine and Meziane 2017) and the European 'scramble for Africa' in the late nineteenth century introduced several of the European and Arabic languages that still serve as lingua franca and national languages on the continent. Over the centuries, African people have adopted some of the customs, technological advancements and new lifestyles of their former colonial masters. In more recent times, Africa has leapfrogged older technology to embrace the latest advancements, such as mobile phones and solar-powered electricity.

Centuries of slavery, colonialism and apartheid preceded the period of independence. Following on the 'first dance of freedom'[2] in the 1960s, the new African nation states experimented briefly with various styles of self-rule in what has been called the 'third wave' of democracy (See Huntington 1991; Diamond 2008; Diamond and Plattner 2010).

---

[2]The title of a chapter in Meredith's (2011, p. 162) history of Africa.

This tumultuous history will have left its imprint on expectations and perceptions of personal well-being.[3] Given the diversity found on the continent, it is natural to expect that there will be large differences among African countries in both life evaluations and likely reasons for these differences. Africa watchers frequently note how different the situations are from one African country to the next. Contrary to the once commonly held view that Africa is a single entity or 'brand', each country in fact has unique features that distinguish it from its neighbours.[4] Veteran Africa journalist and University of Kent professor Somerville (2013) speaks of 'different histories' of the African continent.

For this reason, there is likely to be a multitude of approaches for examining how the people of sub-Saharan Africa experience personal and collective well-being. We can only begin to search for plausible factors that may have promoted or undermined Africa's potential for happiness and satisfaction with life. Somerville (2013) reminds us that we should use many different lenses through which to observe and evaluate Africa's performances.

1.2.1 Patchwork of Countries

Games (2015) refers to the 'patchwork of countries that make up Africa'. Responsible for this patchwork is the nineteenth century 'scramble for Africa' that created borders that cut across ethnicities and ancient polities (see Meredith 2011). In the interest of political stability, the African Union, formed in 2002 with the objectives of promoting peace and democracy on the continent, supports the maintenance of country borders as imposed by the colonial powers. South Sudan, which gained its independence from Sudan in 2011, is an exception.

Over the past decades, outsiders have viewed the quality of life of African people from a number of different perspectives. There have been many frames of reference for the narrative of Africa since independence, ranging from the dismissive 'basket case', to the 'structural adjustment' imposed by the International Monetary Fund during the 1980s, followed by 'debt forgiveness' in the 1990s. The 'Africa Rising' narrative in the new millennium was followed by the global economic recession; and lately Africa has become part of the so-called 'war on terror'. Each of these narratives foregrounds on a different set of factors that may determine the fortunes of Africa and its people.

---

[3]For reports on Africa's quality of life and well-being from an historical perspective, see Tiliouine (2015) and Tiliouine and Meziane (2017) on North Africa, and Roberts et al. (2015) and Møller and Roberts (2017) on sub-Saharan Africa.

[4]See Furlonger (2016) commenting on access to African markets in a South African business daily.

1.2.2 'Africa Rising'

In the new millennium, twenty-first century Africa was no longer associated only with 'endless famine, disease, and dictatorship'.[5] The 'Africa Rising' narrative, which overturned earlier stereotypes, projected a continent with a growing urban middle class market with new consumer appetites.[6] Africa's youthfulness promised to be an asset in an increasingly ageing global society. There was talk of the continent's 'demographic dividend' that would see the continent prosper in future. An investment in the education and skilling of Africa's youth would provide substantial returns to the overall economy. The continent's rich mineral wealth had not been exhausted and its agricultural land was still waiting to be exploited. In the new millennium, foreign direct investment in Africa eclipsed development aid for the first time since the colonial era.

References

Anthony, L., with Spence, G. (2012). *The last rhinos*. London: Sidgwick & Jackson.

Baker, A. (2015). Let's prepare for Africa's population surge now—or face the consequences. *Time*, 11 June. http://time.com/3918006/lets-prepare-for-africas-population-surge-now-or-face-the-consequences/.

Diamond, L. J. (2008). *The spirit of democracy: The struggle to build free societies throughout the world*. New York: Times Books.

Diamond, L. J., & Plattner, M. F. (2010). *Democratization in Africa: Progress and retreat*. Baltimore, Maryland: Johns Hopkins University Press.

Furlonger, D. (2016). Global brands learn Africa is not a country. *Business Day*, Johannesburg, 16 March, p. 13.

Games, D. (2015). Hold your hats—next year will be a rocky ride for Africa. *Business Day*, Johannesburg, 7 December, p. 11.

Huntington, S. P. (1991). *The third wave: Democratization in the late twentieth century*. Norman, Oklahoma: University of Oklahoma Press.

Meredith, M. (2011). *The state of Africa: A history of the continent since independence*. London: Simon & Schuster.

Møller, V., & Roberts, B. (2017). New beginnings in an ancient region: Well-being in Sub-Saharan Africa. In R.J. Estes & M.J. Sirgy (Eds.), *The Pursuit of well-being: The untold global history* (pp. 161–215), International Handbooks of Quality-of-Life Research. Springer International Publishing Switzerland.

Oppenheimer, S. (2003). *Out of Africa's Eden: The peopling of the world*. Johannesburg: Jonathan Ball.

Roberts, B. J., Gordon, S. L., Struwig, J., & Møller, V. (2015). Shadow of the sun: The distribution of wellbeing in sub-Saharan Africa. In W. Glatzer, V. Møller, L. Camfield, & M. Rojas (Eds.), *Global handbook of quality of life: Exploration of well-being of nations and continents* (pp. 531–568). Dordrecht: Springer.

---

[5]See the article on 'Africa Rising' by Baker (2015), the *TIME's* Africa correspondent.

[6]See, for example, political scientist Southall's (2016) portrait of South Africa's emergent black middle class.

Somerville, K. (2013). Framing news in Africa—How journalists approach stories and reinforce stereotypes. *The Conversation*, 26 February. http://africanarguments.org/2013/02/26/framing-news-in-africa-%E2%80%93-how-journalists-approach-stories-and-reinforce-stereotypes-%E2%80%93-by-keith-somerville/.

Southall, R. (2016). *The new black middle class in South Africa*. Auckland Park: Jacana & Dunkeld.

Tiliouine, H. (2015). Quality of life and wellbeing in North Africa – Algeria, Egypt, Libya, Morocco and Tunisia. In W. Glatzer, V. Møller, L. Camfield, & M. Rojas (Eds.), *Global handbook of quality of life: Exploration of well-being of nations and continents* (pp. 507–530). Dordrecht: Springer.

Tiliouine, H., & Meziane, M. (2017). The history of well-being in the Middle East and North Africa (MENA). In R.J. Estes & M.J. Sirgy (Eds.), *The Pursuit of Well-Being: The Untold Global History* (pp. 523–563), International Handbooks of Quality-of-Life Research. Springer International Publishing Switzerland.

Chapter 2
Documenting Well-Being in Sub-Saharan Africa

Abstract We outline the difficulty of sourcing information on African people's well-being in the past. Most documentation is either imprinted in stone, or in historic records kept by outsiders to the continent. It is only recently that African people's own evaluations of their life quality have been recorded. We introduce two home-grown initiatives that track the well-being of sub-Saharan people and the quality of governance in Africa.

Keywords Sub-Saharan Africa · Well-being · Historical records · Archaeology · Oral history

2.1 Early Records of African Well-Being

There is a dearth of reliable written evidence on African well-being in ancient times. The archaeological record is the main source of information on the early history of the continent. In sub-Saharan Africa, genealogy and history have been transmitted orally from generation to generation. Even today, some African people can name their ancestors as far back as eight or ten generations.

The first written records on sub-Saharan well-being saw Africa through the lens of outsiders, mainly traders, explorers, and adventurers, who produced assessments of the continent's material and developmental successes and failures from their own points of view. In the late nineteenth and early twentieth centuries, ethnologists and also missionaries conducted more scholarly studies of African customs and life styles, and collected oral histories from Africans.

It is only with the advent of the social indicators movement in the 1960s (which we shall come to later), that African well-being has been measured systematically and captured in a range of both subjective and objective indicators and indices. Subjective indicators rely on an individual's own judgement whereas objective measures are factual information. We draw on both objective and subjective indicators to trace trends in well-being, in order to give a rounded picture of quality of life.

© Springer Nature Switzerland AG 2021   9
V. Møller and B. J. Roberts, *Quality of Life and Human Well-Being in Sub-Saharan Africa*,
Human Well-Being Research and Policy Making,
https://doi.org/10.1007/978-3-030-65788-8_2

2.2 Home-Grown Monitoring Initiatives

To date, the collection of social indicators in Africa has been carried out mainly under the auspices of international organisations, and there have been problems with data quality and unequal coverage of countries in the region.

More recently, home-grown monitoring initiatives have gained momentum. The Afrobarometer launched its first survey in 1999 and now covers some 34 sub-Saharan countries. The barometer's main focus is on material well-being and the deepening of democracy; its proxy index of 'lived poverty" serves as its measure of material well-being (Mattes 2008).

The Mo Ibrahim Foundation's (2016) index of good governance in Africa is a further home-grown project that aims to keep track of accountable leadership that serves the people. Some of the measures included in the index are based on Afrobarometer items.

References

Mattes, R. (2008). The material and political bases of lived poverty in Africa: Insights from the Afrobarometer. In V. Møller, D. Huschka, & A.C. Michalos (Eds.), *Barometers of quality of life around the globe: How are we doing? Social Indicators Research Series 33* (pp. 161–185). Dordrecht: Springer.

Mo Ibrahim Foundation (2016). *A Decade of African Governance 2006–2016: 2016 Ibrahim Index of African Governance Index Report.* http://s.mo.ibrahim.foundation/u/2016/10/01184917/2016-Index-Report.pdf?_g. Accessed October 31, 2016.

Chapter 3
Looking Back in Time: African Well-Being Over the Centuries

Abstract In this chapter, we present a time line of different historical periods in sub-Saharan Africa, starting from the time when the majority of the population in the region were foragers, to the present times. Reader's (Africa: A biography of the continent. London: Hamish Hamilton, 1997) extensive biography of the African continent is one of our main sources. We sum up the earliest advances in humanity's adaptation to the African environment, then cover the ancient period from 2000 BCE (before the Common Era) to 500 CE, followed by the rise of powerful kingdoms between 500 to 1500 CE. We describe the age of explorers in the fifteenth century, the slave trade of the sixteenth to nineteenth centuries, the scramble for Africa in the late 1800s, and colonial rule in the nineteenth and twentieth centuries. The modern era commences with the 'wind of change' that swept through Africa in the 1960s, followed by independence in the 1970s to 1990s, and 'Africa Rising' in the twenty-first century. We reflect on African life chances and population growth as key indicators of well-being in each of these periods.

Keywords Sub-Saharan Africa · African ancient history · Atlantic slave trade · Colonial period · African independence · Population growth

3.1 Introduction

Historians often distinguish between periods that afforded the people living in Africa different life chances that impacted on well-being: pre-history, ancient times, the age of discovery, the Atlantic slave trade, the colonial period, and independence. We shall consider population growth as an indicator of well-being in each of these periods. Throughout history, Africa's population growth has been subjected to the interrelated constraints of food production, availability of labour, fertility, and disease.

© Springer Nature Switzerland AG 2021
V. Møller and B. J. Roberts, *Quality of Life and Human Well-Being in Sub-Saharan Africa*,
Human Well-Being Research and Policy Making,
https://doi.org/10.1007/978-3-030-65788-8_3

3.2 Pre-history: *'The World Until Yesterday'*[1]

Initially, all humans were nomadic hunter-gatherers who obtained most of their food from wild plants and animals. Foragers survived longer in sub-Saharan Africa than elsewhere, and their subsistence mode of life was one of humanity's most successful adaptations. Technical advances, such as the weighted digging stick that aided foraging, arrow tips, and spear heads that allowed people to hunt rather than scavenge for meat, were likely prompted by threats to food security during times of scarcity (Reader 1997, p. 153). In time, some of these groups became herders and agriculturalists. Some herders developed lactose tolerance to increase food security derived from their herds.

3.3 Ancient Sub-Saharan Africa—2000 BCE to 500 CE

Early African history is mainly recorded in the archaeological evidence. Ancient sub-Saharan Africa was essentially an unknown territory, often referred to by Westerners as 'darkest' Africa. However, the archaeological records tell of early civilisations that date back to 2000 BCE. In East Africa, the Nubian Kushite are believed to be the first people to have made practical use of iron. In West Africa, the agricultural civilisation of Nok that emerged in present-day northern Nigeria, produced terracotta sculpture (500 BCE–200 CE) of high quality. The Niger River was one of the most fertile areas, giving rise to civilisations located in present-day Mali as early as 250 BCE. Its inhabitants produced food surpluses of dried fish, grains, and oil that could be exchanged for essential goods, such as salt, through the trans-Sahara trade route (History of Sub-Saharan Africa 2015).

The predominantly agriculturist Bantu (meaning 'people') slowly moved from their cradleland in West Africa, across the continent and down the eastern coast of sub-Saharan Africa. They brought iron-smelting technology with them that revolutionised agricultural production. By 200 to 300 CE, Bantu-speaking farmers had reached the southern tip of the continent in the area around present-day Cape Town where they gradually displaced San (Bushmen) hunter-gatherers and the Khoi pastoralists (Wilson 2009). As a consequence, the Bantu language group, one of five main language groups in Africa, became dominant in large areas of sub-Saharan Africa.

3.4 Ancient Sub-Saharan Africa—500 to 1500 CE

Recent archaeological excavations have produced evidence of complex societies in West, East, and southern Africa that prospered for several centuries.

---

[1]The title of Diamond's (2012) work on traditional societies.

In West Africa, a succession of powerful kingdoms emerged in the fertile areas between the Senegal and Niger rivers, and later in the tropical coastal forest regions. One example is the ancient settlement of Jenne-Jeno, situated on the fertile inland delta of the Niger River southwest of Timbuktu[2] in present-day Mali. Jenne-Jeno's inhabitants, farmers, pastoralists and fishermen, made use of the annual flood regime to live in a loose symbiotic society. The farmers cultivated indigenous rice varieties that are still grown in the region today. At its height in 800 CE, the Niger inland delta may have supported a population of some 27,000.

In East Africa, the ancient Kingdom of Kush was situated on the island of Meroë where the Blue Nile and the White Nile meet in present-day Sudan. In the eighth century BCE, the Kushite kings ruled as the pharaohs of the 25th Ethiopian Dynasty. A later Ethiopian civilisation, Aksum, took advantage of high altitude and a nearby port to become a socially stratified settlement that prospered for several centuries. At its zenith in 500 CE, it had some 20,000 inhabitants. The Kushite rulers devised a script based on Egyptian symbols and constructed the Sudan Meroë pyramids, which have been declared a UNESCO heritage site. Aksum was also a literate society of its day that erected stele, monumental inscribed stone pillars.

In southern Africa, the pastoralists of Mapungubwe (ca. 900–1250 CE) and Great Zimbabwe (ca. 1275–1550 CE) took advantage of fertile grasslands to grow large settlements that were socially stratified and had far-flung trade relations.

The sub-Saharan civilisations and kingdoms can be classified as Christian, Islamic, and traditional African. Aksum was the first civilisation to convert to Christianity after 300 CE, about the same time as Rome. Muslim influence came along the trade routes that crossed the Sahara desert to commercial centres such as Timbuktu and went down the east coast of Africa where Arab traders founded city states, including Mombasa, Zanzibar, and Kilwa. The civilisations and dispersed settlements of southern Africa are traditional, in the sense of traditional indigenous cultures (History of Sub-Saharan Africa 2015).

The ancient civilisation of Beta Samati, part of the Empire of Aksum, is one of the most recent archaeological discoveries in sub-Saharan Africa (Harrower et al. 2019). Beta Samati was unearthed only thanks to local residents' suggestion that archaeologists should investigate a hill known to be an important place according to oral tradition, but the residents did not know why (Hunt 2019).

The buried settlement located near Ethiopia's border with Eritrea was inhabited for some 1400 years before vanishing around CE 650. Beta Samati was a key hub of trade and commerce, linking the capital Aksum with the Red Sea and beyond. What makes the discovery of Beta Samati so important is that it spans Aksum's official conversion from polytheism to Christianity and the rise of Islam in Arabia. A basilica found in Beta Samati stems from the fourth or early fifth century CE, making it among the earliest known churches in sub-Saharan Africa. Relics uncovered at the site illustrate the cultural diversity of the civilisation. They include a gold Roman-style ring that features an unusual icon—a symbol of a bull and a soft-stone pendant

---

[2] Timbuktu was to become famous for its ancient manuscripts written in Arabic in the sixteenth to eighteenth centuries.

recovered from outside the basilica with a cross and what appears to be an inscription in ancient Ethiopic that reads 'venerable'. According to lead researcher John Hopkins archaeologist Michael Harrower, 'the ring looks very Roman in its composition and its style but the insignia of that bull's head is very African and is very unlike something you would find in the Mediterranean world and shows the kind of interaction and mixing of these different traditions' (Hunt 2019). Harrower hopes the ring will go on display locally at some point so the local community can benefit from the discovery.

The glory of Africa's ancient past is still reflected in the names chosen by the modern states of Ghana, Mali and Zimbabwe. Where the circumstances were opportune, population numbers in ancient sub-Saharan Africa grew and people flourished. However, the majority of the population still lived in dispersed settlements as agriculturalists and pastoralists.

3.5   The Age of Explorers—Fifteenth Century

When Europeans set out to explore Africa in the fifteenth century, they had no idea they were returning to the land of their distant forebears. It would be another 500 years before genetic evidence would authenticate the African Eve, who was featured on the covers of *Newsweek* and *TIME* in January 1987.

The Portuguese began their exploration of the Atlantic west coast in the mid-fifteenth century. Their aim was to find a trade route to Asia that circumvented the Mediterranean route controlled by Venetian and Saracen traders. A lucrative trade was established on the west coast. In time, trade items included gold, ivory, diamonds, animal hides, bananas, palm oil, and the cola that was to become the main ingredient in the soft drink that conquered the world to spread 'shared happiness'. Slaves became one of the most sought-after trade items. The names given to the coastline on ancient maps identify what West Africa had to offer: the *Grain* Coast in today's Liberia (referring to an African species of pepper known as grains of paradise), the *Ivory* Coast, the *Gold* Coast (today's Ghana), and the *Slave* Coast (Benin and Nigeria). Trading was mainly limited to the coastal area.

Each Portuguese expedition moved further down the coast of Africa. The Portuguese erected stone crosses wherever they made landfall, strung along the coast of the continent 'like charms on a necklace' (Reader 1997, p. 383), but they did not venture into the interior. Africa's unnavigable rivers, vividly portrayed in Conrad's (1985) novel, *Heart of Darkness*, presented a formidable deterrent. The mission of discovering a trade route to Asia was accomplished when Bartholomeu Dias finally circumnavigated the Cape of Good Hope in 1488, enabling Vasco da Gama to sail up the east coast and on to India in 1499. Da Gama's expedition discovered that Arab merchants had already established a trading presence on the east coast of Africa; reportedly, their dhows in the Zambezi delta were laden with gold dust.

In later centuries, the Portuguese introduced new crops to some parts of Africa, such as maize, which was easier to grow than traditional sorghum and millet, and which increased food security in sub-Saharan Africa. They also traded firearms, although one of the earlier popes forbade placing weapons in the 'hands of heathens'.

3.6 The Atlantic and East Coast Slave Trades—Sixteenth to Nineteenth Centuries

The Atlantic slave trade, which was conducted from the sixteenth to the nineteenth century, fed the European appetite for sugar. The majority of slaves brought to the New World were used to produce this labour-intensive crop. Initially, the Portuguese enjoyed a near monopoly of the west coast slave trade; later they were joined by other European nations, mainly the British, French, and Dutch (The Transatlantic Slave Trade 2008). Slaves were obtained with the full and active cooperation of African kings and merchants (Boddy-Evans 2014). In Africa, as elsewhere in the world, slavery was a common practice at that time. Historians note that slavery in African cultures was more like indentured servitude, and slave-status was not always permanent. Unlike the slaves shipped to the Americas, an individual enslaved in Africa could be emancipated, or might escape or be traded back to his own people (The Transatlantic Slave Trade 2008).

It is estimated that up to twelve million African slaves were transported from the west coast of Africa, stretching from Senegal to Angola, to the New World. The conditions of the transport slave route, called the 'Middle Passage', were appalling, and large numbers died en route. Slaves were tightly packed into the holds of ships just like any other type of cargo (The Transatlantic Slave Trade 2008).

The British abolished the slave trade in 1807, but not slavery itself until 1833 (Griffiths 1994, p. 46). By that time, the West African slave economy was so well established that it could not grind to a halt immediately and slaves continued to be used to work plantations. After 1807, ships still involved in the slave trade who attempted to break the British blockade were seized, and Africans on board were freed (The Transatlantic Slave Trade 2008). The relief expressed by a rescued slave testifies to the damage done to body and soul by the Atlantic slave trade. He recalled, *'They took off all the fetters from our feet, and threw them into the water, and they gave us clothes so that we might cover our nakedness, they opened the water casks, that we might drink water to the full, and we also ate food, till we had enough'* (Iliffe 1995, p. 148).

On the east coast of Africa, the Arab slave trade focused on Zanzibar, an ancient intersection for trade and cultural exchange between Africa and the East that predated the arrival of the Portuguese. Unlike their European counterparts, Arab slave traders penetrated deeply into the hinterland (Griffiths 1994, p. 46). Some historians refer to the East Coast slave trade as *Maafa*, which means 'holocaust' or 'great disaster' in Swahili (The Transatlantic Slave Trade 2008). In time, sub-Saharan Africa was caught in a pincer of slave raids from both the east and west into the interior, which often displaced whole villages. Many of the ethnic groups known today probably originated in flights from the slaving wars of the late seventeenth and eighteenth centuries.

In summary, the Atlantic and Indian Oceans slave trades caused distress and dispersions in sub-Saharan Africa. The impact on individual well-being varied: a minority of African kings and traders profited while the lives of millions of slaves were made miserable. Possibly the most negative effect for the region as a whole was that the trade exported from Africa the many hands needed there to provide food security. During the period of slavery, the populations of Europe and the Americas grew exponentially, while the population of Africa remained stagnant.

3.7 Scramble for Africa—Late 1800s

Whatever happens, we have got

The Maxim Gun, and they have not.

Belloc (1907)

In 1876, King Leopold II of Belgium (1825–1909) staked his claim as European leader with interests in Africa, when he presented to the Geographical Conference of Brussels his vision of bringing civilisation to a part of the globe that had not yet been penetrated. A few years later in 1884–1885, the European powers met in Berlin to construct the rules for spheres of influence in Africa. King Leopold held the trump cards for dividing the spoils and claimed the Congo for himself while Portugal, Britain, France, Italy and Germany were left to divide the rest of Africa among themselves. Thus, Leopold became the Sovereign of the Congo Free State without informing the Congolese people. African leaders were not present at the Berlin Conference, nor were they consulted (Reader 1997, p. 581).

Meredith (2011, p. 2) notes that by the time the scramble for Africa was over, 'some 10,000 African polities had been amalgamated into forty European colonies and protectorates.' The only two regions to avoid colonisation were Ethiopia, whose absolute independence and the sovereignty of its emperor were recognised in a treaty of 1896, and Liberia, which had been founded in the 1820s as a home for freed slaves (Moss 2011). Medical and technological advances gave Europeans the upper hand. The discovery of quinine as a prophylactic for malaria in the 1850s made military operations possible even in badly malaria-infested areas. The Maxim machine gun, patented in the year of the Berlin Conference, gave the colonisers superior fire power. A few years later, at the Brussels Convention of 1890, they drove home this advantage by agreeing not to sell weapons to Africans.

African leaders who resisted were either killed, or captured and deported. Rural communities, the majority of the African population, had little choice in the matter. Reader (1997, p. 616) notes that where existing circumstances were oppressive, such as in areas where slavery persisted, people may have welcomed the prospect of a brighter future under European domination. Elsewhere on the continent, resistance to colonial rule was crushed by force or attrition.

3.7.1 Famine and Pestilence of Biblical Proportions

Famine and pestilence may have weakened resistance to conquest. Between 1870 and 1895, most of sub-Saharan Africa experienced exceptional rainfalls and abundant harvests. This time of plenty was followed by a period of drought and famine of biblical proportions, outbreaks of cholera and typhus, and a smallpox epidemic. Sand fleas introduced to Angola from Brazil spread across the continent, and locusts destroyed crops. The rinderpest, brought to sub-Saharan Africa by Italian forces, killed over 90% of all cattle in Africa between 1889 and the early 1900s. It is described as one of the greatest natural calamities to befall the African continent. The epidemic swept away the wealth of tropical Africa and ruined the pastoralist aristocrats. The loss of cattle, a form of wealth that signified both power and prestige, dealt a blow to pride and dignity. A British captain assigned to establish a colonial presence in East Africa noted in his diary that without 'this awful visitation, the advent of the white man had not else been so peaceful' (Davies 1979, p. 17). Sometimes the brutal crushing of insubordination introduced man-made famine and the destruction of herds and way of life, as in the case of the Herero and Nama rebellions in German South-West Africa (1904–1905) and the Maji-Maji rebellions in German East Africa (1905–1906) (Pakenham 1992, pp. 602–628).

3.7.2 Bringing 'Civilisation' to Sub-Saharan Africa

The missionary says that we are the children of God like our white brothers… but just look at us. Dogs, slaves, worse than baboons on the rocks… that is how you treat us.

A Herero to a German settler (Pakenham 1992, p. 602)

The colonialists' civilising project was essentially a commercial venture. A whole generation of Africans bore the initial brunt of the colonial incursions. Under subsequent colonial rule, the African population was obliged to give up land, accede to European demands for labour, accept the initiatives of a cash economy, pay taxes, and submit to foreign law. One of the worst known cases of exploitation during the colonial period took place on the rubber concessions in King Leopold's Belgian Congo. Instead of paying state taxes, villagers in concession areas collected rubber to be used in the production of Michelin tyres. The wild rubber supplies were soon exhausted, so that villagers struggled to fulfil their quotas. Those who could not were flogged, imprisoned, or even shot. Soldiers cut off the hands of those they shot to prove they had not wasted cartridges. Entire regions of the Congo were depopulated as a result of this practice. Technical and agricultural advances were finally instrumental in halting the carnage: The Kodak roll-film camera produced photographic evidence of the atrocities, raising public outrage in Europe, and cultivated latex produced in other parts of the world made the harvesting of wild rubber uneconomical (Pakenham 1992, pp. 585–601; Reader 1997, pp. 574–580).

3.8   Colonial Rule in the Twentieth Century

Initially, the colonies had to be supported by grants; they only became economically self-sufficient by around 1914. There are mixed reports on the impact of colonial rule on the well-being of sub-Saharan people once the economies had become viable. Exploitation of labour continued in the gold and diamond mines of southern Africa, where the migrant labour system severely disrupted family life. But in other areas, colonial administration became more competent and efficient over time and produced benefits of improved infrastructure, hygiene, as well as agricultural, health, and educational services for select groupings of peoples. The law and order introduced by Europeans brought peace to some areas formerly plagued by strife among neighbours (Diamond 2012).

However, the most harmful and lasting legacy of the colonial period in Africa is undisputed. All of the boundaries of present-day sub-Saharan states are artificial. Africa was carved up without regard to geography, ethnicity, or cultural distinctions. Nearly half of the new boundaries were 'geometric lines, lines of latitude and longitude or other straight lines' (Meredith 2011, p. 491). Present-day states in sub-Saharan Africa have inherited problems of access to ports, security, and economic stability. The roads and railways that tend to stop at the colonial borders have accelerated fragmentation rather than establishing communication and trade networks in Africa.

Despite the so-called civilising efforts that accompanied the exploration and colonisation of Africa, and the introduction of more productive crops and labour-saving technology, sub-Saharan Africa did not reach its full growth potential during the period of European presence. By 1900 the population of Africa was about 129 million, an increase from 49 million in 1500. During the same 400 years, the world population, excluding Africa, had increased fourfold, from just under 500 million to almost 2000 million.

3.9   'Wind of Change'[3]—1960s

By the end of the Second World War, the ideological basis for colonialism had been fundamentally weakened, and the socio-economic power of European countries had deteriorated. The small but influential African elite that had been educated abroad was agitating for African self-government and independence. The time had come for the European powers, beginning in Sudan in 1956 and Ghana in 1957, to decolonise their possessions in sub-Saharan Africa. Further decolonisation in the 1960s was achieved with varying degrees of violence. Resistance to the granting of local political emancipation was greatest in colonies where there was a large settler population as in Kenya and in the so-called settler states in the south: South Africa, Zimbabwe,

---

[3] Referring to British Prime Minister Harold Macmillan's landmark 'wind of change' address to the South African parliament on 3 February 1960.

and Namibia. These conflicts proved highly destructive to the economic and social bases of the countries involved.

3.10   Independence—1970s to 1990s

In the first two decades of independence, most states in sub-Saharan Africa adopted a single-party system and discouraged democratic opposition. This approach was defended on the basis of ostensibly creating national unity and political harmony among disparate groups (Meredith 2011). However, the single-party state failed to deliver on political stability. In the past five decades of independence, there have been more than 106 military coups, averaging more than 20 per decade in the 1970s and 1980s (see Griffiths 1994, pp. 80–83). Foreign powers have often continued to play a prominent role—particularly France, who launched 46 military operations in its former colonies between 1960 and 2005. Political instability has often led to violent conflict on the continent. During the period 1950 to 2002, 45 military conflicts have occurred in the region.

In January 1989, urban crowds, composed primarily of students and unpaid civil servants, marched in protest on the streets of Benin's cities. The Benin protestors, who eventually overthrew their authoritarian ruler Mathieu Kérékou, signalled a new phase in African history. Between 1989 and 1994, 38 sub-Saharan African states held competitive elections (Iliffe 1995, p. 299); 33 of the region's 42 undemocratic states saw an increase in civil liberties in the period 1988 to 1992 (Ndulu and O'Connell 1999, p. 49). Military coups became less common on the continent—numbering fewer than 10 during the 2000s—and elections became more familiar. Racial oppression in the white south ended, and political rights were finally obtained by the black Africans in Zimbabwe (1980), Namibia (1990), and South Africa (1994).[4]

Since the overthrow of Mathieu Kérékou, the subcontinent has been part of significant political transition away from authoritarianism. The region is part of what Samuel Huntington called the 'third wave' of democratisation, a period beginning in the late 1980s when many authoritarian regimes underwent a democratic transition (Diamond 2002).

---

[4]For a brief description of this process, see Iliffe (1995, pp. 283–287) and Meredith (2011, pp. 265–283).

To summarise, the transition to democracy in many states of sub-Saharan Africa in the latter half of the twentieth century opened up new opportunities for prosperity in the region. The later colonial period had laid some of the foundations that the post-independent states could build on, to improve health, education, income and self-governance in Africa south of the Sahara in the second half of the century.

3.11 'Africa Rising'—Twenty-First Century

In May 2000, *The Economist*'s cover story presented Africa as 'The Hopeless Continent'. In a complete about-turn, the December 2011 cover of *The Economist* featured 'Africa Rising'. This phrase became the catchword for Africa's prospects of earning a place in the global economy in the new millennium. The narrative speaks of economic growth, investment opportunities, regional markets, and an emergent middle class. New trends were thought to drive change in Africa: a more youthful and affluent population, rapid urbanisation, technological changes and innovation, and agricultural potential. For the first time in history, sub-Saharan Africa was poised to realise its full economic potential, which could translate into prospective gains in well-being.

References

Belloc, H. (1907). The modern traveller. [Poem.] In *Cautionary tales.* [Cited in Reader 1997, p. 619]. London: Duckworth and Co.

Boddy-Evans, A. (2014). The transatlantic slave trade. http://africanhistory.about.com/od/slavery/tp/TransAtlantic001.htm. Accessed July 22, 2015.

Conrad, J. (1985). *Heart of darkness.* [Originally published 1902]. Hammondsworth, Middlesex: Penguin Books.

Davies, J.N.P. (1979). *Pestilence and disease in the history of Africa.* [Raymond Dart Lecture 14]. Johannesburg: Witwatersrand University Press.

Diamond, J. (2012). *The world until yesterday: What we can learn from traditional societies.* London: Penguin Books.

Diamond, L. J. (2002). Thinking about hybrid regimes. *Journal of Democracy, 13*(2), 21–35.

Griffiths, L. I. (1994). *The Atlas of African Affairs* (2nd ed.). London: Routledge.

Harrower, M., Dumitru, I., Perlingieri, C., Nathan, S., Zerue, K., Lamont, J., et al. (2019). Beta Samati: Discovery and excavation of an Aksumite town. *Antiquity, 93*(372), 1534–1552. https://doi.org/10.15184/aqy.2019.84.

History of Sub-Saharan Africa. (2015). *Essential Humanities.* http://www.essential-humanities.net/world-history/sub-saharan-africa/. Accessed August 11, 2015.

Hunt, K. (2019). Archeologists unearth lost town from little-known ancient East African empire. *CNN*, 11 December. https://edition.cnn.com/2019/12/11/africa/ethiopia-buried-town-discovery-beta-samati-scn/index.html. Accessed June 3, 2020.

Iliffe, J. (1995). *Africans: The history of a continent.* Cambridge, UK: Cambridge University Press.

Meredith, M. (2011). *The state of Africa: A history of the continent since independence.* Cape Town: Jonathan Ball Publishers.

Moss, T. J. (2011). *African development: Making sense of the issues and actors* (2nd ed.). Boulder, Colorado: Lynne Rienner.

Ndulu, B., & O'Connell, S. (1999). Governance and growth in sub-Saharan Africa. *The Journal of Economic Perspectives, 13*(3), 41–66.

Pakenham, T. (1992). *The scramble for Africa—1876–1912* (2nd ed.). London: Abacus.

Reader, J. (1997). *Africa: A biography of the continent*. London: Hamish Hamilton.

The Transatlantic Slave Trade (2008). Black History.com. [Online encyclopedia and social network]. http://blackhistory.com/content/61583/the-translatlantic%20-slave-trade. Accessed July 22, 2015.

Wilson, F. (2009). *Dinosaurs, diamonds and democracy: A short history of South Africa*. Cape Town: Umuzi.

Chapter 4
Traditional African Ideas of Achieving the 'Good Life'

Abstract The people of sub-Saharan Africa do not have a common identity, but we have isolated some of the experiences and commonalities that bind people of the region. In this chapter, we focus on African values and virtues that have their roots in the early history of the continent, and that have allowed the people living in sub-Saharan Africa to survive misfortune and to prosper in times of plenty. We describe traditional drivers of well-being in African societies including kinship solidarity, an egalitarian ethic, religious beliefs and resilience to overcome hardships.

Keywords Sub-Saharan Africa · Kinship · Egalitarianism · African *Ubuntu* · Religious beliefs · Resilience · Conservatism

4.1 The Sub-Saharan Quest for Well-Being

The heroism of African history is to be found not in the deeds of kings but in the struggles of ordinary people against the forces of nature and the cruelty of men. (Iliffe 1987, p. 1)

Many African values and virtues that nurture well-being have their roots in the early history of the continent, and in the unusually long duration of traditional and less technological ways of life. The people living on the subcontinent have frequently had to stand together to fight against the natural elements and foreign conquest to survive. As a consequence, the African concept of well-being is based on kinship solidarity, collective prosperity, and an egalitarian ethic that ideally precludes internecine strife.

4.1.1 Community Cohesiveness

'Happiness is not perfected until it is shared' (African proverb)

Kinship has been the dominant social structure in sub-Saharan Africa, as illustrated by the proverb cited above. For most of early history, sub-Saharan Africans

Fig. 4.1 *Happy family.* Sylvester Mubayi, 1975, Harare, Zimbabwe. Private Collection, Møller

lived in smaller groups of nomadic foragers, pastoralists and agriculturalists. Foragers need to travel light, so being limited to few material possessions was critical for nomadic well-being. Mobility was an important strategy to make optimal use of poor soils, seasonal changes in rainfall, and annual disease patterns, as well as to avoid competition for scarce food and other resources. Marriage and exchange relations between kinship groups provided an additional degree of food security. Chieftains with larger followings emerged only when sub-Saharan Africans became agriculturalists and pastoralists. In traditional African societies, there were always checks and balances on how chiefs could exercise their power (Mengisteab 2019). The colonial policy of divide and rule further increased the power of chiefs, where they were co-opted to assist as junior administrators (Fig. 4.1).

4.1.2 An Egalitarian Ethic

Citadels and large monuments, the usual hallmarks of great civilisations according to Mumford (1961), are conspicuous mainly by their absence in many of Africa's early civilisations. Larger civilisations, such as the Kush in Sudan and the Aksum in Ethiopia, were the exception rather than the rule. The non-coercive social hierarchies in early African civilisations, best exemplified by the West African inland-delta settlement of Jenne-Jeno on the Niger described earlier, might be regarded as an adaptation to African conditions of extreme uncertainty, where all hands were needed in the co-operative venture to survive. One explanation offered for the decline of Aksum refers to excessive, unequal consumption by its elite, evidence of which is seen in archaeological artefacts.

4.2 African *Ubuntu*

The African philosophy of *ubuntu* or humaneness (Metz 2014) may be considered a legacy from earlier times, when survival depended on kinship. The communitarian ethic aims to promote community welfare and congenial shared living. All individuals born into a community are implicated in a web of moral obligations, commitments, and duties to be fulfilled in pursuit of the general welfare. Molema (Gyekye 2011) noted that 'the greatest happiness and good of the tribe was the end and aim of each member of the tribe'. Similarly, the anthropologist Monica Wilson (Gyekye 2011) observed that 'the basis of morality is fulfilment of obligation to kinsmen and neighbours, and living in amity with them'. To this day, the domains of life related to family and community relationships are very important for the well-being of people living in sub-Saharan Africa.

4.3 Religion and Resilience

Religious beliefs and practice are an integral part of life in Africa and have played an important role in nurturing resilience and coping skills in times of adversity. Traditional religious beliefs in the ancestors, who guard over the welfare of their descendants, are still important to many people in sub-Saharan Africa. In the 1960s, expectations that traditional African beliefs and rituals would cease to be observed when rural Shona people migrated to the cities in contemporary Zimbabwe proved to be unfounded (see Gelfand 1968). Although Christianity is dominant in large areas of sub-Saharan Africa, particularly in urban areas, the number of Africa's professed Christians who also continue to observe their traditional beliefs and customs may be underreported in official statistics. The church currently plays an important role in many domains of life. For example, the African Independent Churches that split off from South Africa's mainline Christian churches in the nineteenth century have assisted rural people to adapt to urban life in the twentieth century. Many of these churches go by the name of Ethiopian with reference to Africa's first Christians, who never came under colonial rule. More recently, Africa's emergent middle class has turned to the Pentecostal and Evangelical churches for fellowship, mutual support, and prosperity.[1]

---

[1] See Dickow (2012) for a portrait of Pentecostal and Evangelical churches in South Africa.

Muslim beliefs and practices, introduced by Arab traders in Islamic states in ancient times, continue to play a central role in the well-being of people in the northern-most areas of sub-Sahara and on the east coast of Africa. Pious Sufis, the mystical adherents of Islam (Tiliouine and Meziane 2017), were mainly responsible for convincing Africans to convert to Islam—apparently without resorting to the sword. However, religious divides between Christians and Muslims within the state boundaries inherited from the colonial era has caused serious socio-economic and socio-political conflicts, as in the cases of Nigeria, Sudan, and the Central African Republic. In particular, religious tensions between Muslim fundamentalists and Muslims belonging to the predominant, more tolerant form of Islam practised in Africa have caused political instability.

Resilience. Archaeological records show how indigenous knowledge systems helped ancient societies in Africa to deal with the shock of illness and pandemics. There are lessons to be learnt for modern societies in sub-Saharan Africa fighting twenty-first century epidemics and pandemics such as Ebola and the Covid-19 virus.

According to professor of archaeology Shadreck Chirikure, archaeological and historical evidence tell us that African societies have always adopted strategies to deal with pandemics, including burning settlements as a disinfectant and shifting settlements to new locations. For example, at a settlement at the Mapungubwe World Heritage site in the Limpopo Valley of South Africa, which dates back to between CE 1000 and 1200, an unusually high number of 94 burials, including some 76 belonging to infants in the 0–4 age category were found, which suggests the settlement was abruptly abandoned around the same time as these burials. An outbreak of disease will have prompted the community to shift to another location. Similarly, archaeological evidence shows that thriving settlements in the Birim Valley of southern Ghana were abruptly abandoned after centuries of continuous and stable occupation during a period that appears to coincide with the devastation of the Black Death in fourteenth century Europe (Chirikure 2020).

Social distancing was always the first line of defence against disease in ancient times, Chirikure explains. For example, archaeologists' findings at Mwenezi in southern Zimbabwe show that it was a taboo to touch or interfere with remains of the dead, lest diseases be transmitted in this way. The Shona people in the seventeenth and eighteenth centuries isolated those suffering from infectious diseases, such as leprosy, in temporary residential structures so very few people would be exposed to the sick. In some cases, corpses were burnt to avoid spreading the contagion. Southern African communities knew that outbreaks were unpredictable but possible, so they built their settlements in a dispersed fashion to plan ahead. Settlements housed one or two families in a space that allowed people to stay at a distance from each other—but not too far apart to engage in daily care, support and cooperation (Chirikure 2020).

Perhaps the most important lesson that contemporaries can learn from ancient African societies is that 'people organised themselves in ways that made it easier to live with diseases'… 'Life did not stop because of pandemics: populations made decisions and choices to live with them' (Chirikure 2020).

4.4 Conservatism and Self-reliance

Africa's isolation and climatic conditions have favoured conservatism but also self-reliance. Interestingly, the continent's elongated shape may also have played a role as innovations travel faster along degrees of latitude where they can take root because climatic conditions tend to be more similar (Diamond 1998). Many innovations bypassed the subcontinent; others proved to be unsuitable or detrimental to prosperity. For example, trade with Africa that might have brought innovations up the Nile was largely one-sided in favour of ancient Egypt. In the west, the Saharan salt trade brought high-quality salt to the Sahel region of West Africa, but it may also have supported indigenous slavery; porters on the last stretch of the trade route were often enslaved. As for unsuitable innovations, there was little incentive for animal husbandry in earlier times given the abundance of wild animals for protein and the few animals that could be domesticated. For example, the horses brought by Portuguese traders to West Africa did not live long. Domestic animals imported to Africa were susceptible to disease, and providing fodder for them was not cost-efficient. Similarly, the wheel was not suitable for Africa's rough terrain.

4.5 Conclusion

We have reviewed some of the values and virtues that have stood African societies in good stead over centuries. It is possible that Africa's people, at least those of standing, flourished in earlier times, for example, at the height of the early kingdoms and civilisations in West and East Africa, and during Islam's golden age in Africa (see Renima et al. 2016). Going further back in time, Africa's more egalitarian hunter-gatherer societies (Reader 1997), whose expectations of life will have been more modest than those of present-day ones, might have been more contented than contemporary African citizens. We shall never know.

References

Chirikure, S. (2020). Archaeology shows how ancient African societies managed pandemics. *The Conversation*, 14 May. https://theconversation.com/archaeology-shows-how-ancient-african-societies-managed-pandemics-138217. Accessed May 30, 2020.

Gelfand, M. (1968). *African crucible: An ethico-religious study with special reference to the Shona-speaking people.* Wynberg, Cape Town: Juta & Company.

Gyekye, K. (2011). African ethics. In E. N. Zalta (Ed.), *The Stanford encyclopedia of philosophy* (Fall 2011 Ed.). http://plato.stanford.edu/archives/fall2011/entries/african-ethics/. Accessed July 24, 2015.

Diamond, J. (1998). *Guns, germs and steel—A short history of everybody for the last 13,000 years.* London: Vintage.

Dickow, H. (2012). Religion and attitudes towards life in South Africa: Pentecostals, charismatics and reborns. In collaboration with P. Bauerle, Th. Hanf & V. Møller. Baden-Baden, Germany: Nomos. ISBN 978-3-8329-7049-9.

Iliffe, J. (1987). *The African poor: A history*. Cambridge, UK: Cambridge University Press.

Mengisteab, K. (2019). Traditional institutions of governance in Africa. *Oxford research encyclopedias, politics*. https://oxfordre.com/politics/view/10.1093/acrefore/9780190228637.001.0001/acrefore-9780190228637-e-1347. Accessed May 30, 2020.

Metz, T. (2014). *Ubuntu*: The good life. In A. C. Michalos (Ed.), *Encylopedia of quality of life and well-being research* (pp. 6761–6765). New York: Springer.

Mumford, L. (1961). *The city in history: Its origins, its transformations, and its prospects*. London: Secker & Warburg.

Reader, J. (1997). *Africa: A biography of the continent*. London: Hamish Hamilton.

Renima, A., Tiliouine, H., & Estes, R. J. (2016). The Islamic Golden Age: A Story of the Triumph of the Islamic Civilization. In H. Tiliouine & R. J. Estes (Eds.), *The state of social progress of Islamic societies (chapter 2)*. Dordrecht: Springer.

Tiliouine, H., & Meziane, M. (2017). The history of well-being in the Middle East and North Africa (MENA). In: R.J. Estes & M.J. Sirgy (Eds.), *The pursuit of well-being: The untold global history* (pp. 523–563), International Handbooks of Quality-of-Life Research. Springer International Publishing Switzerland.

Chapter 5
Africa at War and Peace

Abstract Conflict avoidance in Africa may have been easier in the continent's early history. In this chapter we review the so-called 'garden of Eden' myth, which maintains that the people of Africa were contented and peaceful until the arrival of explorers and colonial power. There is scant evidence to support this idea; the myth is probably just that. But the good news is that since independence, African states, with a few exceptions, have mainly contained conflict within their borders, and the days of imperial conquest may be over.

Keywords Sub-Saharan Africa · 'Garden of Eden' myth · Peaceful coexistence · War · Violence · Country borders

5.1 Peaceful Coexistence Alongside Violence

The Garden of Eden myth of Africa implies that sub-Saharan Africa was peaceful until it came into contact with external influences. Indeed, conflict-avoidance between groups occupying the same space does seem to have been commonplace in earlier times. For example, Bantu agriculturalists and pastoralists co-existed peacefully with hunter-gatherers on the East African highlands. Archaeological evidence suggests that iron was used for food-production technology rather than for weaponry; food was of paramount importance for survival at the time. The wealth of the great civilisations of Aksum, the Niger inland-delta, and Mapungubwe and Great Zimbabwe was derived from trade rather than conquest. Initially, a papal edict prohibited weapons being traded for goods by the Portuguese explorers, but firearms later became a medium of exchange for slaves in West Africa. The subsequent introduction of guns that were easier to load and whose ignition did not light up at night increased the terror of slave raids (see Reader 1997, p. 143ff.).

Although it may be expedient to blame outsiders for introducing violence to sub-Saharan Africa, there can be no doubt that violence and warfare were in fact commonplace in early African history. Slavery was a common practice in ancient Africa, as it was in other parts of the world at the time. Local chiefs and merchants collaborated with the Atlantic and Arab slave traders, probably in ways that included violent

© Springer Nature Switzerland AG 2021   29
V. Møller and B. J. Roberts, *Quality of Life and Human Well-Being in Sub-Saharan Africa*,
Human Well-Being Research and Policy Making,
https://doi.org/10.1007/978-3-030-65788-8_5

internecine raids. On the other hand, some oral accounts, such as from the !Kung of the Kalahari, suggest that intergroup warfare may actually have been suppressed under colonial rule, and did not reoccur thereafter (Diamond 2012). In the 1950s and 1960s, the response to colonial oppression during the transition to independence was often violent. The Mau Mau insurrection in Kenya is just one example. Currently, one of the main challenges for the new independent governments of sub-Saharan Africa has been to guarantee the safety and security of citizens following decades of colonial rule and suppression of civil rights.

Yuval Noah Harari, in his brief history of humankind, makes the point that 'never before has peace been so prevalent that people cannot even imagine war' (Harari 2011, p. 416). This might be naïve, he notes, but since 1945, with very few exceptions, states no longer invade other states in order to 'conquer and swallow them up'. Since time immemorial such conquests have been the 'bread and butter' of political history and most empires were established in this way. Today, wars are no longer the norm, he states, although limited international wars do occur from time to time and millions do still die in wars. Of importance for our report on well-being in Africa, Harari draws our attention to the fact that 'since African states won their independence in the 1960s and 1970s, very few countries have invaded one another in the hope of conquest (Harari 2011, pp. 414–415).

It may be that countries in Africa, whose borders were drawn arbitrarily, are more preoccupied with creating social cohesion across ethnic and language differences within their borders, in pursuit of political stability and prosperity. We noted earlier that the African Union supports the maintenance of country borders dating back to independence, in order to promote peace rather than conflict in sub-Saharan Africa.

5.2 Summary

In this first part of the book, we have attempted to introduce readers to the early history of the continent and to the many challenges faced by the people living in sub-Saharan Africa, as they pursue their ideas of the good life for themselves and their communities over time.

In the next part of the book, we shall turn to the examination of African well-being in the post-independence period, which coincides with the emergence of the 1960s social indicators movement (Land and Michalos 2018; Møller 2018) that applied the first rigorous measures of quality of life and well-being.

References

Diamond, J. (2012). *The world until yesterday: What we can learn from traditional societies.* London: Penguin Books.
Harari, Y. N. (2011). *Sapiens: A brief history of humankind.* London: Vintage Books.

Land, K. C., & Michalos, A. C. (2018). Fifty years after the social indicators movement: Has the promise been fulfilled? An assessment an agenda for the future. *Social Indicators Research, 135*(3), 835–868. https://doi.org/10.1007/s11205-017-1571-y.

Møller, V. (2018). Whatever happened to social indicators in Africa? Whatever happened indeed! A developing world perspective on the Kenneth C. Land and Alex C. Michalos report on 'fifty years after the social indicators movement'. *Social Indicators Research, 135*(3), 1009–1019. https://doi.org/10.1007/s11205-017-1555-y, http://rdcu.be/opqP.

Reader, J. (1997). *Africa: A biography of the continent*. London: Hamish Hamilton.

Part II
Indicators and Drivers of Well-Being

Food is happiness, Artist unknown. Private collection, Møller

Chapter 6
Basic Needs and Well-Being

Abstract In this chapter we examine trends in well-being and concentrate on progress made in achieving greater prosperity since the time of independence. We focus on three domains of life considered to be universal drivers of well-being: health, education, and income. Good health may be considered a basic condition for human life; education and instruction are a means of adapting to and securing a livelihood in a given environment; and income and access to resources create opportunities to cover basic needs and gain power and prestige. We also examine further socio-political challenges for sub-Saharan Africa. Lastly, we review trends in subjective well-being: how people evaluate their own lives.

Keywords Sub-Saharan Africa · Basic needs · Health · Education · Standard of living · Social progress · Life satisfaction · Positive and negative affect

6.1 Progress in Meeting Basic Needs in Sub-Saharan Africa

The wind of change that swept through the continent in the 1960s raised expectations for the material benefits of freedom. In this section we review whether hopes for a better life have been fulfilled in sub-Saharan Africa over the past decades. We begin with an examination of social indicators relating to health, education, and income, which are considered key to human development. The Millennium Development Goals (MDGs) set benchmarks for achieving better health and education outcomes and eradicating poverty in Africa by 2015, which were supplemented by a broader, ambitious Sustainable Development Goals (SDGs) agenda for 2030. These important domains of life have been affected by many factors over time including climate and ecology, economic boom and bust periods, revolutionary technological innovations, and historical events. As we see, significant progress has been made in improving quality of life in these domains since independence.

6.2   Health: Health Is Happiness

"The word mutakalo in Venda means either happiness or health. So I am happy and I have good health" – Rural focus group participant, Vhembe district, Limpopo, South Africa (Roberts et al. 2014).

6.2.1   Food Equals Happiness

In the Venda language spoken by people living near the border between Zimbabwe and South Africa, health *is* happiness. There is no other word for it. A full belly has been important for both health and happiness in Africa since early times. The introduction of the plough during the Iron Age revolutionised agricultural production in Africa, as did the introduction of maize from the Americas by the Portuguese in the seventeenth and eighteenth centuries. Recent research has found evidence that African pastoralists developed lactose tolerance to take advantage of the milk produced by their herds. Agriculturalists and pastoralists in Africa depend on rainfall. Aptly, Botswana's currency is named *pula*, 'rain' in Setswana, which is precious in a country that is home to the Kalahari Desert. Nutritional limitations kept population numbers at minimal levels in sub-Saharan Africa for most of early history. There were cycles of boom and bust depending on whether climatic conditions were favourable or unfavourable. Populations that boomed when conditions were favourable often became surplus when conditions changed. Until the twenty-first century, sub-Saharan Africa's potential for population growth was never fulfilled.

6.2.2   Africa's Burden of Disease

The many vicious and perfidious diseases and parasites that have preyed on both animals and on humans have always presented threats to life in sub-Saharan Africa. Diseases such as malaria, sleeping sickness, which is caused by a parasite spread by the tsetse fly, and bilharzia sapped energy to grow food and caused widespread infant mortality. One of the main reasons for low population growth in Africa relative to the rest of the world was precisely because the people who moved out of Africa some 100,000 years ago were not exposed to such deadly and crippling diseases (Reader 1997). Some groups that remained in Africa managed to develop immunity or found niches in the ecology where they escaped the clutches of disease. For example, sub-Saharan pastoralists migrated to highlands not infested with the tsetse fly.

In the twentieth century, the improved hygiene introduced during the late colonial era and the discovery of penicillin saved lives. Practical preventive health care measures such as the provision to people living in malaria areas of insecticide-treated sleeping nets have increased life expectancy in the last decades. New threats to health are the human immunodeficiency virus (HIV) that causes AIDS and multi- and extremely drug-resistant tuberculosis. In the new millennium, antiretroviral therapy (ART) has allowed thousands of people with HIV/AIDS to lead normal, productive, fulfilling lives. The drugs currently used to treat Africans infected with tuberculosis (TB) were developed some 40 years ago. Meanwhile, cases of multidrug and extremely drug-resistant TB have emerged. A new combination drug may soon become available that will shorten and simplify treatment regimens for regular TB and be more effective in treating multidrug-resistant TB. Vaccine campaigns increasingly play an important role in protecting lives in sub-Saharan Africa. A new affordable vaccine that has been administered across the 'meningitis A' belt stretching from Senegal to Ethiopia has nearly eliminated the deadly disease that can cause severe brain damage (World Health Organisation 2015a).

6.2.3 The Race Between Research and the Ebola Virus

The outbreak of Ebola in West Africa in December 2013 made headlines around the globe. Between 2014 and 2016, the epidemic swept through Guinea, Sierra Leone, and Liberia, all three West African countries that have porous borders. The epidemic was the largest since the discovery of the virus in 1976 by Belgium scientist Peter Piot. The virus was first detected in a Belgian mission hospital in the Democratic Republic of Congo (DRC), where expectant mothers had been injected with vitamins using the same needle. The research team gave the virus the name of the river Ebola in the northern DRC to avoid attaching stigma to the hospital and the region it served. Unlike other outbreaks, the 2014–16 West African epidemic was the first one that threatened to go out of control and to spread to the densely populated capitals of Guinea, Sierra Leone, and Liberia.

A toxic mix of factors overwhelmed the health services of the West African countries battling to halt the spread of Ebola. For example, Liberia's infrastructure and health services were recovering from a 14-year civil war that had ended in 2003; only 52 doctors were left to serve a population of close to 4 million. As was the case with HIV/AIDS in the 1980s, fear, traditional health beliefs, stigma, and conspiracy theories hindered the first attempts to contain the spread of the disease. According to the World Health Organization, by the time Liberia, the hardest hit state, was declared Ebola free in May 2015, more than 11,000 people had died, and new cases were still being detected in neighbouring Guinea and Sierra Leone (WHO 2015b). Only approximately 30% of patients survived the West African Ebola outbreak.

However, there is also a success story: The few cases of Ebola in Lagos, the sprawling metropolitan area of Nigeria, were swiftly contained thanks to meticulous tracing of all contacts with infected individuals (Ogunsola 2015). With lessons learnt from the West African Ebola epidemic (2014–2016), there was hope that survival rates in the event of new outbreaks would be greater in the future. Indeed, trials with new vaccines were a key factor in containing the next outbreak of Ebola in the DRC in August 2018. One of the vaccine candidates was inherited from the West African Ebola epidemic.

6.2.4   The Response to the DRC Ebola

The DRC has extensive experience with Ebola—there have been more outbreaks in the DRC than in any other country[1]—but the race to keep this latest epidemic from spreading faced new challenges. A simmering guerrilla war was raging in the area and during the long-drawn out presidential elections, the government claimed the Ebola outbreak was used as pretext to prevent over a million voters from participating (Bamford 2019). In February 2019, the medical charity Médicins Sans Frontières (MSF), who had played a key role in ending the 2014 West African outbreak, had to suspend its operations in the DRC owing to its treatment centres being attacked and set alight.

In July 2019, the World Health Organisation declared the current Ebola outbreak in the DRC 'a public health emergency of international concern'. That month the first case had spread to Goma, a city in North Kivu Province of two million and a major international transit hub. There was concern that the epidemic would spread across the DRC's porous borders into neighbouring countries.[2] President Félix Tshisekedi then announced that he would take over the coordination of the country's response to Ebola from his minister of health and appointed an Ebola pioneer to lead the efforts, a strategic decision that was certain to galvanise national and international support, according to public health expert Fallah (2019b). When Liberia's President Ellen Johnson-Sirleaf took over the running of her country's Ebola response in 2014, the number of cases dropped dramatically.

When the DRC was declared Ebola-free on 25 July 2020, the world's second largest outbreak of Ebola had claimed 2287 deaths since 1 August 2018 (WHO 2020). However, as the *TIME*'s special Africa correspondent, Baker (2019), notes, 'progress in defeating Ebola often means taking a step backward for every two steps forward'. No sooner was the DRC declared free of its 10th outbreak of Ebola than the country was faced with multiple outbreaks of diseases: A new outbreak of Ebola in the north west, an ongoing measles outbreak that had already claimed over 6000 deaths, and the Covid-19 pandemic that had reached Africa earlier that year. There were already 4639 confirmed cases of the coronavirus and 101 deaths in the DRC as of 13 June 2020 (Boum 2020).

---

[1]Over the past ten years there have been five outbreaks of Ebola in the DRC, in 2007, 2008–2009, 2012, in 2014, and in 2017 (see Weyer 2017). Boum (2020) reports 10 outbreaks in the past 40 years.

[2]See Dr. Fallah (2019a), Deputy Director of Deputy Director General at Liberia's National Public Health Institute, on the challenges of controlling the cross-country spread of Ebola and lessons learnt from the West African experience.

6.2.5   Responding to the Global Public Health Crisis—The Covid-19 Pandemic

DRC's health experts were confident that the country would be able to face off the Covid-19 pandemic by drawing on its newly developed research capacity in fighting the 2018 outbreak of Ebola (Boum 2020). The country had managed to run clinical trials in the middle of an emergency and conduct its largest-ever vaccine campaign that was a key factor in containing Ebola.[3] According to World Health Organisation's Regional Director of Africa, Dr Matshidiso Moeti, 'the DRC is now better, smarter and faster at responding to Ebola and this is an enduring legacy which is supporting the response to COVID-19 and other outbreaks' (WHO 2020).

As is the case with Ebola, Covid-19 has no cure. Until a vaccine is developed, the virus cannot be eradicated. DRC is among the three sub-Saharan countries prepared to take part in vaccine trials, along with South Africa and Kenya. South Africa commenced with its first Covid-19 vaccine trials in June 2020 while Kenya was still awaiting approval at the time. There had been resistance in Africa to participate in human vaccine trials based on earlier experiences of exploitation and unethical drug trials, as expressed in the '#Africans are not lab rats!' movement. However, there are advantages for vaccine trials to be conducted in Africa. Firstly, it is important to know that the vaccine works in the African population. Furthermore, when a vaccine for Covid-19 becomes available, it is likely to be in short supply globally. Countries that have participated in trials must be given access to the vaccine, which will also be available at more affordable prices.[4]

6.2.6   Life Expectancy in Africa

Despite the AIDS pandemic of the 1980s, the recent outbreaks of Ebola in West Africa and the Democratic Republic of Congo, and the outbreak and global spread of Covid-19 in 2020, the prospects of living a longer and healthier life have never been as good in Africa's history. Life expectancy has improved dramatically in the last decades, which have witnessed a population explosion and the so-called demographic dividend in sub-Saharan Africa.

Increasing life expectancy is a worldwide trend in recent decades, and, for the first time in history, it includes Africa. In 2018, a child born anywhere in the world could expect to live 73 years, a gain of 7 years compared to a child born in 1990. If that child was born in Africa, the gain in life expectancy over the same period would be an additional four years. Significantly, the eleven-year gain in life expectancy in

---

[3]See: DR Congo's deadliest Ebola outbreak declared over. *BBC News Africa.*
   https://www.bbc.com/news/world-africa-53179323 (Accessed 25 June 2020).

[4]See Coronavirus vaccine trials in Africa: What you need to know: https://www.bbc.com/news/av/world-africa-53169928/coronavirus-vaccine-trials-in-africa-what-you-need-to-know (Accessed 24 June 2020).

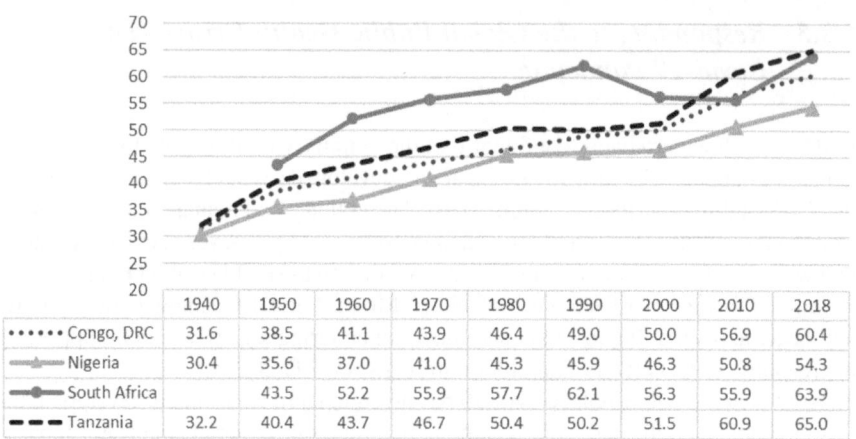

	1940	1950	1960	1970	1980	1990	2000	2010	2018
••••••Congo, DRC	31.6	38.5	41.1	43.9	46.4	49.0	50.0	56.9	60.4
Nigeria	30.4	35.6	37.0	41.0	45.3	45.9	46.3	50.8	54.3
South Africa		43.5	52.2	55.9	57.7	62.1	56.3	55.9	63.9
Tanzania	32.2	40.4	43.7	46.7	50.4	50.2	51.5	60.9	65.0

Fig. 6.1 Progressively longer lives despite AIDS-related setbacks. Changes in life expectancy (in years) in sub-Saharan Africa's more populous countries, 1940–2018 (Data from Clio-infra 2013; World Bank World Development Indicators)

sub-Saharan Africa between 1990 and 2018 occurred despite the effects of the HIV pandemic that continues to beleaguer many countries in the region.

Figure 6.1 shows the dramatic changes in life expectancy in four of sub-Saharan Africa's most populous countries: Nigeria in West Africa, the Democratic Republic of Congo in Central Africa, Tanzania in East Africa, and South Africa, which is located on the southern tip of the continent. A child born in any of these countries in 1940 might expect to live only 30 years, whereas generations born in 2018 could expect to live approximately 55–65 years. The changing pattern in years of life expectancy between 1990 and 2018, characterised by stagnation or decline in the 1990s followed by general improvement in the new millennium, highlights the impact of the HIV pandemic and the significant gains in life expectancy subsequently achieved after the introduction of ART, one of Africa's major success stories.

Global and regional averages tend to conceal substantial cross-national inequalities, and life expectancy is no exception. In 2018, life expectancy in sub-Saharan Africa ranged from a low of 53 years on average in the Central African Republic to a high of around 75 years in the island states of Mauritius, Seychelles, and Cabo Verde. Despite this disturbingly large difference in longevity within the region, there has been a slight narrowing in inequality in life expectancy since the early 1990s, with the range of country values falling from a difference of 36 years to 22 years.

It is instructive to look a little closer at the experience of one of the countries at the bottom end of the ranking in both periods of evaluation, namely Sierra Leone. In 1990, the country was at the tail end of a decade-long civil war, and life expectancy for both newborn boys and girls was a mere 39 years. This value is similar to the longevity recorded in the United States as well as in England and Wales around 1850 or China in 1960. Jumping ahead to 2018, life expectancy in Sierra Leone has increased by sixteen years for newborn children, around double the world average.

These improvements are, however, from a low base, and the health context facing the country is still bleak. The country has some of the world's highest infant and maternal mortality rates; is prone to diseases such as yellow fever, cholera, meningitis, and Lassa fever; and has a relatively small share of the population with access to adequate medical care. The outbreak of the Ebola virus in West Africa in late 2013 resulted in a rapid progression of the disease through Sierra Leone and brought into sharp relief the limitations of the health infrastructure in the country.

Table 6.1 shows that life expectancy exceeds 70 years among both men and women in only three of the 49 sub-Saharan nations, all of which are small-island developing nations (Mauritius, Seychelles, and Cabo Verde). At the lower end of the distribution, we find countries where life expectancy is estimated at less than 55 years. Most of these countries have been affected by conflict and civil war, and Lesotho is among the countries most badly affected by the AIDS pandemic. The table also ranks countries in the region on the basis of the change in life expectancy from 1990 to 2018. A number of low-income countries within sub-Saharan Africa have produced remarkable improvements. Rwanda experienced the world's greatest observed increase in life expectancy, from 33 years in 1990 to 69 years in 2017, an increase of 35 years. Progress was equally impressive in countries such as Ethiopia, Niger, Malawi, Liberia, Uganda, Eritrea, Madagascar and Angola, all of which are ranked in the top countries in terms of change in life expectancy. An important part of the explanation for such impressive strides in human development is success in reducing child mortality rates (WHO 2014, 2019). Improvements in areas such as water and sanitation, child immunisation, public health infrastructure, and maternal and child nutrition have all played a part.

Conversely, the shadow of AIDS features prominently among those countries in the region showing the greatest reversals in life expectancy in recent decades. Lesotho and eSwatini are the only countries in the world, with the exception of Belize, to have experienced aggregate declines in life expectancy in the 1990 to 2018 period. Zimbabwe, South Africa, and Namibia also registered significant AIDS-related declines in life expectancy during the 1990s. Yet, despite such losses, the scaling up of access to ART has begun to yield a significant reduction in AIDS-related deaths in Africa over the last decade-and-a-half, which is a positive development that should translate into further gains in life expectancy across the region in coming years.

6.2.7   Maternal and Child Health

Improving maternal health has become an important global priority, as reflected in the fact that it was adopted as one of the core Millennium Development Goals (MDGs) and Sustainable Development Goals (SDGs). A range of initiatives have been pursued in recent years to bring about sizable and sustainable improvements, especially in relation to maternal deaths. The most recently available trend data cover a period of approximately a quarter century, from 1990 to 2015 (WHO 2015c, 2018a, 2019). There have been commendable strides in addressing maternal mortality, with the maternal mortality ratio (MMR) falling 45% worldwide and 48% in sub-Saharan

Table 6.1 A healthy picture—gains in life expectancy

Top 10 countries in 2018: life expectancy (years)	1960	1990	2000	2018	Change 1990–2000	Change 2000–18	Change 1990–2018
Mauritius	59	69	72	74	2	3	5
Seychelles	–	68	73	73	5	0	5
Cabo Verde	49	65	69	73	4	4	8
São Tomé and Príncipe	50	58	61	70	3	9	12
Botswana	51	59	51	69	−9	19	10
Rwanda	42	33	49	69	15	20	35
Senegal	38	57	58	68	1	10	10
Madagascar	40	51	58	67	7	8	16
Djibouti	44	57	57	67	0	10	10
Kenya	46	57	51	66	−6	15	9
Bottom 10 countries in 2018: life expectancy (years)	1960	1990	2000	2018	Change 1990–2000	Change 2000–18	Change 1990–2018
Equatorial Guinea	37	49	53	58	5	5	10
Guinea-Bissau	38	47	50	58	3	8	11
South Sudan	32	44	49	58	6	8	14
Côte d'Ivoire	37	53	50	57	−4	8	4
Somalia	37	45	51	57	5	6	12
Nigeria	37	46	46	54	0	8	8
Sierra Leone	32	39	39	54	1	15	16
Chad	38	47	48	54	1	6	7
Lesotho	47	60	48	54	−12	6	−6
Central African Republic	36	49	44	53	−5	9	4
Top 10 countries ranked by years gained (1990–2018)	1960	1990	2000	2018	Change 1990–2000	Change 2000–18	Change 1990–2018
Rwanda	43	33	49	69	15	20	35
Ethiopia	38	47	52	66	5	14	19
Niger	35	44	50	62	6	12	18

(continued)

Table 6.1 (continued)

Top 10 countries ranked by years gained (1990–2018)	1960	1990	2000	2018	Change 1990–2000	Change 2000–18	Change 1990–2018
Malawi	37	46	45	64	−1	19	18
Liberia	34	46	52	64	6	12	18
Uganda	44	46	46	63	0	17	17
Eritrea	38	50	55	66	6	11	16
Sierra Leone	32	39	39	54	1	15	16
Madagascar	40	51	58	67	7	8	16
Angola	38	45	47	61	1	14	15
Bottom 10 countries ranked by years gained (1990–2018)	1960	1990	2000	2018	Change 1990–2000	Change 2000–18	Change 1990–2018
Mauritius	59	69	72	74	2	3	5
Togo	40	56	53	61	−2	7	5
Seychelles	–	68	73	73	5	0	5
Côte d'Ivoire	36	53	50	57	−4	8	4
Central African Republic	36	49	44	53	−5	9	4
Zimbabwe	53	58	45	61	−13	17	3
Namibia	46	62	52	63	−9	11	2
South Africa	48	63	56	64	−7	8	1
Eswatini	44	62	47	59	−14	12	−3
Lesotho	48	60	48	54	−12	6	−6
Sub-Saharan Africa, years gained (1990–2018)	*40*	*50*	*50*	*61*	*0*	*11*	*11*

Life expectancy in Africa, 1990 and 2018 (World Bank World Development indicators)
Bold italics represents average for the subregion on this measure

Africa (Fig. 6.2). The MDG target of reducing maternal deaths by three quarters between 1990 and 2015 was achieved in Equatorial Guinea, Cabo Verde, and Rwanda, and countries such as Ethiopia, Eritrea, Angola, and Mozambique came close to attaining this milestone. Yet, despite such gains, in 2015 the maternal mortality ratio for the region was still around two-and-a-half times the world average (546 compared to 216), and 66% of the women who died that year from complications during pregnancy or childbirth (201,000 of 303,000) came from sub-Saharan Africa (WHO 2015c, 2018a). Although 43 of the 49 countries in the region have maternal mortality ratios below the global average, vast inequalities in maternal health are

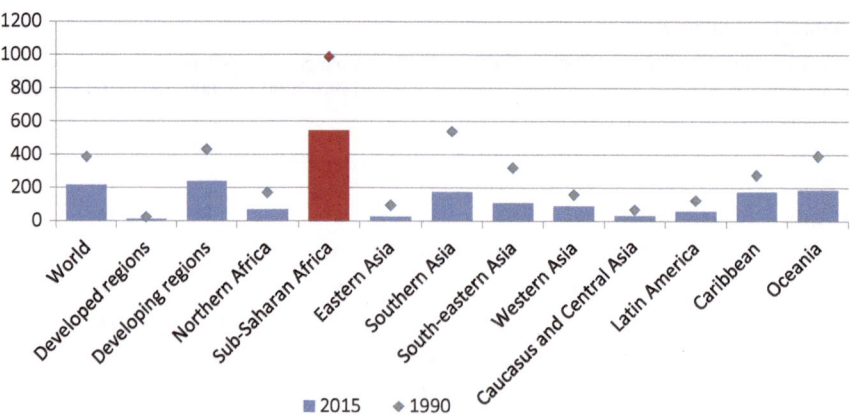

Fig. 6.2 Maternal health improving in sub-Saharan Africa, but at an insufficient pace to meet global targets. Regional trends in maternal mortality, 1990–2015, number of maternal deaths per 100,000 live births (WHO 2015c, 2018a)

evident across the region. For example, in Mauritius the MMR in 2015 (53 per 100,000) was only a tenth of the regional average and a quarter of the global average, while the MMR in Sierra Leone (1360 per 100,000) was more than double the regional average and six times higher than the global average.

The core SDG maternal health target for 2030 is 'to reduce the global maternal mortality ratio to less than 70 per 100 000 live births'. Achieving this would require an eight-fold reduction in the 2015 level of maternal mortality in the region. If the same rate of change observed between 1990 and 2015 is maintained up until 2030, the maternal mortality ratio for sub-Saharan Africa would end up being around 280 per 100,000 live births. Although this would miss the target by a considerable degree, what is key is ensuring sustained progress in improving maternal health across Africa. In particular, this will require significant investments in improving access to modern methods of contraception, ensuring that women of reproductive age receive high quality care from a skilled health professional before, during and after childbirth. The case of Nigeria, the region's most populous country, conveys the scale of this challenge. The country has the fourth highest MMR in the sub-Saharan Africa region (814 per 100,000 in 2015), which is partly a reflection of a high unmet need for family planning (only 43% of women being satisfied) and a relatively low share of births being delivered by a skilled attendant (43%) (WHO 2019). Yet the regional experience since the early 1990s has demonstrated that impressive gains can be made if there is sufficient political will to design, invest in, and monitor maternal health programmes, together with concerted efforts to address women's economic empowerment and educational attainment (ibid.).

One of the reasons for the positive achievements in life expectancy described earlier relates to the improvement in child survival that is evident in the region, particularly since 2000 (WHO 2014, 2019). Between 1990 and 2000, the under-five mortality rate in the African region fell from 173 to 154 deaths per 100,000 live births, a decline of approximately 11% or an average of barely 1% per year. By contrast, between 2000 and 2017, the child mortality rate dropped 52% to 74 deaths per 100,000 live births. Countries such as Rwanda, Malawi, Senegal and Uganda reduced the under-five mortality rate by two thirds between 2000 and 2017, and for 39 of the 49 countries in the region there was at least a 40% reduction in child mortality over this period. If this pace of change is maintained, then as many as 33 out of 49 countries would in the region could be considered to be on track to meet the SDG target of reducing child mortality to at least as low as 25 per 1000 live births by 2030. The challenge is likely to still remain acute in countries such as Somalia, Central African Republic, Chad, Lesotho, Benin and Mauritania, where child mortality rates are likely to remain at more than 50 per 1000 live births by 2030 based on current projections. Yet, even in these instances, mortality rates fell by between a quarter and a third since the turn of the century. These are laudable developments, but it is sobering to remember that in 2017 alone, 2.7 million children died in sub-Saharan Africa, equivalent to half of the total number of child deaths worldwide.

Internationally, the last two decades have seen a transition in the primary causes of premature death and disability among children away from communicable diseases toward noncommunicable lifestyle diseases affecting the adult population. Sub-Saharan Africa is somewhat exceptional in this regard, with infectious and parasitic diseases (especially HIV, tuberculosis, and malaria) together with maternal, newborn, and nutritional conditions still accounting for about 70% of premature deaths in 2012 (WHO 2014). Though these conditions are still among the top-ranked conditions in the region's burden of disease, there are again positive signs of change. Although the AIDS pandemic has had devastating consequences for many sub-Saharan African countries over the last 30 years,[5] in many instances the pandemic peaked in the mid-2000s. The result of this peak, coupled with the rapid scaling up of access to ART, has meant that the number of years lost declined by slightly more than a fifth (22%) between 2005 and 2010. In 2017, 93% of all malaria-related deaths (403,000 out of 435,000) occurred in sub-Saharan Africa, and the disease was responsible for a fifth of all childhood deaths (WHO 2018b). Around half of all malaria deaths reported globally remain concentrated in six African nations, namely Nigeria, the Democratic Republic of the Congo, Burkina Faso, Tanzania, Sierra Leone and Niger. Despite the staggering number of malaria-related deaths still occurring in the region, commendable strides have been made in expanding malaria control programmes involving interventions such as insecticide-treated bed nets, indoor spraying, preventive treatment during pregnancy, and antimalarial drugs. Such efforts translated into a 38% reduction in malaria mortality rates in Africa between 2010 and 2017 (WHO 2018b). Vaccinating children against measles has also been successful. In 1990, immunisation rates for measles across the continent stood at 58%, a figure that fell to 53% in 2000. The drive to improve vaccination rates in Africa since 2000 has seen single-dose measles vaccination coverage increase to 70% by 2017 and an 86% drop in measles-related deaths from 320,000 in 2000 to 43,000 in 2017. However, as of 2017, only

---

[5]Evident in the more than threefold increase in the number of years lost to premature death and disability between 1990 and 2010.

26 African countries had introduced a second dose of measles vaccine into their immunisation schedule, resulting in second-dose vaccination coverage standing at only 25%. Continued efforts to achieve and maintain high rates of vaccination, especially in countries such as Nigeria, Somalia, and the Central African Republic, will hopefully bring further gains in reducing preventable childhood deaths.

Although communicable diseases still predominate as causes of illness and death in the region, the relative contribution of noncommunicable lifestyle diseases has grown (from 18% in 2000 to 29% in 2016). For instance, the number of deaths from cardiovascular diseases such as strokes and heart disease increased by 27% between 2000 and 2016; the number of cases of diabetes and depression is also rising, especially in middle income countries in the region. This emerging threat is imposing an added burden on health systems that are already strained under the demands imposed by communicable diseases. Road injuries and interpersonal violence also display an increasing trend.

Although efforts to fight high-profile diseases such as HIV/AIDS, TB, and malaria have received the greatest attention in recent years, diseases that have been neglected continue to take lives. Polio, which has been eradicated in most of the world, has recently reappeared in West Africa because some parents refuse to inoculate their children on religious grounds.

In summary, although considerable health challenges remain in sub-Saharan Africa, the fairly impressive gains that have been achieved in recent decades are producing important quality-of-life gains through longer and healthier lives.

6.3   Education in Sub-Saharan Africa: A Class Act?

Worldwide, countries are far more concerned about improving the quality of life of their citizens than they were a hundred years ago. The most corrupt and inefficient of countries in Africa are still providing services of a quality and extent far in advance of any country in the world prior to the Industrial Revolution. (Kenny 2012)

From an historical perspective, formal schooling was a late innovation in most regions of sub-Saharan Africa. Africa's oral tradition had served as the sole means of communication and transmission of knowledge in most of sub-Saharan Africa until the nineteenth century. The task of carrying out the civilising project that had justified the scramble for Africa was delegated to missionaries who proceeded to build schools, churches, and hospitals and transcribed many local African languages. The few missionary-educated Africans who had studied abroad became the leaders of Africa's independence movements in the 1950s and 1960s and the first heads of states. In the 1930s, just four institutions offered those among sub-Saharan Africa's 165 million inhabitants who were eligible an education that met university-entrance standards (Reader 1997, p. 666). Education, considered a prerequisite for democracy, represented an important MDG for sub-Saharan Africa between 2000 and 2015, a priority that continues to form a critical component of the SDGs and indeed the

Table 6.2 Signs of convergence in primary school enrolment (Benavot and Riddle 1988; World Bank 2020)

	Unadjusted primary school enrolment rates (%)			Net primary enrolment rates (%)			
	1870	1900	1930	1990	2000	2010	2016
Sub-Saharan Africa	17	15	15	53	60	74	78
United States	72	95	93	99	95	93	95
United Kingdom	49	74	82	100	100	98	100
Germany	67	73	73	–	99	98	99
	Ratio of Enrolment in Sub-Saharan Africa (SSA) to Other Countries						
SSA: United States	0.23	0.16	0.16	0.53	0.63	0.80	0.82
SSA: United Kingdom	0.34	0.20	0.18	0.53	0.60	0.76	0.78
SSA: Germany	0.25	0.20	0.21	–	0.60	0.76	0.78

SSA Sub-Saharan Africa

African Union's Agenda 2063. Since the 1960s, illiterate African parents have made great sacrifices to send their children to school so that levels of education have risen rapidly from one generation to the next. Furthermore, urbanisation has increased access to schooling.

As with health, if one adopts a longer historical perspective when looking at patterns and trends, it is evident that sub-Saharan Africa has experienced notable growth in certain core educational indicators and has begun to narrow the gap relative to leading countries. Although it is again important to recognise the multiple challenges that remain in bringing about greater parity with other world regions, this fact should not overshadow the appreciable progress that has been forged.

6.3.1 School Enrolment

With regard to basic education, the region was unable to reach the ambitious Education for All goal of universal primary education by 2015, with a net enrolment ratio of 77% in that year. This number does nonetheless represent an increase of approximately 25 percentage points relative to 1990 (53%). By pushing further backward and comparing recent educational statistics to those covering the period prior to World War II (see Table 6.2), one is left with a clearer sense of the convergence that has occurred in relation to basic access to education in the region relative to other key high income countries.[6] Over the half century between 1870 and 1930, during the time of colonial education in Africa, levels of primary school across the

---

[6]Some caution needs to be taken in directly comparing enrolment patterns in the 1870 to 1930 period to those in the 1990 to 2016 interval, especially because of the different types of enrolment measures used. If gross rather than net enrolment ratios are used for recent trends, the impression of convergence is even more apparent.

region ranged from three to six times below that of countries such as the United States, the United Kingdom, and Germany. In the decades following independence, sub-Saharan African nations pursued major educational reforms and major initiatives to promote education, which yielded remarkable results. Some concern has, however, been expressed about the fact that primary enrolment has remained relatively unchanged since 2008 (rising only from 74 to 78% between 2008 and 2016). This finding is partly attributable to population growth, which has seen the numbers of primary and lower secondary school age children increase by around a third since 2000 and the out-of-school population in the region remain constant in a narrow range between 35 and 37 million children since the mid-2000s.

Although the share of primary school-age children out of school fell from 40 to 21% between 2000 and 2017, corresponding to a reduction from 44 to 37 million children, the slowdown in momentum in getting such children to school is worrisome because estimates suggest that half of these children will never receive any formal education. Nigeria, Sudan, Ethiopia, Tanzania, South Sudan, Niger, Kenya and Mali each have more than a million out-of-school children.

The abolition of school fees in accordance with the Dakar Framework has been instrumental in bolstering enrolment in certain contexts. For instance, when Burundi abolished school fees in 2005, the effect was an increase in net primary enrolment from 54% in 2004 to 74% in 2006; by 2017, the figure had risen to an impressive 97% (UNESCO 2014; World Bank 2020).

Slightly over half of the sub-Saharan African countries that had enrolment ratios below 80% in 2000 were still in the same position in 2016, placing them among the countries furthest from achieving universal primary enrolment. The countries are Burkina Faso, Central African Republic, Chad, Djibouti, Equatorial Guinea, Eritrea, the Gambia, Guinea, Liberia, Mali, Mauritania, Niger, Senegal and Sudan. However, other countries in the subcontinent exhibit encouraging signs of progress, and nine countries that had primary enrolment levels below the 80% threshold in 2000 managed to achieve this milestone by 2016. Most dramatic is the case of Burundi, where enrolment rose from 42 to 97% over the period, while in Ethiopia the enrolment figure increased from 40 to 85%. Even in cases where the 80% primary enrolment level was not reached, some countries still managed impressive gains, with Burkina Faso, Niger and Guinea improving more than 30 percentage points.

6.3.2 Quality Education and Learning Outcomes

With the adoption of the Sustainable Development Goals, the educational emphasis has begun to focus more substantively on issues of quality learning outcomes rather than just school enrolment. This is crucial in ensuring that opportunities for upward socioeconomic mobility are realised in coming decades, especially among poorer nations. The priority is for policymakers to 'ensure inclusive and equitable quality education and promote lifelong learning opportunities for all'. The status quo is nonetheless worrying, with large shares of children and adolescents falling short of

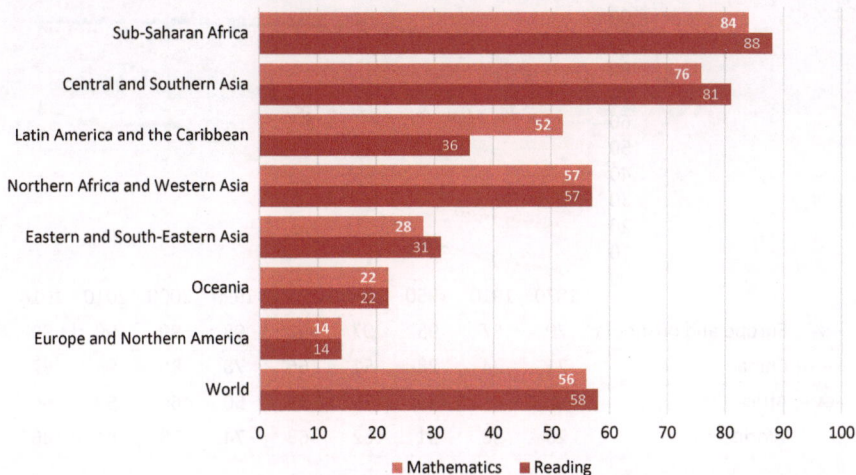

Fig. 6.3 Critical improvements needed in relation to quality learning outcomes. Percentage of children and adolescents *not* achieving minimum level of proficiency in reading and mathematics, 2015 (%) (UNECSO 2017, p. 7, based on UIS UNESCO MPL data)

minimum proficiency standards in respect of reading and mathematics. In 2015, 88% of children of primary and lower secondary school age were not suitably proficient in reading, while 84% failed to achieve the minimum required level of proficiency in mathematics (Fig. 6.3). This will require a big policy push in the coming ten to fifteen years in relation to promoting basic literacy and numeracy among young Africans if the region is to improve the skills base of the economically active population and strategically position itself to take advantage of the rapid technological advancements that are beginning to reshape the character of employment.

Literacy is deemed a fundamental human right and the basis for addressing deprivation and for promoting societal participation. The extension of access to primary education to sizable shares of the population in African countries since independence has brought about general advances in the ability to read and write. Between 1870 and 1910, less than a tenth of African citizens were literate, a figure that rose to a mere 15% by 1950. This figure doubled to 29% over the next 20 years and doubled again to 60% by 2000. Progress has been more modest on aggregate since 2000, rising a few percentage points to 64% by 2016. Although literacy in sub-Saharan Africa still lags behind that of other regions, we again see that disparities in literacy have narrowed significantly (Fig. 6.4). The literacy rate in Africa was 19 times lower than that of Europe and its offshoots in 1870, around six times lower in 1950, and only one-and-a-half times lower by the turn of the century.

Despite overall improvement in the adult literacy rate in sub-Saharan Africa since 1990, this period has also been characterised by growth in the absolute number of illiterate persons aged 15 years and older, rising 55% between 1990 and 2016 (from 127.8 to 198.3 million) due primarily to continuing population growth. In 2016, around one in four (26.4%) of the world's illiterate adults were found in the region.

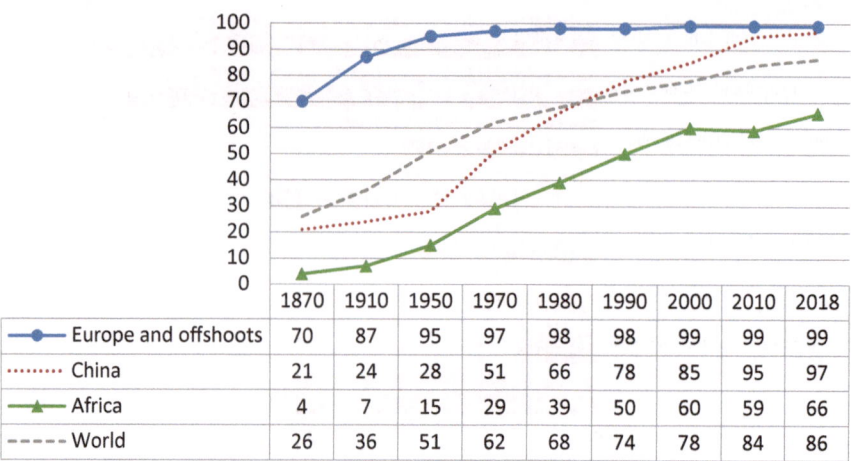

Fig. 6.4 Substantive gains in literacy, but regional, gender and quality concerns remain. Average adult literacy rates, 1870–2016 (%) (data from Morrison and Murtin 2005; World Bank 2020)

Close to half of the region's illiterate are concentrated in three countries—Nigeria, Ethiopia, and the Democratic Republic of Congo. Furthermore, low literacy rates (below 50%) are still found in sixteen countries, most of which are in West Africa (Fig. 6.5), with less than a third of adults literate in Chad, South Sudan, Niger, Guinea, and Sierra Leone.

Female illiteracy in sub-Saharan Africa is a particular challenge, and around three fifths of illiterate persons in the region are women. In 15 of the 46 countries (33%) in the region with available data, the female literacy rate falls below the 50% threshold (Fig. 6.6). The situation in Chad, Guinea, Mali, Central African Republic and South

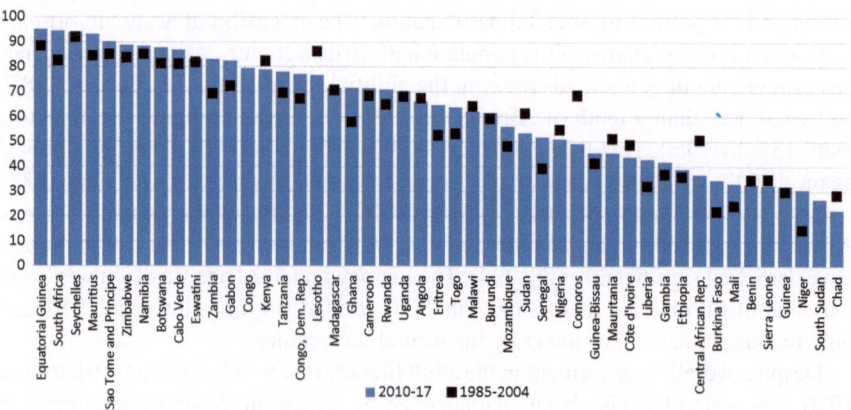

Fig. 6.5 A sizeable disparity exists in levels of adult literacy across sub-Saharan Africa. Adult literacy rate, population 15+ years, both sexes (%) (data from UNESCO UIS 2019)

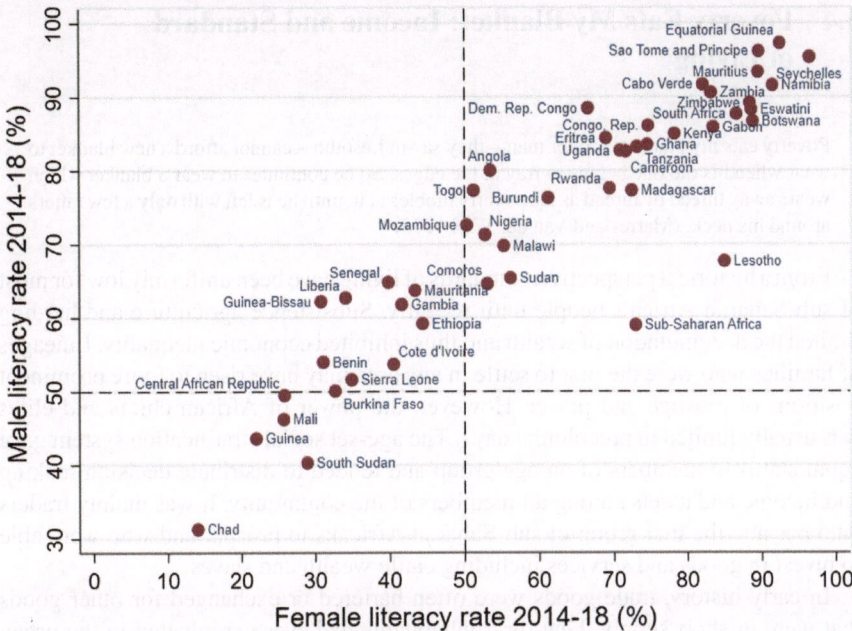

Fig. 6.6 Gender gaps in adult literacy persist across sub-Saharan Africa. Male and female literacy rates in sub-Saharan Africa, population 15+ years, 2013–18 (%) (data from UNESCO UIS 2019)

Sudan is more alarming: The female literacy rate does not even exceed 30%, and the literacy rate among men is approximately double that of women in all countries excepting South Sudan. The prospects of a rapid change in this scenario are unlikely, given that the same patterns are reflected among young women aged 15 to 24 years. Young women in half of the 15 countries exhibit literacy levels below 50% and below 60% in a further four cases, with less than a quarter able to read and write in the four lowest ranked countries. A threat to female literacy gains in northeast Nigeria is the militant Islamist movement of Boko Haram (*Western education is forbidden*) that abducted women and kidnapped 276 schoolgirls in 2014. In some of the northern states of Nigeria, less than 5% of women can read and write.

Therefore, despite appreciable generational gains among women in countries such as Sierra Leone, Ethiopia and Senegal, efforts to further bolster literacy and bring greater gender parity in literacy levels will take at least another generation to materialise in sub-regions such as West Africa that are presently lagging behind.

6.4 Poverty Eats My Blanket: Income and Standard of Living

Poverty eats my blanket. A poor man—they say in Lesotho—cannot afford a new blanket to wear when his old one begins to fray at the edges. So he continues to wear a blanket which wears away thread by thread as his poverty nibbles at it, until he is left with only a few tatters around his neck. (Marres and Van der Wiel 1975)

From a historical perspective, standards of living have been uniformly low for most of sub-Saharan Africa's people until recently. Subsistence agriculture and herding limited the accumulation of wealth and thus inhibited economic inequality. Lineages of families who were the first to settle in any area may have risen to more prominent positions of prestige and power. However, the power of African chiefs and elites was usually limited in precolonial days. The age-set social stratification system gave equal status to members of an age group and tended to distribute decision making and income and assets among all members of the community. It was mainly traders who became the first group of sub-Saharan Africans to prosper and who were able to invest in goods and services including cattle wealth and slaves.

In early history, trade goods were often bartered or exchanged for other goods that were in short supply. Few rural inhabitants had ever participated in the urban cash economy until the hut tax was introduced during the colonial period to ensure a regular supply of labour for the gold and diamond mines of southern Africa and for farms in the highlands of East Africa in the nineteenth and twentieth centuries. The hut tax, which had to be paid in cash, forced men to leave their homes to seek work in the mines or on plantations for little pay. In southern Africa, the migrant labour system, which divided families for most of the year but provided a source of cash income, became a way of life for a large sector of the population. Former herders and agriculturalists turned migrant workers sent remittances to their families in the rural areas and invested any savings in cattle. In recent decades, the situation in most of sub-Saharan Africa has changed dramatically. Participation in the wage economy has increased rapidly since independence. In parallel, living standards have risen as more people have moved to urban centres to find work in industry, manufacturing, and services. However, expectations of improved living standards have also increased for citizens in Africa's fledgling democracies. Large pockets of poverty still exist where people live below the subsistence minimum in informal urban settlements and rural areas.

6.4.1 Social Welfare in the Twenty-First Century—'My Family Eat This Money Too.'[7]

Large numbers of sub-Saharan people were left behind in the new scramble for wealth during the 1980s and 1990s that enriched ruling elites and their cronies (Meredith 2014). Rapid urbanisation has put enormous pressure on traditional ways of coping with adversity. The kinship system of mutual aid and support is overstretched, particularly when falling back on subsistence agriculture as a lifeline is no longer an option. It has been an embarrassment for independent Africa to have to rely regularly on external aid to feed its starving people in times of famine or civil war. In the new millennium, sub-Saharan countries are attempting to look after their poor and vulnerable themselves. Historically, South Africa took the lead in providing social protection for the new white poor who were displaced after the brutal South Africa War (1899–1902). South Africa's social pension, an unconditional cash transfer to impoverished whites first introduced in 1928, was gradually extended to black pensioners and disabled people. The amounts paid out to beneficiaries were equalised in 1993, on the eve of the country's transition to democracy. A new child support grant was introduced during Nelson Mandela's first years as president of the new democracy (1994–1999). Social pensions and cash grants currently reach approximately one third of the South African population. Namibia introduced its social pension in 1949 and Mauritius followed suit in 1958. By 2010, nine sub-Saharan states were paying old-age and disability pensions and 20 were providing some form of social assistance to the poor and vulnerable (Barrientos and Nino-Zarazua 2010). In the 2010s there has been a focus on cash transfer programmes in approximately ten countries, with a concentration in Eastern and southern Africa (Handa et al. 2018). Assistance comes in different forms, such as cash grants to poor and child-headed AIDS households, pensions for the aged and disabled, and work guarantees or public works programmes for the unemployed. In some cases, cash transfers are tied to the conditions that infants be vaccinated and school-age children be enrolled in school, resulting in improved child nutrition and survival rates as well as the alleviation of poverty. In line with Africa's traditional mutual support system, pension-sharing is widespread, and cash grants often support whole families.

6.4.2 Poles Apart: Income Divergence and Quality of Life

In 1997, Harvard economist Lant Pritchett published an influential study entitled 'Divergence, big time,' which outlined how advanced capitalist nations experienced rapid long-run growth in per capita income between 1870 and 1990 while poorer, developing countries exhibited stagnating economic performance over this period (Pritchett 1997). The effect of these patterns of change was a mounting divergence

---

[7]A reference to the sharing of welfare grants in multi-generational African families (Møller and Sotshongaye 1996).

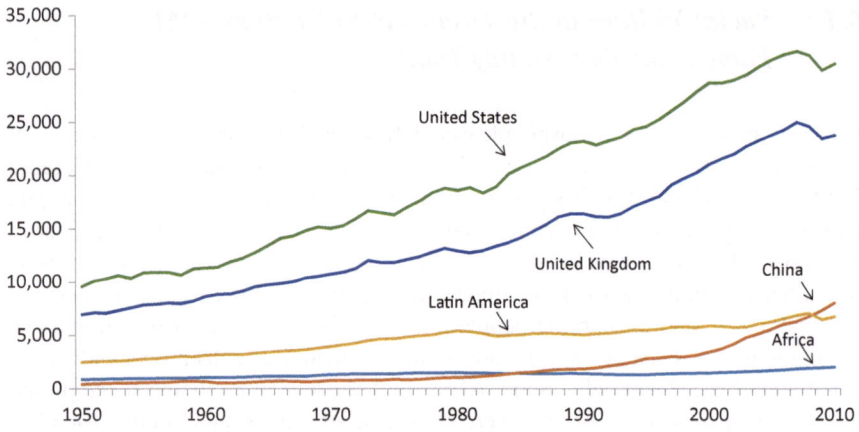

Fig. 6.7 Big divergence in income growth between sub-Saharan Africa and other world regions, though some signs of progress since 2000. Real GDP per person in select countries and continents (in 1990 dollars), 1950–2010 (Bolt and Van Zanden 2013—Maddison project database)

prior to the end of World War II and limited signs of convergence in recent decades, despite the rise of China and India (Fig. 6.7). Going back to the beginning of the second millennium (1000 CE), the level of estimated gross domestic product per capita (in 1990 international $) in both Africa and Western Europe was indistinguishable at around $400 per person. By the eve of the African era of independence in 1950, Western Europe was five times richer than Africa. Jumping ahead another half-century, we find that the gap has widened immeasurably, with average income in Western Europe thirteen times that of Africa. Recent growth in Africa closed the relative gap to a 10-fold difference by 2010, but the overarching pattern remains.

Africa did exhibit modest growth in per capita incomes between 1820 and 1980, increasing threefold over this period but stagnating over the next two decades, before slowly improving after the turn of the millennium. Even if one compares African income growth with that of other developing countries such as Brazil, China, and India, it is apparent that the region has tended to lag behind (Bolt and Van Zanden 2013).

Within and between countries in the region, economic inequality and impoverishment remain salient development challenges. Figure 6.8 presents the range of Gini coefficients for 46 sub-Saharan African countries with available data around year 2010. The inequality measures have been ranked from the least unequal (São Tomé and Príncipe, 30.8; Mali, 33.0 and Mauritania, 33.7) to the most unequal economy (South Africa, 63.0). None of the countries have coefficients below 30; four have values exceeding 55, whereas fifteen of the 46 countries fall below the developing country mean of 39.8. The graph also highlights the region's most populated nations, showing that South Africa has exceptionally high inequality levels (the highest globally); Nigeria and the Democratic Republic of Congo lie in more intermediate positions; and Tanzania and Ethiopia exhibit relatively low levels on

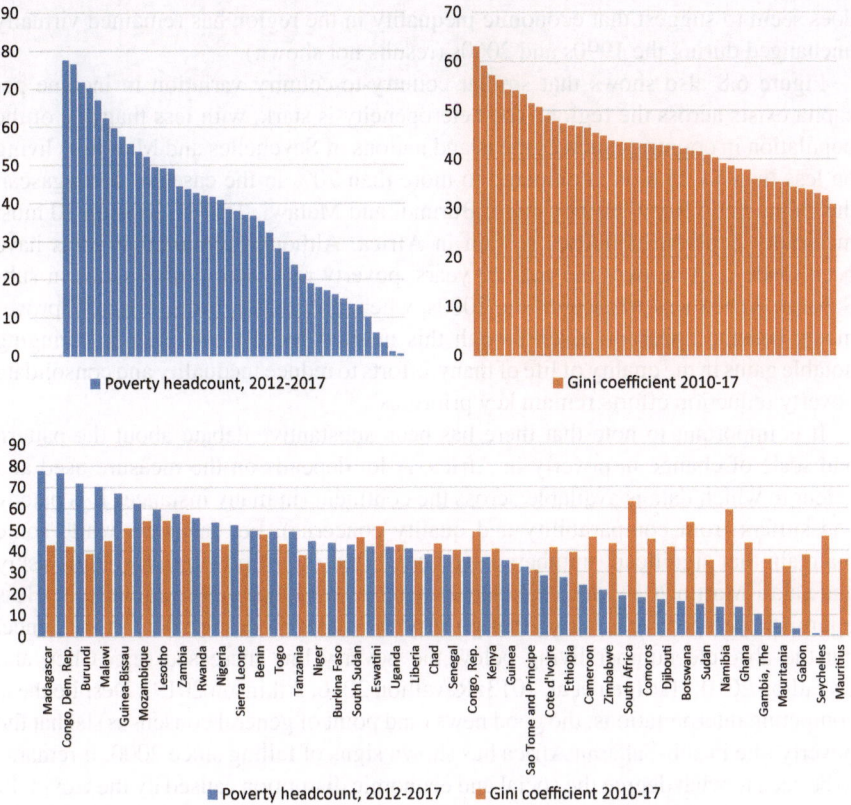

Fig. 6.8 Considerable polarisation within the sub-Saharan Africa region in respect of poverty and inequality levels. Gini index for the distribution of household consumption per capita in sub-Saharan Africa, 2010–17. The Gini index measures the extent to which the distribution of income (or, in some cases, consumption expenditure) among individuals or households within an economy deviates from a perfectly equal distribution. A Gini index of 0 represents perfect equality, while an index of 100 implies perfect inequality. Poverty headcount ratio in sub-Saharan African countries, 2012–17. Poverty computed over the distribution of consumption/income per capita with the purchasing power parity-adjusted $1.25-a-day line. The two graphs in the top panel display the spread in country poverty and inequality values, ranked from highest to lowest. The graph is bottom panel displays the poverty and inequality values for each country, with countries sorted in descending order by their poverty headcount ratios (Data from the World Bank 2019). Four countries had Gini index values but no poverty headcount estimates, and are not displayed in the bottom panel. The countries and corresponding Gini values are the Central African Republic (56.2), Cabo Verde (47.2), Angola (42.7) and Mali (33.0)

inequality. The spread of Gini coefficient values across the region is considerable, the largest dispersion of any of the world's regions, although almost all highly unequal societies with Gini coefficients above 50 are located on the continent (Alvaredo and Gasparini 2015). Although constrained by the availability of data, the evidence does seem to suggest that economic inequality in the region has remained virtually unchanged during the 1990s and 2000s (results not shown).

Figure 6.8 also shows that similar country-to-country variation in income per capita exists across the region. The heterogeneity is stark, with less than 1% of the population in countries such as the island nations of Seychelles and Mauritius living on less than $1.25 a day compared to more than 70% in the cases of Madagascar, the Democratic Republic of Congo, Burundi and Malawi. The world's top 10 most materially deprived countries remain in Africa. Although remarkable gains have been made in Asia over the past 30 years, poverty reduction performance in sub-Saharan Africa was weak until the 2000s, when discernible, broad-based improvements became apparent. Even though this news is indeed encouraging, bringing notable gains in the quality of life of many, efforts to reduce inequality and consolidate poverty reduction efforts remain key priorities.

It is important to note that there has been substantive debate about the pattern and scale of change in poverty in Africa. A lot depends on the measure used and extent to which data is available across the continent (in many instances it is patchy and suffers from comparability and quality concerns). For instance, while some maintain that significant numbers have been lifted out of poverty (e.g. Pinkovskiy and Sala-i-Martin 2014) other scholars have tended to adopt a more circumspect, less optimistic perspective, arguing that poverty showed a modest decline in incidence, but the absolute number living below the poverty line increased (e.g. Chen and Ravallion 2010; Harttgen et al. 2013; Ravallion 2016; Atkinson 2019). Despite these competing interpretations, the good news (and point of general consensus) is that the poverty rate in sub-Saharan Africa has shown signs of falling since 2000. It remains to be seen to what degree the social and economic disruption caused by the Covid-19 pandemic, which spread rapidly across the globe since its outbreak in late 2019, will erode these gains.

6.5 Social Progress in Review

Since the wave of independence in Africa more than half a century ago, interest has been growing in monitoring societal progress to determine how well countries are faring relative to the vision for reform and long-term development that was articulated. Indicators and data abound with which to provide an overarching sense of the state of social progress in sub-Saharan Africa toward ensuring well-being and quality of life for its diverse population. One of the most comprehensive review measures of objective well-being is the Index of Social Progress—or the WISP as its statistically weighted version is known—developed by Richard Estes (see Estes 2015, and Chapter 6.23 in Sirgy et al. 2017, pp. 144–149). The index consists of 10 sub-indices encompassing 41 individual social indicators. The aim of such a composite measure is to encompass all major aspects of societal economic development including educational status, health, gender equality, social welfare nets, and cultural diversity. The use of such an index, which has been collected since 1970, allows the researcher to

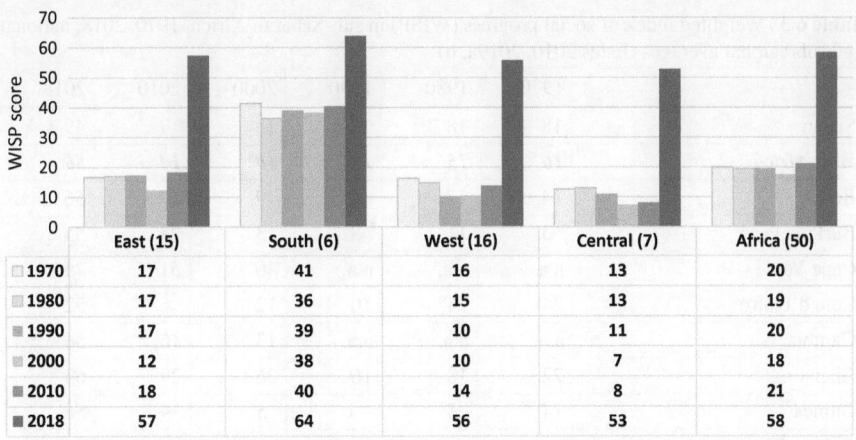

	East (15)	South (6)	West (16)	Central (7)	Africa (50)
1970	17	41	16	13	20
1980	17	36	15	13	19
1990	17	39	10	11	20
2000	12	38	10	7	18
2010	18	40	14	8	21
2018	57	64	56	53	58

Fig. 6.9 Large gains in social progress in Africa and its sub-regions since 2000 compared with preceding decades. Average weighted index of social progress (WISP) scores by sub-regions of sub-Saharan Africa, and the continent 1970-2018. The African average includes the WISP scores for six North African countries. Figures in brackets represent number of countries included in calculating the average WISP scores (Estes 2019a, b)

measure the capacity of nations to provide for the basic social and material needs for their citizens.

A review of a half century of progress using the WISP data reveals that sub-Saharan Africa has consistently ranked the least socially developed world region over the 1970 to 2020 period, reflecting the appreciable development challenges facing many individual nations. Social progress for much of the continent in fact declined between 1970 and 1980 and only began to rebound after 2000. The recovery experienced during the 2000s was profound enough for Estes (2012a, p. 439) to remark that 'Africa's recent social gains [in the last 10 years] nonetheless are impressive.' More dramatic improvements were achieved since 2010, marking a distinct departure from the stagnation of previous decades (Fig. 6.9). These changes have occurred among some of the more socially disadvantaged African nations, driven in part by the successes of the resolute commitments to societal well-being made by governments and a range of domestic and international non-state actors in pursuit of the Millennium Development Goals and the vision of a better life enshrined in national development plans.

In 2018, a majority of sub-Saharan African countries had WISP scores well below the world average of 73 (Table 6.3), ranging from a low of 41 in the Central African Republic to a high of 75 in Mauritius. To convey the scale of progress since 2010, the corresponding spread of values in 2010 was −11 through to 60, signifying considerable advances among poorer, lowest ranked nations in the region, together with smaller but clear gains among the top ranked nations. Significant sub-regional differences in social progress have historically existed in sub-Saharan Africa, though a relative convergence in sub-regional WISP scores has taken place since 2010 (Fig. 6.9).

Table 6.3 Weighted index of social progress (WISP) in sub-Saharan Africa, 1970–2018, national and subregional averages (Estes 2010, 2019a, b)

	1970	1980	1990	2000	2010	2018
Sudan	18	18	13	13	7	49
West Africa	*16*	*15*	*10*	*10*	*14*	*56*
Benin	14	17	8	19	19	56
Burkina Faso	3	11	8	3	23	55
Cape Verde	n.a.	n.a.	n.a.	40	51	75
Côte d'Ivoire	24	24	16	12	6	52
Gambia	n.a.	n.a.	n.a.	13	16	56
Ghana	22	18	16	26	29	63
Guinea	14	5	−1	5	9	56
Guinea-Bissau	n.a.	n.a.	n.a.	−4	−3	56
Liberia	24	20	12	−6	−11	56
Mali	13	8	4	13	16	52
Mauritania	23	10	13	12	20	58
Niger	6	8	3	−4	9	50
Nigeria	6	26	11	14	4	48
Senegal	27	18	24	19	22	58
Sierra Leone	25	12	2	−10	0	48
Togo	9	13	17	14	11	55
East Africa	*17*	*17*	*17*	*12*	*18*	*57*
Burundi	5	8	18	3	10	58
Comoros	n.a.	n.a.	n.a.	22	20	65
Djibouti	n.a.	n.a.	n.a.	12	14	59
Eritrea	n.a.	n.a.	n.a.	−15	−7	55
Ethiopia	4	−10	−10	−12	15	51
Kenya	27	26	24	12	24	61
Madagascar	30	31	23	19	24	59
Malawi	11	4	13	9	27	57
Mauritius	n.a.	56	67	61	60	75
Mozambique	n.a.	2	−4	4	11	55
Rwanda	17	18	21	19	24	59
Seychelles	n.a.	n.a.	n.a.	n.a.	n.a.	n.a.
Somalia	19	10	1	1	−4	48
South Sudan	n.a.	n.a.	n.a.	n.a.	n.a.	n.a.
Tanzania	12	20	15	20	22	54
Uganda	14	14	12	7	12	49

(continued)

Table 6.3 (continued)

	1970	1980	1990	2000	2010	2018
Zambia	27	25	28	22	21	54
Central Africa	*13*	*13*	*11*	*7*	*8*	*53*
Angola	n.a.	5	−3	−10	−4	52
Cameroon	23	22	21	15	14	54
Central African Rep.	10	12	9	2	3	41
Chad	3	−4	−2	−4	−7	47
Congo	n.a.	22	27	22	17	59
Congo, Dem. Rep.	15	21	14	−2	2	54
Equatorial Guinea	n.a.	n.a.	n.a.	n.a.	n.a.	n.a.
Gabon	n.a.	n.a.	n.a.	28	30	62
São Tomé and Príncipe	n.a.	n.a.	n.a.	n.a.	n.a.	n.a.
Southern Africa	*41*	*36*	*39*	*38*	*40*	*64*
Botswana	n.a.	n.a.	n.a.	44	50	70
Lesotho	n.a.	36	36	36	46	64
Namibia	n.a.	n.a.	n.a.	36	46	67
South Africa	51	43	44	52	51	74
Eswatini	n.a.	n.a.	n.a.	37	33	58
Zimbabwe	32	29	37	24	23	51
Africa (incl. North Africa)	*20*	*19*	*20*	*18*	*21*	*58*

Bold italics represents subregional averages

By 2018, southern Africa (64) had only slightly higher average WISP scores than East Africa (57), West Africa (56), and Central Africa (53). These values represent a significant improvement over the last 10 years. The difference in average WISP score between the highest ranked sub-region (southern Africa) and the other three sub-regions narrowed by at least two-thirds between 2010 and 2018.

Recent conflicts in sub-Saharan Africa, particularly civil conflict, made it impossible for millions of Africans to pursue happiness and improve the quality of their lives. In a notable study on failing states, Estes (2012b, p. 577) found that social development 'requires peace, or at least minimum levels of positive social, political, and economic stability.' Indeed, Estes further argued that a failing state will have a negative impact on the quality of life in neighbouring states. As the results show, those states that have become entrenched in civil conflict in the recent past tended to have low social development.

Civil strife was particularly common to West Africa during the 1990s and 2000s. A majority of West African countries experienced a decline in their WISP scores between 1970 and 2000, and the average for the sub-region fell from 16 in 1970 to 10 in 2000, although some progress was made between 2000 and 2010 when the WISP score increased to 14, followed by the rapid increase to 56 by 2018.

Those Western African countries (Chad, Sierra Leone, Liberia, and Côte d'Ivoire) directly involved in civil war experienced extreme deteriorations in social progress during the 2000s, though significant improvements were experienced after 2010. Much of central Africa is also recovering from civil wars that occurred in the 1990s and 2000s, and the sub-region had a low WISP average of 8 in 2010, with the Democratic Republic of the Congo, the Central African Republic, and Angola scoring below this sub-regional average. Without exception, each of these countries recorded unprecedented upswings in social progress during the 2010s.

Most countries in sub-Saharan Africa that achieved greater political stability also experienced increased social development. Ethiopia, for instance, made significant improvements in social development, albeit from a low base. The country's WISP score increased from -12 in 2000 to 15 in 2010. This increase was caused primarily by the end of the prolonged civil disorder of the authoritarian Mengistu era in 1994 and the constitutional and agricultural reforms of the democratic Meles era. By 2018, the country's WISP score was 51. However, not all transitions to democracy coincided with increases in social progress. Nigeria, plagued by disputed elections since the transition from military rule in 1999, experienced a reversal of social development, declining from 26 in 1980 to 4 in 2010. Fortunately, there has been a process of recovery and achievement during the 2010s, with the WISP score increasing to 48 in 2018.

The case of Nigeria demonstrates that even when civil war is avoided, other factors can reverse social development. Estes (2010) suggested that other contributing factors are the rapid spread of infectious and communicable diseases (such as HIV/AIDS), the underinvestment and, in some cases, declining investment in health, education, and social welfare by some countries as well as an inability to overcome serious infrastructure limitations, particularly within the region's landlocked states. Zimbabwe, for example, suffered considerable economic (and subsequent social) decline following a poorly managed land reform programme that destroyed the country's leading export-producing agricultural sector. As a result, Zimbabwe was the only country in southern Africa to suffer a substantial decline in its WISP score (falling from a high of 37 in 1990 to 23 in 2010). Like other countries in the region, the 2010s brought definite advances, with the WISP score rising to 51 by 2018. The question remains whether drought, food insecurity, rampant inflation, power cuts and growing discontent with President Emmerson Mnangagwa will erode this progress in coming years.

6.5.1   Subjective Well-Being

With the exception of South Africa, and to a lesser degree Nigeria, research into subjective well-being in sub-Saharan Africa has tended to trail more objective analysis of quality of life during the post-independence period. Following influential cross-national undertakings of the 1960s and 1970s, progress in surveying subjective well-being in Africa proceeded at a rather slow pace until the late 1990s and early

2000s. The World Values Survey series, established in 1981, has measured subjective well-being on a bidecennial basis using a single-item overall life satisfaction question based on a 10-point scale. Only Nigeria and South Africa were included in the survey during the first three waves of the survey, though this increased to nine countries in Wave 5 (2005–2007). The latest rounds of interviewing (Wave 6 from 2010–2014 and Wave 7 from 2017–2020) focused on dramatically increasing sub-Saharan African participation. However, Wave 6 eventually only managed to include five countries from the region, and by mid-2020 only five countries had again completed surveying for Wave 7. The economic consequences of the Covid-19 pandemic are likely to damper the prospects of significant regional expansion.

Other global survey series that have gained prominence since the end of the twentieth century, such as the Gallup World Poll and the Pew Global Attitudes Surveys, are characterised by a greater representation of African countries, but relatively small sample sizes, sampling problems, and inconsistent country participation are some of the limitations experienced to date. Similarly, at the regional level, the Afrobarometer survey series, which was established in the late 1990s, comprised 12 countries as part of its first wave (1999–2001) and managed to expand to at least 22 nations by its fifth round (2011–2013), and to around 35 countries in the sixth and seventh rounds (2014–2015 and 2016–2018 respectively). The series, however, does not contain a direct measure of subjective well-being, though analysts have attempted to overcome this by examining proxy measures such as lived poverty or optimism (Mattes 2008). Although these developments have resulted in significant advances in our understanding of social attitudes in Africa and the extent to which this approximates or diverges from other countries and regions, there remains much room for building on this initial engagement.

6.5.2 Overall Life Satisfaction

Data on overall life satisfaction for sub-Saharan Africa are generally less readily available than other forms of happiness measures, though the World Database of Happiness has compiled available empirical evidence for 41 sub-Saharan African nations, with a coverage that focuses predominantly on the period 2000 to 2019. We find an appreciable spread in national averages. Based on average data collected during the 2000s, the highest rating was observed in Malawi, which at 6.2, was nearly two-and-a-half times higher than the lowest rating of 2.6 in Togo (Table 6.4). Globally, Togo was the lowest ranked of 149 nations in the database, whereas Costa Rica had the highest score (8.5). Another finding from this period was that relatively few countries in the sub-Saharan region recorded mean scores above the scale midpoint (5.0). Only Malawi, South Africa, Nigeria, Djibouti, Chad, and Namibia fell into this category. The overall average level of satisfaction for the set of sub-Saharan African countries with available data was 4.4, which was below that of North Africa (5.6) and the world average (5.9).

Table 6.4 Average life satisfaction in sub-Saharan African countries, 2000–2009 and 2010–2018 compared (mean on a 0–10 scale, ranked from highest to lowest based on 2010–2019 scores) (Veenhoven n.d.)

	Satisfaction with life, average 2000–09	Satisfaction with life, average 2010–18	Change between the two decades
Rwanda	4.3	6.1	1.8
South Africa	5.8	6.0	0.2
Mauritius	–	5.9	–
Nigeria	5.7	5.8	0.1
Ghana	5.2	5.7	0.5
Somalia	–	5.4	–
Mozambique	3.8	5.3	1.5
Zimbabwe	3.0	5.3	2.3
Namibia	5.2	5.2	0.0
Eswatini	–	5.2	–
Zambia	5.0	5.2	0.2
Cameroon	3.9	4.8	0.9
Sierra Leone	3.5	4.8	1.3
Ethiopia	4.2	4.7	0.5
Mauritania	4.9	4.7	−0.2
Angola	4.3	4.6	0.3
Congo, Dem. Rep.	4.4	4.6	0.2
Djibouti	5.7	4.6	−1.1
Kenya	3.7	4.6	0.9
Lesotho	–	4.6	–
Sudan	5.0	4.6	−0.4
Congo (Brazzaville)	3.7	4.5	0.8
Gabon	–	4.5	–
Liberia	4.3	4.5	0.2
Mali	4.7	4.3	−0.4
Senegal	4.5	4.3	−0.2
Uganda	4.8	4.3	−0.5
Burkina Faso	4.4	4.2	−0.2
Malawi	6.2	4.2	−2.0
Niger	3.8	4.2	0.4
Chad	5.4	4.1	−1.3
Côte d'Ivoire	4.4	4.1	−0.3
Guinea	4.5	4.1	−0.4

(continued)

Table 6.4 (continued)

	Satisfaction with life, average 2000–09	Satisfaction with life, average 2010–18	Change between the two decades
Botswana	4.7	4.0	−0.7
Comoros	–	4.0	–
Madagascar	3.7	3.9	0.2
Burundi	2.9	3.8	0.9
Benin	3.0	3.7	0.7
Tanzania	2.8	3.7	0.9
Central African Republic	4.6	3.4	−1.2
South Sudan	–	3.4	–
Togo	2.6	3.4	0.8

The happiness scores across the sub-continent for the 2010 to 2018 period follow a similar tendency, arguably with a modest improvement. The range in scores varies from a high in Rwanda (6.1), which is 1.8 times higher than the lowest recorded mean level of happiness in Togo and South Sudan (both 3.4). While the number of countries with average happiness levels above the scale midpoint has increased to eleven, three-quarters of countries fall below. The regional average of 4.6, while marginally higher than that of the 2000s, still remains lower than North Africa (5.3) and the global average of 5.9 for the 162 countries with available data.

6.5.3 Cantril Ladder of Life Scale

The most commonly used measure of happiness in the region asks respondents to rate their life on an 11-step Cantril ladder scale that ranges from what they perceive to be the worst possible life (0) to the best possible life imaginable (10). In Fig. 6.10 we present ranked averages for 43 sub-Saharan African countries based on 2017/18 data from the Gallup World Poll, building on earlier regional analysis (Roberts et al. 2015). In terms of the pattern of responses within the region, we again found a considerable degree of variation in contentment, ranging from a low of 2.8 in South Sudan to a high of 5.9 in Mauritius. Only Mauritius, Angola, Ghana, Congo (Brazzaville), Somalia, Nigeria and Cameroon had a mean score exceeding the midpoint of the scale, with 9 countries recording an average score that was below four on the 0 to 10 scale. A simple mean score was calculated for all the countries as well as for each of the four sub-regions. The lowest score was found in eastern Africa (4.12), followed by southern Africa (4.30), with a moderately higher average in western and central Africa (4.76 and 4.80 respectively). Relative to 2011/12, there has been a slight gain

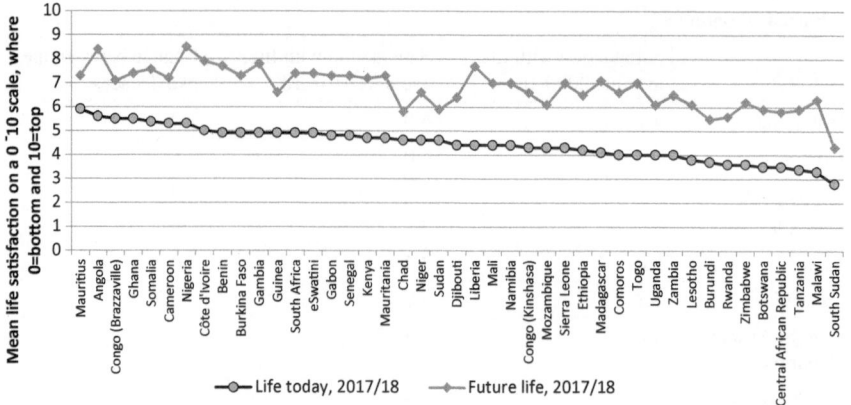

Fig. 6.10 A consistently optimistic outlook across Africa despite relatively low levels of content-ment with life at present in many nations. Average contentment for select sub-Saharan African countries, ranked by current life ratings. Life today and Life in 5 years are measured using the Cantril ladder questions with respondents asked to choose a rung on a 0–10 ladder. All countries use data from Gallup World Poll covering the 2017/18 period, with seven exceptions: Angola, Burundi, Comoros, Djibouti, Sudan and eSwatini are point estimates from 2011/12, while the esti-mates for Somalia are from 2015/16. All data are weighted so that the results are representative of the adult population in each country. Data supplied by Jay Loschky, Gallup regional research director for Africa

in present life evaluations in central and western Africa, and modest reversals in southern and eastern Africa.[8]

The Gallup data also include prospective evaluations, with the national averages displayed in Fig. 6.10. It is immediately apparent that considerable optimism exists among sub-Saharan African countries concerning life improvements in the medium term. Contentment in the region, based on simple all-country averages in 2017/18, is expected to rise from the present 4.5 to 6.8 over the 5-year interval, an increase of more than 50%. On the basis of these future evaluations, only one nation has an average score below the midpoint of the ladder (South Sudan) with 23 countries reporting a value of seven and above. It is interesting to note that substantive anticipated gains in contentment with life can even be found among citizens living in even some of the harshest socio-political contexts.

The South Sudan example is perhaps most telling. As with overall life satisfac-tion, the 2017/18 Gallup data indicate that the country possesses the lowest level of contentment worldwide. At the time of surveying, citizens of this landlocked Central-Eastern African nation were thoroughly discontent with life. After gaining inde-pendence from Sudan in mid-2011, following an agreement that ended the longest running civil war (21 years from 1983 to 2005), the country sadly became embroiled in another civil war between government and opposition forces that lasted from

---

[8]The mean score for life today in central Africa rose from 4.30 to 4.80, and from 4.08 to 4.76 in western Africa. Conversely, contentment with life decreased from 4.44 to 4.12 in eastern Africa and from 4.92 to 4.30 in southern Africa.

2013 to early 2020, killing an estimated 400,000 people and displacing a further 4 million. Famine, water scarcity, a high malaria burden, and widespread material deprivation contribute to some of the worst health indicators globally. Yet, despite this unimaginable suffering, the mean future rating on the ladder scale for South Sudanese is 4.3, which is 1.5 steps (54%) higher than the present evaluation. The future score ranks the lowest of the 43 sub-Saharan countries with data, but this is a significant hope for improved quality of life in a 5-year period. It is this 'happiness in hardship' (Veenhoven 2005) that strikes one in the comparative examination of happiness in the subcontinent: the remarkable resilience that is encountered in the face of considerable personal and societal adversity.

6.5.4 Positive Experiences Outweigh the Negative

The Gallup World Poll has also fielded a series of questions concerning the positive and negative feelings experienced by respondents on the day prior to interviewing. From the results, a positive experience index is constructed on the basis of the respondents' reported well-being yesterday with regard to feeling well-rested, being treated with respect all day, smiling or laughing a lot, learning or doing something interesting, experiencing enjoyment or love, feeling proud about something that they did, and expressing a general desire for more days like yesterday. Gallup also constructs a negative experience index on the basis of the reported experience of physical pain, worry, sadness, stress, anger, and depression. Examining such experiences rather than other types of evaluations of life, such as happiness, we find that the share reporting positive emotions exceeds the share with negative feelings for all 39 sub-Saharan African countries with available data in 2019 (Fig. 6.11). As such, all affect balance scores (positive experience index minus negative experience index) for these nations are positive, with a regional mean of +33.1, ranging from +1 in Central African Republic to +66 in Mauritius.

From a comparative perspective, the sub-Saharan Africa region has an average affect balance score (+33.1) that exceeds that found in South Asia (+17.8) and the Middle East and North Africa (+26.4), and is moderately below Europe and central Asia (+46.0). The highest affect balance scores are found in East Asia and the Pacific (+55.5), North America (+55.4) and in Latin America and the Caribbean (+50.7). Sub-Saharan Africa therefore has a higher average affect balance score than one might expect given the multiple social challenges that continue to beleaguer the subcontinent. This score, as in Latin America, is buoyed partly by a fairly high level of positive feelings reported among the region's population. Slightly over two fifths of the sub-Saharan African countries (17 out of 39) had a positive experience score exceeding 70, with the highest scores evident in Niger (82), Mauritius (81), South Africa (81), Senegal (79) and eSwatini (78), whereas only two African countries (Sierra Leone, 51, and Malawi, 54) were in the bottom 10 countries in terms of positive emotions worldwide. In addition, those regions of the world with the lowest rankings include countries that face lower than average positive affect

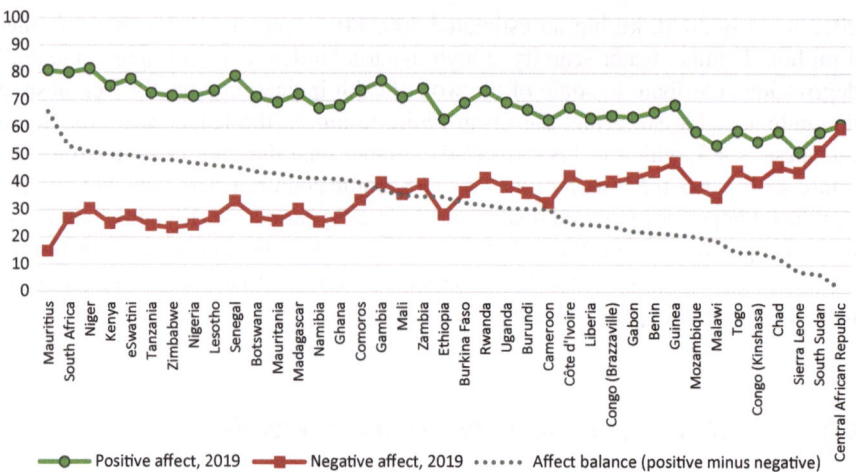

Fig. 6.11 Positive emotional experiences outweigh the negative across 39 sub-Saharan African countries in 2019, suggesting resilience despite hardship. Positive and negative experiences in sub-Saharan Africa in 2019, ranked by the size of the gap between the two indices. All data represented use Gallup World Poll 2019 data for Positive Experience Index and Negative Experience Index, with the following exceptions: 2018 estimates for Burundi, Gabon, and 2017 estimates for Central African Republic, Congo (Kinshasa), and South Sudan (Gallup 2019; Heliwell et al. 2020)

coupled with a high degree of negative emotion. This situation exists in nations such as Lebanon (−17),[9] Tunisia (+11) and Iran (+15) in the Middle East and North Africa; Afghanistan (−15), Bangladesh (+17) and Nepal (+18) in South Asia; and Turkey (+5) and Armenia (+13) in Europe and central Asia. Individuals living in the Central African Republic (+2), South Sudan (+7), Sierra Leone (+8), Chad (+13), Togo (+15) and Guinea (+21) are similarly predisposed toward experiencing a high level of negative emotion on a daily basis, and all six countries are in the top third of the negative emotion distribution. The resilience of sub-Saharan Africans to social and economic hardship is evident from the Positive and Negative Experience Index data.

6.6   Conclusion: Impressive Progress But Not Necessarily the African Miracle

This chapter examined the nature and extent of progress that has been made in meeting the basic needs of citizens across sub-Saharan Africa over recent decades. Taking

[9]Lebanon has the lowest affect balance score of 148 countries in the 2019 Gallup World Poll and is one of only two countries with a negative overall score (the other being Afghanistan). This result is attributable to a high level of negative affect (49) in contrast with an exceptionally low experience of positive emotion (32).

a longer perspective, it becomes apparent that, in spite of the pressing and appreciable challenges that remain in ensuring that such needs are effectively responded to, personal quality of life improved - substantive gains have in fact been achieved. Quality of physical health in the region has improved on aggregate. Greater life expectancy has been secured even among the poorest nations and among countries significantly affected by AIDS and other significant disease burdens, while maternal and child mortality rates have displayed improving tendencies. On the educational front, primary school enrolment rose appreciably in the 1990s and 2000s, followed by slower progress in the 2010s. A focus on quality learning outcomes (such as proficiency in reading and mathematics) is one of the next critical aspects warranting attention. In both health and education, these unprecedented developments have produced relative convergence between sub-Saharan Africa and higher income regions and nations, which is encouraging from a quality-of-life perspective.

A less sanguine picture emerges in terms of income. The same degree of convergence has not occurred and poverty, unemployment and inequality remain an inescapable part of the lived reality for millions across the continent (Kenny 2012). Despite success stories such as Botswana and Mauritius in the 1970s and 1980s, and countries such as Ethiopia and Rwanda from the 1990s onwards (Studwell 2019), many countries in sub-Saharan Africa continue to have extremely low real per capita incomes. On a more promising note, there have been important experiments in the field of social protection, with intensifying efforts to provide basic safety nets to the vulnerable and socially disadvantaged. Furthermore, the fact that the strides in non-income dimensions were attained despite the relative lack of substantive income growth further underscores the nature of the achievement. The resilience of Africans in the face of complex socio-economic difficulties is also striking. This is reflected in a consistently optimistic future outlook across county contexts despite fairly low levels of contentment with life at present, and with reported positive emotional experiences generally outweighing the negative.

The next chapter engages with the themes of democracy, good governance and well-being. The role of the state and, executive leadership in particular, is integral to any discussion of quality of life and well-being. It is an issue that has received much attention across sub-Saharan Africa, no more so than during the Covid-19 pandemic, where the quality of political leadership came to be regarded as a critical factor shaping the scale of health, economic and other effects and the trajectory of the post-pandemic society.

References

Alvaredo, F., & Gasparini, L. (2015). Recent trends in inequality and poverty in developing countries. In A. B. Atkinson & F. Bourguignon (Eds.), *Handbook of income distribution* (Vol. 2A, pp. 697–805). Oxford: North-Holland.

Atkinson, A. B. (2019). *Measuring poverty around the world*. Princeton, New Jersey: Princeton University Press.

Baker, A. (2019). Congo attacks raise fear of Ebola's spread. *TIME*, Vol. 193, No. 10, March 18, p. 10.

Bamford, C. (2019). Why Ebola is proving hard to beat in the DRC. *The Conversation*, December 18. https://theconversation.com/why-ebola-is-proving-hard-to-beat-in-the-drc-109017. Accessed June 14, 2019.

Barrientos, A., & Nino-Zarazua, M. (2010). *Effects of non-contributory social transfers in developing countries. A compendium.* Geneva: International Labour Office Social Security Department.

Benavot, A., & Riddle, P. (1988). The expansion of primary education, 1870–1940: Trends and issues. *Sociology of Education*, 191–210.

Bolt, J., & Van Zanden, J.L. (2013) *The first update of the Maddison Project: Re-estimating growth before 1820.* Maddison-Project Working Paper WP-4. Groningen, The Netherlands: The Groningen Growth and Development Centre, University of Groningen.

Boum, Y. (2020). The coping mechanisms the DRC is putting in place as it faces Ebola, measles and COVID-19. *The Conversation* 22 June. https://theconversation.com/the-coping-mechanisms-the-drc-is-putting-in-place-as-it-faces-ebola-measles-and-covid-19-140756.

Chen, S., & Ravallion, M. (2010). The developing world is poorer than we thought, but no less successful in the fight against poverty. *The Quarterly Journal of Economics, 125*(4), 1577–1625. https://doi.org/10.1162/qjec.2010.125.4.1577.

Estes, R. J. (2010). The world social situation: Development challenges at the outset of a new century. *Social Indicators Research, 98*, 363–402.

Estes, R. J. (2012a). Economies in transitions: Revisiting challenges in quality of life. In K. C. Land, A. C. Michalos, & M. J. Sirgy (Eds.), *Handbook of social indicators and quality of life research* (pp. 433–457). Dordrecht: Springer.

Estes, R. J. (2012b). "Failed" and "failing" states: Is quality of life possible? In K. C. Land, A. C. Michalos, & M. J. Sirgy (Eds.), *Handbook of social indicators and quality of life research* (pp. 555–580). Dordrecht: Springer.

Estes, R. J. (2015). Development trends among the world's socially least developed countries (SLDCs): Reasons for cautious optimism. In B. Spooner (Ed.), *Globalization in progress: Understanding and working with world urbanization* (pp. 23–70). Philadelphia: University of Pennsylvania Press.

Estes, R. J. (2019a). *Social indicators research series Vol. 78. The social progress of nations revisited, 1970–2020: 50 years of development challenges and accomplishments.* Cham, Switzerland: Springer.

Estes, R. J. (2019b). The social progress of nations revisited. *Social Indicators Research, 144*(2), 539–574.

Fallah, M. (2019a). How Africa's porous borders make it difficult to contain Ebola. *The Conversation*, 15 June. https://theconversation.com/how-africas-porous-borders-make-it-difficult-to-contain-ebola-118719.

Fallah, M. (2019b). Tshisekedi has taken over the DRC's Ebola response. How he can make a difference. *The Conversation*, 11 August. https://theconversation.com/tshisekedi-has-taken-over-the-drcs-ebola-response-how-he-can-make-a-difference-121595.

Gallup, (2019). *2019 Gallup global emotions report.* Washington, D. C.: Gallup.

Handa, S., Daidone, S., Peterman, A., Davis, B., Pereira, A., Palermo, T., et al. (2018). Myth-busting? Confronting six common perceptions about unconditional cash transfers as a poverty reduction strategy in Africa. *The World Bank Research Observer, 33*(2), 259–298.

Harttgen, K., Klasen, S., & Vollmer, S. (2013). An African growth miracle? Or: what do asset indices tell us about trends in economic performance? *Review of Income and Wealth, 59*, S37–S61.

Helliwell, J., Layard, R., Sachs, J., & De Neve, J. E. (2020). World happiness report 2020. *New York: Sustainable Development Solutions Network.* https://worldhappiness.report/ed/2020/.

Kenny, C. (2012). *Getting Better: Why global development is succeeding—and how we can improve the world even more.* New York: Basic Books.

Marres, P. J., & Van der Wiel, A. (1975). *Poverty eats my blanket. A poverty study: The case of Lesotho*. Maseru, Lesotho: Government of Lesotho.

Mattes, R. (2008). The material and political bases of lived poverty in Africa: Insights from the Afrobarometer. In V. Møller, D. Huschka, & A.C. Michalos (Eds.), *Social Indicators Research Series 33. Barometers of quality of life around the globe: How are we doing?* (pp. 161–185). Dordrecht: Springer.

Meredith, M. (2014). *The Fortunes of Africa: A 5,000-year history of wealth, greed and endeavour*. London: Simon & Schuster with Johannesburg/Cape Town: Jonathan Ball Publishers.

Møller, V., & Sotshongaye, A. (1996). 'My family eat this money too': Pension sharing and self-respect among Zulu grandmothers. *Southern African Journal of Gerontology 5*(2), 9–19. http://journal.ru.ac.za/index.php/sajog/article/view/97/76.

Ogunsola, F. (2015). *How Nigeria beat the Ebola virus in three months*. https://theconversation.com/how-nigeria-beat-the-ebola-virus-in-three-months-41372. Accessed June 14, 2019.

Pinkovskiy, M., & Sala-i-Martin, X. (2014). Africa is on time. *Journal of Economic Growth, 19*(3), 311–338.

Pritchett, L. (1997). Divergence, big time. *The Journal of Economic Perspectives, 11*(3), 3–17.

Ravallion, M. (2016). *The economics of poverty: History, measurement, and policy*. Oxford: Oxford University Press.

Reader, J. (1997). *Africa: A biography of the continent*. London: Hamish Hamilton.

Roberts, B. J., Magidimisha, H. H., & Møller, V. (2014). *Trying to take the lid off: Qualitative insights into the South African Tshivenda translation of the Personal Wellbeing Index*. Paper presented at the XII International Society for Quality of Life Studies (ISQOLS) Conference, Free University, Berlin, 15–18 September.

Roberts, B. J., Gordon, S. L., Struwig, J., & Møller, V. (2015). Shadow of the sun: The distribution of wellbeing in sub-Saharan Africa. In W. Glatzer, V. Møller, L. Camfield, & M. Rojas (Eds.), *Global handbook of quality of life: Exploration of well-being of nations and continents* (pp. 531–568). Dordrecht: Springer.

Sirgy, M.J., Estes, R.J., & Selian, A.N. (2017). How we measure well-being: The data behind the history of well-being. In: R. J. Estes & M. Joseph Sirgy (Eds.), *The Pursuit of human well-being: The untold global history* (pp. 135–157). Springer International Publishing Switzerland.

Studwell, J. (2019). *Success stories can change the course of Africa's development*. Overseas Development Institute (ODI), 31 July. https://www.odi.org/blogs/10775-success-stories-can-change-course-africa-s-development.

UNESCO. (2014). *Progress in getting all children to school stalls but some countries show the way forward* (Policy Paper 14/Fact Sheet 28). Paris: UNESCO. https://en.unesco.org/gem-report/progress-getting-all-children-school-stalls-some-countries-show-way. Accessed July 31, 2020.

UNESCO. (2017). *More than one-half of children and adolescents are not learning worldwide* (Fact Sheet 46). Paris: UNESCO, September. http://uis.unesco.org/sites/default/files/documents/fs46-more-than-half-children-not-learning-en-2017.pdf. Accessed July 31, 2020.

Veenhoven, R. (n.d.). The World Database of Happiness: Archive of research findings on subjective enjoyment of life. Erasmus University Rotterdam.

Veenhoven, R. (2005). Happiness in hardship. In L. Bruni & P. L. Porta (Eds.), *Economics and happiness: Framing the analysis* (pp. 243–266). Oxford: Oxford University Press.

Weyer, J. (2017). Speed and co-ordination are key to curbing the DRC's Ebola outbreak. *The Conversation*, May 16. https://theconversation.com/speed-and-co-ordination-are-key-to-curbing-the-drcs-ebola-outbreak-77727.

World Bank (2020) *World development indicators*. Washington, D.C.: World Bank. https://databank.worldbank.org/source/world-development-indicators. Accessed July 30, 2020.

World Health Organization (WHO). (2014). *World health statistics 2014*. Geneva: WHO. https://www.who.int/gho/publications/world_health_statistics/2014/en/. Accessed February 5, 2019.

World Health Organization (WHO). (2015a). *Affordable and effective vaccine brings Africa close to elimination of meningitis A*. https://www.who.int/features/2015/meningitis-africa-elimination/en/. Accessed June 29, 2020.

World Health Organization (WHO). (2015b). Ebola Situation Report 3 June 2015. Geneva: WHO. https://www.who.int/csr/disease/ebola/situation-reports/archive/en/. Accessed June 14, 2019.

World Health Organization (WHO). (2015c). *Trends in maternal mortality: 1990–2015: estimates from WHO, UNICEF, UNFPA, World Bank Group and the United Nations Population Division.* Geneva: WHO. https://www.who.int/reproductivehealth/publications/monitoring/maternal-mortality-2015/en/. Accessed February 5, 2019.

World Health Organization (WHO). (2018a). *World health statistics 2018: Monitoring health for the SDGs.* Geneva: WHO. https://www.who.int/gho/publications/world_health_statistics/2018/en/. Accessed February 5, 2019.

World Health Organization (WHO). (2018b). *World malaria report 2018.* Geneva: WHO. https://www.who.int/malaria/publications/world-malaria-report-2018/report/en/. Accessed February 5, 2019.

World Health Organization (WHO). (2019). *World health statistics 2019: Monitoring health for the SDGs.* Geneva: WHO. https://www.who.int/gho/publications/world_health_statistics/2019/en/. Accessed August 26, 2019.

World Health Organization (WHO). (2020). 10th Ebola outbreak in the Democratic Republic of the Congo declared over; vigilance against flare-ups and support for survivors must continue. https://www.who.int/news-room/detail/25-06-2020-10th-ebola-outbreak-in-the-democratic-republic-of-the-congo-declared-over-vigilance-against-flare-ups-and-support-for-survivors-must-continue. Accessed June 25, 2020.

Chapter 7
Democracy, Good Governance, and the Promise of Prosperity

Abstract In this chapter, we review how citizens see positive changes in their lives under democracy. We report on attitudes to democracy and citizen evaluations of good governance in the new millennium. We also discuss threats to an inclusive African democracy, in the form of authoritarian leaders (Africa's so-called 'Big Men'), patronage systems, and corruption, all of which may have negative impacts on well-being on the continent.

Keywords Sub-Saharan Africa · Good governance · Supply and demand for democracy · Trust · Corruption · Infrastructure · 'Big Men' · Authoritarian rule

7.1 Africa's Quest for Positive Change

The winds of change that swept through the continent in the late 1950s and early 1960s brought independence to formerly subjugated peoples and the anticipation of a better life. An international study conducted by Gallup-Kettering in the 1970s asked respondents world-wide if they thought they would be happier if things could be changed about their lives. The desire for change was greatest by far in newly liberated sub-Saharan Africa. Some 90% of African respondents wished for change in their lives, and the vast majority in this group wanted not a 'few' but 'many' things to change to improve their lives.[1] On gaining independence from colonial rule, most countries on the continent experimented with democratic rule that was to restore dignity and freedom for Africa's people.

---

[1] Of the 90% in the sub-Saharan sample who wished for change in their lives, 67% wanted 'many things' to change, 22% 'just a few' things. The question on the 'extent of change necessary for a happier life' read: 'Thinking about how your life is going now, do you think you would be happier if things could be changed about your life? (If yes) Would you like many things about your life changed or just a few things? See Table VI in the Gallup-Kettering Global Survey (1976) summary volume's reprint of: Human Needs and Satisfactions, Mankind: The Global Survey and the Third World, Blue Supplement to the "Monthly Public Opinion Surveys" of the Indian Institute of Public Opinion, Vol. XXI, Nos. 9 and 10. http://worlddatabaseofhappiness.eur.nl/hap_bib/freetexts/~Gallup_Kettering_1976k.pdf.

© Springer Nature Switzerland AG 2021
V. Møller and B. J. Roberts, *Quality of Life and Human Well-Being in Sub-Saharan Africa*,
Human Well-Being Research and Policy Making,
https://doi.org/10.1007/978-3-030-65788-8_7

7.2 Democracy as a Work in Progress

Africa is said to have embraced democracy 'in fits and starts' since the winds of change blew through the continent in the 1960s. The newly independent states adopted the Western liberal democratic systems of their former colonial masters, which meant having a constitution, allowing political parties, and holding regular elections. However, as political scientist Mtimkulu (2015) notes, elections did not become a permanent feature in the new democracies. Instead, Africa experienced three decades of 'democratic drought', and authoritarian rule became the order of the day. By the end of the 1980s, only Botswana, The Gambia and Mauritius still had democratic systems. It was only in the 1990s that democracy was generally restored. Today, the vast majority of Africa's countries are multiparty democracies, at least in name if not entirely in practice.

Why should democracy be important for African well-being? One argument is that Africa's approach to democracy focuses on 'horizontal equality' among diverse cultural and ethnic groups, rather than on 'individual' or vertical rights. Noting that Africans live on the world's 'most ethnically diverse and fractious continent', Stremlau (2016) argues that Africa's democracies need to cater to the needs of multiple groups in society. Thus, Africa's democracy project might be said to be in tune with a continent that has always nurtured collectivist values, such as African humanism, which ensured societal well-being in the past and still continues to do so today.

The African Union's Vision 2063 envisages a prosperous and peaceful Africa that promotes democratic governance. Free and fair elections are seen as a test of the strength of Africa's democracies (Akokpari 2004). In 2019, almost one in four sub-Saharan countries was due to hold elections (Africa Wikipedia 2019). Elections matter for democracy in Africa; when conducted well, they bring hope for a brighter future (Diatta 2018). With each election, citizens gain experience in how democracy should work. For example, in Sierra Leone, the impact of election debates among candidates increased voters' political knowledge making them more likely to vote along policy rather than ethnic lines, as tends to be common in sub-Saharan Africa (Logan 2017). Non-partisan citizen observers and monitoring groups, such as the West Africa Election Observers Network, are increasingly involved in election monitoring. In Ghana, some 4000 people were trained and deployed to cover the 2012 presidential and parliamentary elections (Logan 2017).

In their book 'Democracy Works', Greg Mills, former Nigerian president Olusegun Obasanjo, Jeffrey Herbst, and Tendai Biti note that precisely because democratisation is so difficult and failure not unexpected, African countries will continue to have to experiment with new and different democratic forms. In fact, differentiation among countries over the last 50 years has become starker (Mills et al. 2019, p. 93). For example, whereas Ghana has developed a political culture where incumbents transfer power peacefully when they lose the vote, other countries, such as Burundi, the Democratic Republic of Congo (DRC) and Somalia, struggle just to sustain basic institutions and hold peaceful elections in the first place. Ghana's

success in getting such peaceful transitions to 'stick' is due to a long process of incre-
mentalism over two decades, rather than a 'sudden democratic moment' (Mills et al.
2019, p. 123).

7.3 Africa's 'Third Liberation'—Good Governance

Starting in the mid-1970s, more than 60 countries around the world made transitions
to democracy in what has been termed a 'third wave' of democratisation (Huntington 1991), a process of change that indelibly influenced sub-Saharan Africa in
its own new wave from the early 1990s onward. Longstanding authoritarian rule,
characterised by military and one-party states as well as by dominant leaders, was
challenged, and multiparty electoral competition was established in countries such
as South Africa, Benin, Ivory Coast, Gabon and Zambia. The influence of these
changes also spread to other regimes spanning the continent, from Niger and Togo
in West Africa, through the Congo in Central Africa, and even to the island nations
of Madagascar, São Tomé and Príncipe, and Cabo Verde. At the beginning of the
1990s, only the three countries of Botswana, The Gambia and Mauritius could be
classified as democracies; by the close of that decade only two of 48 countries in the
region had *not* held national competitive, multiparty elections (Diamond and Plattner 2010). The rise of democracy on the continent has therefore seen a significant
change in the nature of political transitions. The often violent overthrow of leaders
that typified the 1960s through 1980s has been increasingly replaced with peaceful
exits, the imposition of limits on terms of office, and the gradual demise of one-party
states.

To provide a sense of the changing nature of freedom in the region over recent
decades, we make use of the cumulative findings of the Freedom House series,
Freedom in the World (Freedom House 2020). This annual report series assesses the
state of freedom across the countries of the world, by rating each in terms of the state
of political rights as well as of civil liberties. In each instance, a 1 to 7 ratings scale
is used, where 1 represents the most free and 7, the least free. These scores are, in
turn, premised on 25 detailed indicators. The average of the political rights and civil
liberties scores is finally used to classify a country or territory as Free, Partly Free, or
Not Free.[2] The pattern of freedom in sub-Saharan Africa over the last 40 years clearly
reflects the processes of democratisation that have occurred, as well as the advance
of civil and political rights in public opinion and legal practice (Fig. 7.1). In 1973,
less than a tenth of countries in the region were deemed Free by Freedom House,
while 23% were designated as Partly Free and the remaining majority were Not Free
(Freedom House 2014). Distinct progress is evident between 1973 and 2003, with
the share of countries in sub-Saharan Africa that are deemed Not Free halving, and
the corresponding shares that are Free or Partly Free exhibiting improving trends.

---

[2]More information on the Freedom House methodology can be found at https://freedomhouse.org/
reports/freedom-world/freedom-world-research-methodology.

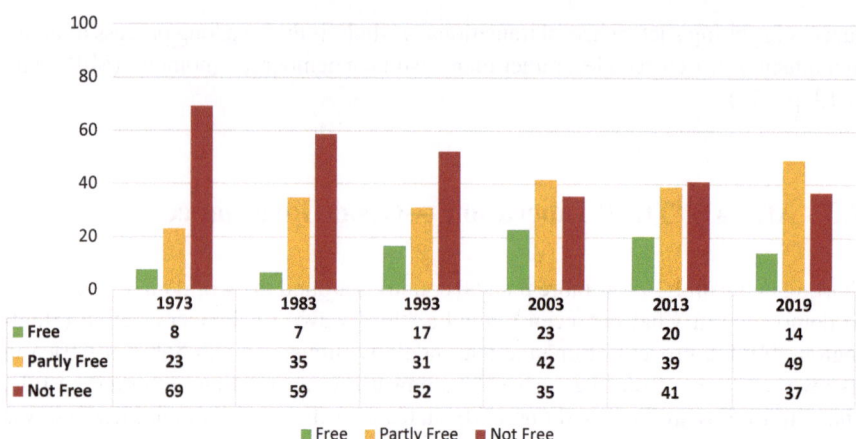

	1973	1983	1993	2003	2013	2019
Free	8	7	17	23	20	14
Partly Free	23	35	31	42	39	49
Not Free	69	59	52	35	41	37

Fig. 7.1 Progress in freedom since the 1970s, though indications of democratic recession evident since the early 2000s. Trends in freedom in sub-Saharan Africa over the 1973 to 2019 period, based on the percentage of countries that are classified as 'free', 'partly free' and 'not free' (Data based on calculations from Freedom House 2020)

Despite such accomplishments, the Freedom House measures for the decade between 2003 and 2013 provided early warning signs of democratic recession in the region. This period was generally one of heightened volatility, with declines precipitated by coups, insurgencies, political instability, terrorism, and reversals in terms of freedom of expression and association. Nevertheless, these losses occurred alongside gains in countries such as Côte d'Ivoire, Madagascar and Mali, due mainly to recovery after coups and conflict (Freedom House 2014). For the first time in four decades, the share of countries categorised as Not Free demonstrated an upward tendency, whereas the share that was Free or Partly Free declined modestly. Between 2013 and 2019, this democratic reversal continued, with the share of countries classified as Free falling from 20 to 14%, and the share regarded as Partly Free increasing (from 39 to 49%). Although the share of countries designated as Not Free reduced slightly from 41 to 37%, the fact that slightly over a third of counties in the region remain classified as such is troubling. Notable gains following leadership change occurred in Ethiopia, Angola and the Gambia. Conversely, a reversal in freedom took place in Benin following flawed elections, while countries such as Tanzania, Zimbabwe, and Uganda witnessed a narrowing in the space for independent civic and political activity. Continuing long-term rule spanning more than three decades in countries such as Cameroon, Equatorial Guinea, the Republic of the Congo, and Uganda is also a source of unease.

7.3.1 Quality of Governance

> If ... African countries are to achieve sustainable development, democracy cannot stand still, and freedom alone will not be enough. Democratic institutions will have to work better to control corruption and constrain the exercise of power, so that the chief business of government becomes the delivery of public goods, not private ones. (Diamond 2008, p. 262).

As noted above, Africa has undergone successive liberations, first from colonialism and then from the autocratic rulers that often followed on colonial rule. Now that Africa has liberated itself from both, African countries are advised to achieve the so-called 'third liberation', that is, to free themselves from poor governance in order to accelerate development and create jobs for prosperity (Mills and Herbst 2012). International evidence suggests there is a strong link between good governance and well-being. Societies that have high levels of well-being tend to be economically developed, to have effective governments with low levels of corruption, to have high levels of trust, and to be able to meet citizens' basic needs for food and health.[3]

Apart from the spread, as well as the ebbs and flows of democracy in the region, another important aspect of developmental progress that has a bearing on individual and collective well-being in sub-Saharan Africa is the quality of governance. The Brookings Institute economist Daniel Kaufmann and his World Bank colleagues have identified six core dimensions with which to evaluate the nature of governance in any given country. The first of these is voice and accountability, which links closely with the Freedom House focus on basic civil liberties as well as the ability to participate in the selection of government. The other aspects are political stability and absence of violence or terrorism; government effectiveness (in providing public service, public administration, and policy formulation and implementation); regulatory quality (in terms of enabling and promoting private sector development); the rule of law; and, lastly the control of corruption. The latter four dimensions could be thought of collectively as an indication of 'state quality' (Diamond 2008). Available indicators, compiled to inform this multidimensional definition of quality governance, and covering 1996 to 2018, tend to portray sub-Saharan Africa in a fairly unfavourable light (Kaufmann and Kraay 2020).

In 2018, sub-Saharan Africa ranked at the low end of the 30th percentile on governance measures (Fig. 7.2a), faring marginally better on indicators of political stability and accountability than on the other four components of state quality. Yet, with the exception of the Middle East and North Africa, the African continent fell behind other world regions on the basis of these indices. These averages also mask considerable variations among different countries within the region. If one concentrates on sub-Saharan Africa's five largest countries, which account for close to half of the

---

[3] Here we refer to observations on the importance of good governance for citizen well-being in Helliwell and Huang (2008), the volume on well-being for public policy edited by Diener et al. (2009, p. 60), and an OECD working paper that traces the linkages between good governance and national well-being (Helliwell et al. 2014). Similarly, an Institute for Security Studies African Futures scenario links gains in effective governance with poverty reduction on the continent (Aucoin and Donnenfeld 2016).

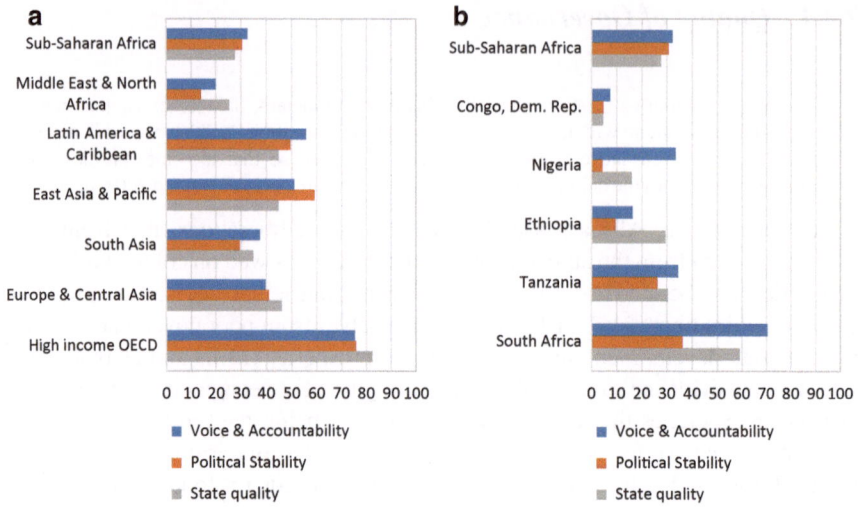

Fig. 7.2 **a** Sub-Saharan Africa lags behind other world regions based on different dimensions of governance, and **b** is characterised by significant within-region variation. World Governance Indicators rankings by world region, 2018 (Data from Kaufmann and Kraay 2020). **b** World Governance Indicators rankings among the five largest sub-Saharan African countries, 2018 (Data from Kaufmann and Kraay 2020)

region's population, it is immediately apparent how appreciably the quality of governance varies across nations (Fig. 7.2b). Whereas the percentile rankings for South Africa approximated those of Eastern Europe, the DRC and Nigeria had worse governance scores than the region as a whole; Ethiopia also had voice and accountability and political stability scores below the sub-Saharan average. Tanzania fared moderately better than the rest of the region on the different dimensions of governance. Across the region, the control of corruption in particular is of concern.

Although politics across the continent has become less violent and more institutionalised in character over the last two decades, at the same time many democracies remain fragile and beleaguered by quality concerns, affected in particular by corrupt practices, clientelism, and authoritarian leadership (Diamond and Plattner 2010).

7.3.2   Supply and Demand for Democracy, and Citizen Well-Being

Alongside the complex patterns of progress and reversal that have occurred following the democratic experiments in Africa since the 1990s, it is interesting to observe the resolute public appetite for democracy. Afrobarometer surveys have found that the most commonly held understanding of democracy in Africa relates to civil liberties,

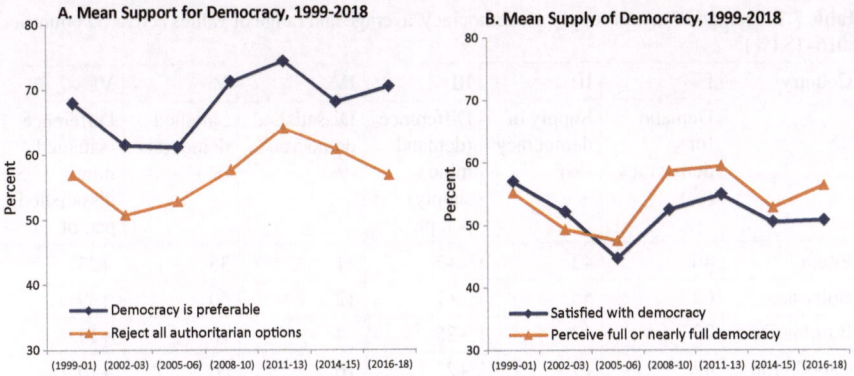

Fig. 7.3 Trends in the demand for and supply of democracy, 12 sub-Saharan African countries, 1999–2018. Data from Afrobarometer rounds 1 to 7 (Afrobarometer 2019)

especially freedom of speech (Afrobarometer 2002). Successive rounds of this cross-national survey series also show that Africans consider democracy to be preferable to any other form of government,[4] rejecting authoritarian alternatives including one-party, military and one-man rule (see Fig. 7.3a left). According to our analysis of Round 7 of Afrobarometer (2016/18), more than two-thirds (68%) of people across the sub-Saharan Africa region believe that democracy is preferable to any other form of government, and around three quarters disapprove of 'big man' politics (78%), one-party rule (74%), and military rule (72%). There is similar support for constitutional limits to terms of office (75%). These beliefs convey a deeply rooted demand for democracy and an appreciation of the benefits it brings to citizens, and they represent a trend that has remained relatively resilient since the inception of the survey series in the late 1990s.

Despite this good news, Mattes (2019) draws attention to certain worrying aspects about this commitment or 'demand' for democracy. His assessment is based on the Afrobarometer aggregate demand for democracy measure, which is constructed by combining support for democracy with rejection of all three forms of authoritarian rule. Firstly, barely two-fifths (42%) simultaneously agree that democracy is preferable *and* reject 'big man' politics, one-party rule, as well as military rule. Secondly, the variance in this multidimensional commitment to democracy is appreciable, ranging from a high of around two-thirds of citizens in countries such as Zambia and Mauritius to less than a quarter in South Africa (23%), Burkina Faso (23%), eSwatini (23%), Madagascar (22%), Mozambique (21%), and Lesotho (19%) (see Table 7.1, Column I). Finally, in terms of trends over time, short-term decline in demand for democracy occurred in 14 countries between 2014/15 and 2016/18, while only 7 recorded increasing demand. This pattern persists if the trends are extended

---

[4]See also Mattes and Bratton (2016) and Mattes (2019) on Afrobarometer surveys of demand for democracy in Africa.

Table 7.1 Demand for, and supply of, democracy, average and range of values across 32 countries, 2016–18 (%)

Country	I	II	III	IV	V	VI
	Demand for democracy (%)	Supply of democracy (%)	Difference (demand minus supply) pct. pt.	Dissatisfied democrats (%)	Satisfied democrats (%)	Difference (satisfied minus dissatisfied) pct. pt.
Benin	46	43	+3	11	35	+25
Botswana	62	55	+7	12	50	+39
Burkina Faso	22	47	−25	4	18	+14
Cabo Verde	42	19	+23	16	26	+10
Cameroon	30	21	+9	16	15	−1
Côte d'Ivoire	54	34	+20	22	32	+10
eSwatini	23	20	+3	11	12	+1
Gabon	50	6	+45	42	8	−34
Gambia	52	48	+3	7	45	+38
Ghana	52	70	−18	3	49	+46
Guinea	44	23	+20	20	24	+5
Kenya	46	48	−2	8	38	+29
Lesotho	19	25	−6	7	12	+4
Liberia	42	32	+10	11	31	+20
Madagascar	22	7	+15	15	7	−9
Malawi	39	25	+14	17	22	+5
Mali	40	28	+12	18	22	+4
Mauritius	66	49	+17	15	51	+36
Mozambique	21	35	−13	5	16	+12
Namibia	39	57	−18	5	34	+29
Niger	34	27	+7	13	22	+9
Nigeria	43	32	+11	16	27	+11
São Tomé and Príncipe	41	13	+28	19	22	+3
Senegal	58	45	+13	14	43	+29
Sierra Leone	53	60	−7	8	45	+37
South Africa	23	26	−3	9	14	+5
Sudan	28	15	+13	19	9	−10
Tanzania	55	68	−14	7	48	+41
Togo	46	12	+35	33	13	−20
Uganda	59	39	+20	22	37	+15
Zambia	67	44	+23	22	45	+22

(continued)

Table 7.1 (continued)

Country	I	II	III	IV	V	VI
	Demand for democracy (%)	Supply of democracy (%)	Difference (demand minus supply) pct. pt.	Dissatisfied democrats (%)	Satisfied democrats (%)	Difference (satisfied minus dissatisfied) pct. pt.
Zimbabwe	44	33	+11	29	15	−14
32-country average	43	35	+9	15	28	+14
Highest value	67	70	+45	42	51	+46
Lowest value	19	6	−25	3	7	−34

Source Afrobarometer Round 7

Note: 'Demand for democracy' refers to the percentage that prefer democracy and reject all 3 authoritarian alternatives. 'Supply of democracy' refers to the percentage that believe their country is a democracy (full or with minor flaws) and are very or fairly satisfied with democracy. 'Dissatisfied democrats' are "those who demand democracy but are dissatisfied with the performance of democracy" (Mattes, p.22), while 'satisfied democrats' are the share that demand democracy minus the share of dissatisfied democrats. 'Pct. pt.' refers to percentage point differences

back further to 2011/13, but do improve if one examines the country-level trajectories for those with data spanning more than a decade.

On average, public evaluations of the supply of democracy in the region tend to be more critical in nature than the demand for democracy. In 2016/18 only 43% of citizens across 32 sub-Saharan African countries expressed satisfaction with the way democracy is functioning in practice. The corresponding figure stands at 51% for the 12 countries with data across all seven rounds of the Afrobarometer survey series, fluctuating over the two-decade period in a narrow range between 45 and 57% (Fig. 7.3b right). The share of citizens that viewed their country as a full democracy or a democracy with minor flaws stood at a rather middling 52% across all 32 countries in 2016/18. This increases to 56% if we again narrow our focus to the 12 countries with data across all rounds of surveying, with the figure varying between 48% and 59% between 1999 and 2018.

As with the demand for democracy, citizen beliefs about whether they are being supplied with democracy in practice diverge substantially across sub-Saharan Africa. Combining the share that believe their country is a full democracy or democracy with minor problems with the share fairly or very satisfied with the functioning of democracy in the country (the two indictors displayed in Fig. 7.3b) into a single measure of the perceived supply of democracy, we find an astounding 64-percentage point difference between the highest and lowest recoded country values (Table 7.1, Column II). Only five of the 32 countries with 2016/18 data in Afrobarometer Round 7 had democratic performance evaluation scores exceeding 50% on average. These were Ghana (70%), Tanzania (68%), Sierra Leone (60%), Namibia (57%) and Botswana (55%). While barely more than a third (35%) of citizens provided positive evaluations across the region as a whole, in six countries this dropped to less than two in ten feeling they were being supplied with democracy, namely in Gabon (6%), Madagascar (7%), Togo (12%), São Tomé and Príncipe (13%), Sudan (15%), Cabo Verde (19%).

Mattes (2019, p. 16) looks at long-term trends in the perceived supply of democracy over a decade or more. He finds that, despite fluctuations, there has been a distinct upward tendency in seven countries (Ghana, Tanzania, Botswana, Burkina Faso, Namibia, Zambia, and Zimbabwe). Conversely, long-term decline views on the supply of democracy are evident in Mozambique, Mali, Madagascar, and Kenya.

The demand for democracy has not always been matched by a perceived supply of democracy over the course of twenty years. Noteworthy is that the share of sub-Saharan African citizens that favour democratic rule (in Fig. 7.3a) outweighs the share that are satisfied with democracy and regard their country as a democracy (see Fig. 7.3b right). Although there have been ebbs and flows in public opinion in the region over time, with a particularly disconcerting fall in the rejection of authoritarian options in the last decade, the general pattern of demand for democracy exceeding perceived supply remains true for now. The obvious gap between the demand for and evaluation of the supply of democracy suggests that important democratic deficits exist within the region. These deficits reflect disillusionment with the manner in which democracy is delivering upon the expectations of the mass public. By extension, as the example of the Arab Spring has taught us, these statistics also serve as a signal to the elected of their responsibility to the voting public and the potential consequences of failing to live up to this mandate.

In 2016/18, the share of citizens across the region who felt they were being supplied with an acceptable level of democracy (35%) falls short of the 43% who voiced a pro-democratic demand across the 32 countries. Eighteen of these countries display a similar predisposition (positive values in Table 7.1, Column III), with demand exceeding supply to a sizable degree in Gabon (+45), Togo (+35), São Tomé and Príncipe (+28), Zambia (+23) and Cabo Verde (+23) in particular. This unmet demand for greater democracy is likely to translate into increasing pressure on leaders for progressive change. At the other end of the spectrum, we find a subset of countries where the proportion who feel they are getting democracy exceeds the proportion demanding democracy. These are contexts with an apparent oversupply of democracy, which has been linked to disproportionate shares of 'uncritical democrats' (Chaligha et al. 2002; Keulder and Wiese 2005; Mattes and Shenga 2013; Mattes 2019). The most prominent examples (negative values in Table 7.1, Column III) include Burkina Faso (−25), Namibia (−18), Ghana (−18), Tanzania (−14), and Mozambique (−13).

7.3.3 'Dissatisfied Democrats' as Positive Force for Change?

Beyond this overall weighing up of the regional and country-level demand for democracy and perceived supply of democracy, scholars such as Mattes (2019) argue that ultimately the concept of 'dissatisfied democrats' at the individual level may matter more fundamentally for democratisation and democratic consolidation. This term refers to citizens who are committed to democracy but are simultaneously discontent with the present functioning of the political system in their country. Such citizens are said to be more inclined to demand accountability from leadership, support effective legislatures and independent courts, oppose political interference in democratic spaces, and engage in political action to protect and defend rights and liberties. They are also likely to represent a positive force for democratic change, especially when coupled with other contextual factors such as strong legislatures and courts, democratic commitments among elites, and where the space for opposition politics is not restricted.

On average, the share of adult citizens across sub-Saharan Africa that are dissatisfied democrats stood at only around 15% in 2016/18, with a larger share (28%) presenting as satisfied democrats (Table 7.1, Columns IV and V). The share of the adult public that presents as dissatisfied democrats tends to be higher is countries in the region that are classified by Freedom House as "not free" or "hybrid regimes" and lower in liberal and electoral democracies. In the liberal democracies, there are no instances where the share of dissatisfied democrats exceeds the proportion that are satisfied democrats (negative values in Table 7.1, Column VI). In some instances, the relatively low share of dissatisfied democrats in liberal and electoral democracies is a potential worry for democratic consolidation. For example, South Africa displays relatively low shares of both dissatisfied democrats (9%) and satisfied democrats (14%). The survey round occurred several months after President Zuma resigned and his deputy, Cyril Ramaphosa, was sworn into office. The Zuma administration came to be characterised by so-called 'state capture' involving widespread political corruption. The relatively low shares of both dissatisfied and satisfied democrats points to the potential damage that may have been done to the government-public relationship and the public's faith in the democratic system. Equally troubling is the high share or satisfied relative to dissatisfied democrats in a country such as Tanzania, despite indications of a decline in governance, with President Magufuli's populist tendencies and the intimidation of opposition parties, and arrest of critical journalists. In cases such as these, having dissatisfied democrats would be important in holding the elected to account and motivating for change. By contrast, in certain countries deemed 'not free', such as Gabon, Zimbabwe and Togo, large shares of dissatisfied democrats substantially exceed the share of satisfied democrats. This suggests perhaps an ongoing contestation between democratic and autocratic forces within these nations (Mattes 2019).

7.3.4 Trust and Corruption

Citizens' trust in their country's leaders will contribute to political stability in democratic societies, while lack of trust may undermine the strength of institutions that ensure basic freedoms. Corruption at any level of governance will restrict economic growth, the development of infrastructure, and delivery of services to citizens.

Perceptions of the trustworthiness and honesty attributed to Africa's leaders and civil servants vary across the continent (see Table 7.2, middle). Highest and lowest values differ by at least 50 percentage points between countries. Within countries, trust in the president is consistently greater than trust in other members of the ruling party (São Tomé and Príncipe is the only exception, though the difference is marginal in South Africa[5] and Malawi[6]). Similarly, government officials are consistently seen to be more corrupt than those in the office of the president (Mauritius, São Tomé and Príncipe, Sudan and Malawi are exceptions).

On average, 54% of respondents across all countries surveyed by Afrobarometer thought corruption had increased in their country in the past year, while barely one in three (34%) approved of their government's efforts to fight corruption (see Table 7.2 bottom). Although the regional average has not increased much between Rounds 6 and 7 of Afrobarometer (from 2014/15 to 2016/18), there are certain countries where there has been substantial growth in approval for government anti-corruption efforts. The largest increase in public support for state-led anti-corruption efforts was in Sierra Leone, which increased from 19 to 66% (+47 percentage points) over this period. This has much to do with presidential terms of office. The ascendancy of President Koroma in 2007 saw a strong anti-corruption focus that seems to have won public favour, with the share saying government was doing well in its handling of corruption standing at 54% in 2011/13, far higher than the sub-Saharan average of 36%. The president's second five-year term in office following his successful re-election in late 2012 saw public views on corruption efforts collapsing to a mere 19% in 2014/15. This latter survey occurred during a time when alleged misappropriation of Ebola relief funds was being exposed. With the transition to President Bio in 2018,

---

[5] In South Africa, President Jacob Zuma's presidency (2009–2018) was tainted by corruption scandals. In particular, there was popular outrage when he claimed that upgrades to his rural homestead, at the expense of taxpayers, were for national security purposes rather than his own benefit. A case in point was a swimming pool said to be needed for fire-fighting purposes. South Africa's strong institutions were instrumental in his resigning and leaving power before the end of his second term. Corruption has also become a key issue during the Ramaphosa administration's (2018–) handling of the Coronavirus pandemic, with alleged tender fraud in the awarding of lucrative contracts of Covid-19 emergency response goods and services to family members of senior ranking ruling party members and leaders in the Executive. This has resulted in strong demands for the President to take decisive action.

[6] Malawi's Vice President Joyce Banda was installed as Malawi's first and Africa's second woman president on 7 April 2012, following the unexpected death of President Bingu wa Mutharika. During her short period in office, Joyce Banda's government became embroiled in a 'Cashgate' scandal implicating government officials in syphoning off millions from the budget. The scandal is likely to have tarnished Banda's reputation. For example, a study found that households in informal settlements of Lilongwe, the capital of Malawi, were more likely to blame Cashgate for their food insecurity than other factors such as the floods that led to a decline in food production (Riley and Chilanga 2018). After only two years in power, Banda lost deeply flawed elections to Bingu wa Mutharika's brother, Peter Mutharika, in 2014. Banda's successor has also suffered public criticism. In 2018, thousands of citizens in six cities were involved in protests against corruption and Peter Mutharika's government. Mutharika was replaced by Lazarus Chakwera in June 2020, following a court nullification of the 2019 election due to widespread irregularities, although the latter faced early criticism over alleged favouritism and nepotism in Cabinet appointments.

Table 7.2 Support for Authoritarian rule in sub-Saharan Africa, political trust, and perceived corruption, average and range of values across 34 countries, 2016–18 (%)

	African average	Lowest value	Highest value	Diff high to low	Three highest percentages	Three lowest percentages
Authoritarian rule						
Reject one-man rule	79	41	92	51	BEN, TZA, BWA	MOZ, MDG, ZAF
Support one-man rule	11	3	30	27	MOZ, ZAF, NGA	MUS, ZBA, GBA
Agree that constitution should limit president to a maximum of two terms	75	54	91	37	GAB, TZA, TGO	MOZ, LSO, ZAF
Political trust						
Trust president somewhat/a lot	52	27	73	46	SEN, TZA, GHA	MUS, GAB, STP
Trust ruling party somewhat/a lot	43	14	67	53	SLE, TZA, MOZ	GAB, SDN, MUS
Perceived corruption						
All/most of government officials corrupt	38	12	75	63	GAB, CAM, TGO	TZA, MUS, STP
All/most of those in office of president corrupt	33	4	71	67	GAB, TGO, SDN	TZA, CPV, GBA
Corruption increased a lot/somewhat in last year	54	10	82	72	SDN, GAB, NAM	TZA, BFA, GBA
Government doing very/fairly well in fighting corruption	34	10	71	61	TZA, SLE, LSO	MDG, GAB, SDN

Source Afrobarometer Round 7

Note: *BEN* Benin; *BFA* Burkina Faso; *BWA* Botswana; *CAM* Cameroon; *CPV* Cabo Verde; *GAB* Gabon; *GBA* Gambia; *GHA* Ghana; *LSO* Lesotho; *MDG* Madagascar; *MOZ* Mozambique; *MUS* Mauritius; *NAM* Namibia; *NER* Niger; *NGA* Nigeria; *SDN* Sudan; *SEN* Senegal; *SLE* Sierra Leone; *STP* São Tomé and Príncipe; *TGO* Togo; *TZA* Tanzania; *ZAF* South Africa; *ZBA* Zambia

a few months before Afrobarometer Round 7, there was an upsurge in confidence to 66%. His subsequent anti-corruption drive is likely to continue to resonate with the public.

Nigeria represents a similar case, with the increase from 22 to 59% (+38 percentage points) believing that government is faring well in anti-corruption efforts probably likely to partly reflect the transition from the Jonathan to the Buhari presidency in 2015. The latter's war against corruption and efforts in dealing with the *Boko Haram* terrorist group and securing the release of the kidnapped Chibok girls seems to found resonance with the Nigerian public. Other examples of significant gains in appraisal of government anti-corruption efforts following recent leadership change include Ghana with the ascendency of President Akufo-Addo in 2017 (+35 percentage points) and Tanzania following the incumbency of President Magufuli in 2015 (+34 percentage points).

Despite the promise of change that new leadership tends to inspire among African citizens, the experiences of high profile changes of leaders and governments across the region during the latter half of the 2010s serve as a cautionary note and suggest a need to temper expectations of rapid political and economic transformation. The Bertelsmann Transformation Index Africa Report 2020 (BTI) examined trends in 44 African nations between 2017 and 2019 and concluded that, while leadership change generates an initial surge of optimism, enduring political challenges and constraints ultimately mean that the more likely outcome will be continuity than progressive change (Cheeseman 2020). The report suggests that in countries such as Angola, Ethiopia, Sierra Leone, Zimbabwe, South Africa, Nigeria, Tanzania and Kenya, the hope for reform vested in new leaders was met with initial progress but these gains have tended to be limited or short-lived. Concern is mounting over human rights abuses in Ethiopia, Nigeria, Tanzania and Zimbabwe, including the repression of peaceful protest action and the arrest of political activists and journalists in the latter in mid-2020. This has raised questions about the personalisation of power, as well as whether, in line with the title of the BTI Report, there has been 'a changing of the guards' rather than a genuine 'change of systems'.

Another noteworthy observation drawing on Table 7.2 is that corruption might be easier to contain in smaller island states, such as Cabo Verde, Mauritius and São Tomé and Príncipe. In these settings, Afrobarometer respondents on average indicated there was less corruption among officials and the Office of the President or approved of their governments' fight against corruption. Yet, it is not all sandy beaches and azure skies in the island nations. There is nonetheless a higher than average concern that corruption increased in the year prior to interviewing in both Mauritius and São Tomé and Príncipe. In Mauritius, despite the perception that corruption is not widespread, there is exceptionally low and rapidly declining trust in the president, prime minister and the ruling party. Trust in these political institutions halved between 2014 and 2017. Although corruption in Mauritius remains low in regional perspective, nepotism and cronyism are a source of unease (Rahman 2019). A prominent example of this was the passing of the office of prime minister by Sir Anerood Jugnauth to his son Pravind in 2017. In terms of political corruption, former President Ammenah Gurib-Fakim was implicated in a high-profile credit card fraud scandal, which surfaced in early 2017 and led to her eventual resignation in March 2018. Incidents such as these have adversely affected the political support vested by the public in the political system. The resignation of Gurib-Fakim is nonetheless taken as a positive sign for accountability and democratic functioning in this liberal democracy.

Despite the far-reaching impacts of corrupt practices on societies across the region, many citizens display resilience in the face of such challenges. One possible indication of this is the relative lack of effect of corruption perceptions on electoral behaviour. In a comparative analysis of corruption and political behaviour across Africa, Latin America and European Bank for Construction and Development (EBRD) countries, Rose and Peiffer (2019, pp. 133–134) found that experiences of bribery and perceptions of corruption have little or no substantive effect on individual decisions to go and vote. In the African context, the scholars rely on Afrobarometer data to show that paying a bribe, the ranking of corruption as a top national problem, and views on whether corruption is increasing or decreasing all exert no statistically significant effect on voting. The only exception is the depressing effect on electoral behaviour of perceiving political institutions as corrupt. In this instance, regarding the executive, parliament, officials and local government as corrupt produced on average a 9 percentage point decline in the likelihood of voting. This effect was not present in Latin America or EBRD countries in Europe, Asia and the Middle East and North Africa. The evidence also does not support the argument that people regarding corruption as a key problem become more politically involved as a way of rooting out political corruption. Another study on the electoral consequences of corruption perceptions in South Africa (Roberts et al. 2020b) also revealed that viewing corruption as one of the most important problems in the country does not diminish the intention to vote. Discontent with government anti-corruption efforts did however reduce planned electoral participation by 14 percentage points relative to those satisfied with state efforts in this regard.

While this inclination of African citizens to vote irrespective of corruption might reflect sheer determination, the influence of other factors, such as party loyalty, ideology and traits of the party system operating in countries, could arguably also be at play (Dahlberg and Solevid 2016; Charron and Bågenholm 2016; Rose and Peiffer 2019). In contrast with the slight electoral effect, the Rose and Peiffer study demonstrates convincingly that corruption experiences and perceptions are more likely to produce a large corrosive effect on trust in government. Whether citizens across the region will increasingly use the power of their vote as a means of punishing corruption in government and demand greater accountability remains to be seen.

7.3.5 Good Governance and Covid-19

The factors responsible for successful pandemic responses have been state capacity, social trust, and leadership. Countries with all three—a competent state apparatus, a government that citizens trust and listen to, and effective leaders—have performed impressively, limiting the damage they have suffered. (Fukuyama 2020, p. 26)

The World Health Organization (WHO) declared COVID-19 a pandemic on 11 March 2020, pointing to the over 118,000 cases of the coronavirus illness in over 110 countries and territories around the world and the sustained risk of further global spread (Ducharme 2020). The organisation warned that nearly a quarter of a billion Africans could contract the coronavirus in the first year of the pandemic, with between 150,000 and 190,000 of them dying.[7] The virus had arrived later in Africa than elsewhere, which allowed sub-Saharan societies a little more time to prepare for the pandemic. However, most public health systems in the region were already under strain with the burden of endemic diseases such as malaria, and widespread TB and HIV/AIDS. Regional economies had not recovered fully from the last global recession and health systems generally were underfunded and understaffed. On the other hand, as described in an earlier chapter, West African countries and the DRC had gained valuable experience fighting Ebola outbreaks, which would better equip the response to Covid-19 in the region.

Good governance in Africa was put to the test during the Covid-19 pandemic. None of the continent's post-independence constitutions will have anticipated the need to deal with a health emergency as serious as a global pandemic. Little was known about the virus, so political leaders had to rely on good judgement to make the right decisions. In times of crisis, trust in leaders would be essential, if they were to gain the support of citizens asked to sacrifice personal freedoms to stop the virus from spreading.

There is consensus among political scientists and commentators that democracies have fared better than non-democracies in handling the corona pandemic. With reference to economist Nobel laureate Amartya Sen's treatise on response to famines, Hamilton (2020) notes that democracy is uniquely placed to engender good judgements. Political leaders 'judge best when they listen to their populations and learn from science'. Referring to rumours and conspiracy theories about Covid-19 circulating on social media, Friedman (2020) notes that democracies may not protect citizens from the virus, but they can hold their leaders accountable for their actions. 'One of democracy's strengths is that it allows its critics to complain about it loudly'. People in authoritarian societies, who do not feel part of the system, are more likely to struggle with the virus.

In line with the quote by Fukuyama at the beginning of this section, a survey conducted among the South African public during the country's lockdown found trust in good governance matters in times of crisis. Confidence of the president's performance was associated with greater willingness of citizens to sacrifice their

---

[7] See https://www.bbc.com/news/world-africa-52702838 (Accessed 20 May 2020).

human rights and adapt their behaviour to fight the virus. Citizens who stated they trusted the president were more prepared than others to wear a face mask in public in line with lockdown prescriptions to stop the spread of the virus (Roberts et al. 2020a).

In contrast, Tanzanian President John Magufuli's idiosyncratic and autocratic style of leadership was widely criticised for putting the health of his people and those in neighbouring countries at risk during the coronavirus. Magufuli downplayed the threat of the Covid-19 and dismissed the need for scientific consultation (Kwayu 2020). Tests were faulty, he claimed, as samples of fruit and goats had also tested positive. Instead, he recommended the use of local remedies to treat the disease and encouraged congregational worship—God would answer the prayers of Tanzanians against the pandemic. By mid-June 2020, President Magufuli stated Covid-19 had been widely defeated; prayers had ended the virus in his country. However, there was no information on the true level of infections, as the Tanzanian government had not released official data on the coronavirus. Transmission of the virus across Tanzania's open borders was of particular concern to neighbouring countries. People travelling out of Tanzania and into Kenya, Zambia and Uganda, including truck drivers transporting goods, were tested for the virus. In some cases, travellers testing positive were sent back to Tanzania (Awami 2020; Mwai and Giles 2020).

7.3.6 Crisis Governance During Covid-19

The Covid-19 pandemic that took the world by surprise in early 2020 would affect both the material and psychological well-being of citizens in all countries south of the Sahara. Following the lead of China, the first country to be infected with Covid-19 in the city of Wuhan, and later European epicentres of the pandemic, most countries in sub-Saharan Africa introduced restrictions on movement in their countries to delay infection rates from soaring out of control before public health services were prepared to cope with a surge in numbers of positive cases requiring isolation and hospitalisation. The challenge to African leaders posed by the coronavirus lockdown was to weigh 'lives against livelihoods', that is to consider how to fight the virus to save lives while ensuring the country's economy did not collapse under the weight of restrictions on market and business activities.

The long-standing debate on the advantages of an unconditional basic income grant was revived in many parts of the world in the time of the coronavirus (Shanahan and Smith 2020). The Covid-19 pandemic also prompted renewed focus on government transfers in both cash and kind to assist sub-Saharan households with food security during the lockdown period. A large proportion of people in the region work in the informal sectors of the economy and live from hand to mouth. Also hard hit by the lockdown were small businesses and the self-employed. Some countries pledged to give citizens money each month to help them through the Covid-19 crisis (Gqubule 2020). For example, the South Africa government introduced a special coronavirus grant to assist low-income households not benefiting from the country's social safety net to put food on the table during the lockdown period. A number of economists regard the Covid-19 pandemic as an opportunity to rethink the value of the basic income grant as a permanent social security solution (see Gqubule 2020; Shanahan and Smith 2020; Sunday Times 2020).

7.4 Well-Being and the Material Underpinnings of Democracy

Given the continent's history of colonialism, there was hope that democracy would restore dignity to African people and improve their life circumstances. Africa's independence promised material benefits—the decent standard of living that provides dignity. It is important to note that African citizens expect much more of their democracies than just civil liberties such as free freedom of speech and free and fair elections.

The briefing paper on the first round of Afrobarometer surveys conducted in 12 countries in 2001 (Afrobarometer 2002) reported that the democracy concept was understood mainly as civil liberties. However, in practice, people want democracy to deliver basic services such as water, electricity, housing and education, even more strongly than they insist on regular elections, majority rule, competing political parties, and freedom to criticise the government.

It is telling that an improved or decent standard of living was the greatest hope expressed by Nigerians participating in Cantril's classic study of citizen concerns in the 1960s. Among the 13 countries from different world regions participating in the study, Nigeria was selected to represent sub-Saharan Africa. Before voicing their concerns and giving their life evaluations, 69% of Nigerian respondents stated they aspired to a better standard of living, while 60% worried that they might not achieve a decent standard of living (Cantril 1965, p. 75). Fast forward to 1996 and we find that South Africa's post-apartheid constitution affirms the democratic value of human dignity as a human right. The embodiment of this new-found dignity under democracy is the provision of free housing and basic services for South Africa's under-served poorer households. Many of our surveys show that the owners of so-called RDP (Reconstruction and Development Programme) houses are both proud to have a decent roof over their heads and grateful to the ruling African National Congress government for caring for their well-being.

7.4.1 Waiting for the 'End of Poverty'[8] Under Democracy

In the new millennium, the Afrobarometer uses the Lived Poverty Index[9] to measure experienced freedom from deprivation in everyday life. Respondents are asked whether they have gone without five basic necessities in the preceding year, specifically food, clean water, health care (medicines or medical treatment), cooking fuel, and a cash income in the home. On average across the 32 sub-Saharan countries, participating in Round 7 of Afrobarometer (2016/18), large shares were still struggling to secure even the most basic needs required to lead a decent quality of life. In the face of a severe unemployment challenge, 81% reported going without a cash income at least once. Around half experienced shortages of necessary health care (54%), clean water (50%), and food (49%) at least once during the 12 months prior to being interviewed, while 39% went without cooking fuel on one or more occasions.

The overall Lived Poverty Index is constructed by averaging together responses to the five items, producing a 0 to 4 scale, where 0 signifies no deprivation in any of the domains and 4 represents constant absence of all five basic necessities. As Fig. 7.4 reveals, the sub-Saharan African average for the 32 countries in 2016/18 was 1.25 on the index, ranging from a relatively nominal 0.16 in Mauritius to 1.96 in Guinea and 1.95 in Gabon. Severe lived poverty, based on the frequent experience of a lack of one or more of the five basic necessities is also prevalent in a number of countries across the region (Fig. 7.5). This ranges from a low of 3% experiencing one of more forms of severe deprivation to more than 70% in the cases of Guinea, Niger, Gabon, Togo, Lesotho, Madagascar and Benin.

Evidence suggests that there exists a negative association between well-being and lived poverty. For instance, based on analysis of the early Afrobarometer rounds, Bratton (2006) found that respondents' self-placement on the Cantril ladder of well-being tended to increase as their level of lived poverty decreased. Similarly, Møller et al. (2017, pp. 95–96) examined Afrobarometer Round 6 (2013/14) data and Gallup World Poll ladder-of-life data (2013/15) and were able to demonstrate that African countries that experienced less lived poverty generally reported higher levels of happiness. Their analysis also suggested that changes in both lived poverty and happiness over time are associated. For example, Zimbabwe, formerly a breadbasket in southern African and since then often regarded as a failed state, where unemployment and poverty are endemic and political strife and repression are commonplace, experienced some poverty relief in daily life in the decade between 2005 and 2015, possibly owing to a very brief respite from harsh economic hardship and political instability, thanks to a coalition government. The drop in the country's lived poverty

---

[8] Referring to development economist Sachs' (2005) book by that title.

[9] Afrobarometer's Lived Poverty Index is an experiential measure that is based on a series of survey questions about how frequently people actually go without five basic necessities during the course of a year. Respondents report how often (just once or twice, several times, many times, always) they or a member of their family have gone without enough food, clean water for home use, medicines or medical treatment, cooking fuel, and cash income. See Mattes (2008, 2019) and www.afrobarom eter.org.

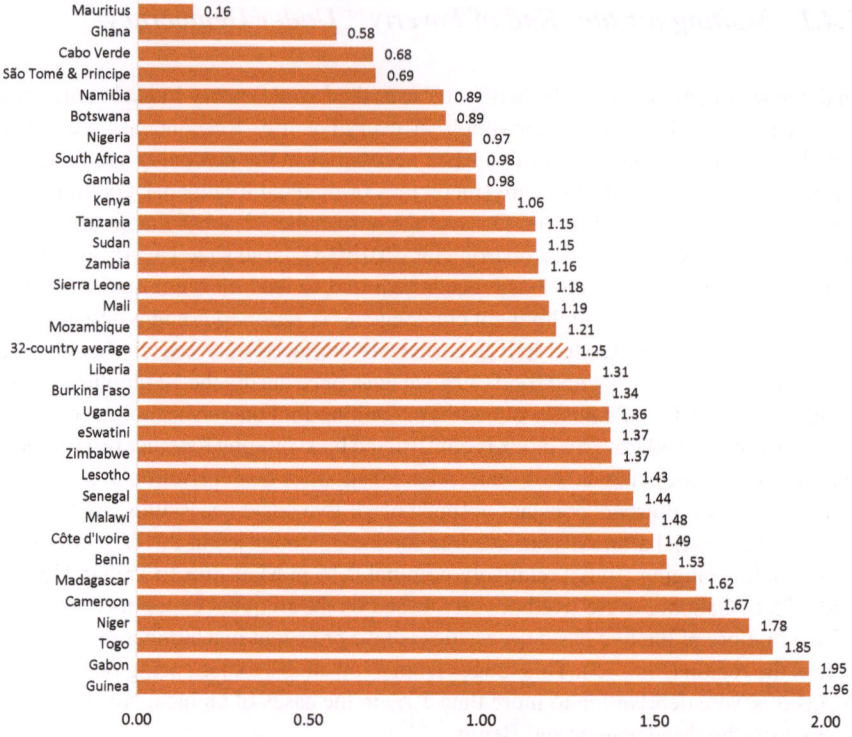

Fig. 7.4 Lived poverty index scores for 32 sub-Saharan African countries, 2016/2018. Data from Afrobarometer round 7 (Afrobarometer 2019). Lived poverty index (LPI) scores reflect average deprivation of five basic necessities on a scale of 0 (no deprivation) to 4 (constant absence of all basic necessities)

score of 0.61 points over this period was matched by a corresponding increase of 0.64 points in its happiness score.

7.4.2 Well-Being and Infrastructure Development

Developing the continent's infrastructure is a major challenge for African countries. The upkeep of infrastructure inherited from the colonial days has not kept pace with population growth since the 1960s. The Programme for Infrastructure Development in Africa estimated in 2016 that the continent would need to invest up to $93 billion a year until 2020 for capital investment and maintenance (Gernetzky 2016). Where there is an expectation that democracy will provide not only freedom but also better living conditions for ordinary people, Africa's huge backlog of infrastructure may play an even more important role in determining personal well-being.

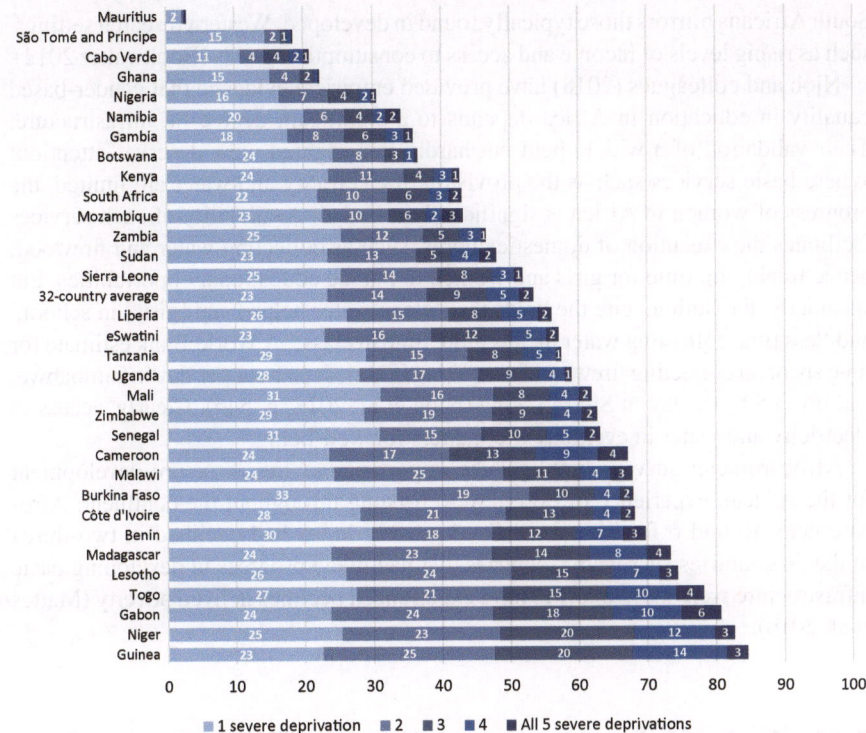

Fig. 7.5 Severe lived poverty for 32 sub-Saharan African countries, 2016/2018. Data from Afrobarometer round 7 (Afrobarometer 2019). Severe lived poverty reflects the frequent experience (many times/always) in the year prior to interviewing of one or more of the five basic necessities

Afrobarometer reports that on average, across 35 African countries in Round 6, only about two-thirds of the people live in communities with an electric grid (65%) and/or piped water infrastructure (63%), and less than one in three have adequate sewage disposal (30%), while more than three times as many have access to cellular phone service (93%). Only about half (54%) live in zones with tarred or paved roads. Regional comparisons across the continent show that sub-Saharan Africa lags behind North Africa in making all five of these services available to citizens (Afrobarometer 2016; Mitullah et al. 2016). The availability of infrastructure may be one of the factors reflected in North Africa's higher than average happiness ratings on the continent, according to Gallup World Poll happiness ratings (Møller et al. 2017, p. 86).

It is telling that in 1994 the government of South Africa, the last country on the continent to gain its independence, promised a 'better life' to meet its newly enfranchised black citizens' aspirations for housing, running water, and electricity. Some twenty-five years later, there is still a marked difference between what determines happiness among black and white South Africans, respectively. Economists found that better access to infrastructure and public goods increased happiness among black South Africans, while determinants of the happiness among mainly wealthier white

South Africans mirrors those typically found in developed, Western research settings, such as rising levels of income and access to consumption goods (Bookwalter 2012).

Njoh and colleagues (2018) have provided empirical evidence that gender-based equality in education in Africa depends to a significant degree on infrastructure. Their validation of a widely-held but hardly interrogated view deserves attention: Where basic services such as the provision of electricity and water are limited, the progress of women in Africa is significantly retarded. Availability of such services facilitates the execution of domestic chores, such as collecting water and firewood, hence freeing up time for girls and women to pursue educational opportunities. Put succinctly, the authors cite the point that 'clean water helps keep [girls] in school,' and 'less time collecting water means more time in class.' A World Bank estimate for time spent on collecting firewood for cooking is almost an hour per day in Zimbabwe, and up to 5 h per day in Sierra Leone (Njoh et al. 2018, p. 546). Clearly, access to electricity and water in everyday life matters for well-being.

Afrobarometer surveys highlight the importance of infrastructure development for the African experience of everyday well-being throughout the continent. Afrobarometer Round 6 found that the lived poverty index had declined in two-thirds of the 36 countries surveyed. Countries that had made progress in developing basic infrastructure were more likely to have experienced declines in lived poverty (Mattes et al. 2016).

7.4.3 Lack of Infrastructure and Threats to Democracy

While poor infrastructure and lack of service delivery may contribute to everyday lived poverty and depressed happiness, it may also undermine Africa's democracy project. A case in point is South Africa's relatively new democracy. An Afrobarometer Round 6 survey conducted there suggests that South African citizens might be willing to give up their democratic rights in favour of improvements to their living conditions. While almost two-thirds (64%) of South African respondents thought that democracy was preferable to any other kind of government, a similarly high percentage (62%) stated they would be 'very willing' or 'willing' to give up regular elections to live under a non-elected government capable of ensuring law and order and service delivery.[10] The growing global trend towards authoritarianism could lead to a resurgence of such regimes in Africa.[11]

---

[10]See Afrobarometer (2015, p. 22) for results relating to conditional support for democracy in South Africa amid rising discontent at the time of the Zuma presidency (2009–2018), which was characterised by mismanagement, inconsistent policy-making, and corruption scandals. See also Afrobarometer Dispatch No. 71 by Lekalake (2016) on declining support for democracy and rising discontent with implementation.

[11]See Foa and Mounk (2017) on the global rise in citizens wishing for a strong leader in their paper on signs of democratic deconsolidation.

7.5 Africa's 'Big Men', Authoritarian Regimes, and Discontent

7.5.1 The 'Wind that Shakes Africa's Coconut Trees'

The end of the Cold War and the demise of the Soviet Union may have been a factor in setting the stage for a dramatic turn away from one-party autocracy in Africa. Although the challenge to authoritarianism in many African states may have preceded the fall of the Berlin Wall in 1989, and the disintegration of the communist union, external dynamics may have played a secondary role in the collapse of Africa's authoritarian regimes. Western governments no longer had any need to support corrupt autocrats, such as Mobutu, Doe, Banda, and Bongo,[12] who provided political stability or assistance in the 'war on terror'. President Bongo of Gabon is said to have described the end of the Cold War as 'a wind from the East that is shaking the coconut trees' (Somerville 2017, pp. 212–213).

The late 1980s and the early 1990s saw an upsurge in demonstrations, strikes and demands for democracy and accountability in many African states, where citizens had grown impatient with the incompetence and corruption of their leaders. Eleven heads of states were removed from power as protests escalated and by 1992, eighteen heads of state had lost power. Others who remained had 'to change their tune' (Somerville 2017, p. 213). For example, Felix Houphouët-Boigny of Côte d'Ivoire bowed to domestic pressure and to demands from French President Mitterand that Francophone countries become more democratic or risk cuts in aid (Somerville 2017, p. 213).

7.5.2 The Ibrahim Prize for Good Governance

Three decades after democracy's restoration in the 1990s, Africa's democratic process is still very fragile. While the two-term presidency is now the norm—some few countries allow for seven-year terms—leaders have nevertheless found ways to persuade the electorate to make exceptions. After the winds shook the coconut trees, some former autocratic leaders adapted to the new system of rules by ostensibly organising multi-party elections while using state power, media control and coercion by party thugs and security forces to ensure that the outcomes favoured them (Somerville 2017, p. 213). Although the era of military coups, dictatorships and blatant authoritarianism may be over in Africa, there are still a number of African leaders who resort to more subtle manipulations of electoral and constitutional mechanisms to delay relinquishing power.

---

[12]Mobutu Sese Seko was president of Zaire/the Democratic Republic of the Congo from 1965 to 1997; Samuel Doe ruled Liberia from 1980 to 1990; Dr. Hastings Kamuzu Banda was Malawi's autocratic ruler from 1966 to 1994 although he had hoped to rule for life; and Omar Bongo was in power in Gabon from 1967 to 2009.

In 2020, the Covid-19 pandemic upset the democratic process in countries that were scheduled for elections that year. In Ethiopia, the decision by Prime Minister Abiy to postpone the elections indefinitely created a constitutional crisis, as the five-year terms of the federal and regional legislatures would expire that year. Some analysts interpreted Abiy's decision as reflecting authoritarian aspirations to become the 'Big Man' of Ethiopia at any cost (Berhe 2020). Malawi's incumbent President Mutharika's decision to hold elections during the pandemic was criticised for putting citizens at risk for contracting the virus in order for him to stay in power.

The Ibrahim Prize for good governance in Africa, instituted by the Mo Ibrahim Foundation in 2006, is awarded to former African leaders who have honoured their countries' constitutionally mandated term limits, and have dedicated their rule to improving people's lives. Only five winners have been selected since the prize was launched, if we discount President Nelson Mandela of South Africa, who was named the inaugural Honorary Laureate in 2007. The Ibrahim Prize has been awarded to President Joaquim Chissano of Mozambique (2007), President Festus Mogae of Botswana (2008), President Pedro Pires of Cabo Verde (2011), President Hifikepunye Pohamba of Namibia (2014), and most recently, in 2017, President Ellen Johnson Sirleaf (of Liberia).

Johnson Sirleaf served two terms as president of Liberia, from 2006 to 2017. In its citation, the prize committee praised 'her exceptional and transformative leadership, in the face of unprecedented and renewed challenges, to lead Liberia's recovery following many years of devastating civil war'.[13] During Sirleaf's term in office, the country faced the challenge of fighting the worst outbreak of Ebola that swept through her country and its two neighbouring ones in West Africa between 2014 and 2016. Noteworthy is that Sirleaf was the first woman to serve as president of a sub-Saharan country and is the only female recipient of the prestigious Ibrahim award so far.

7.5.3   The Curse of Third-Termism

'As Africans we don't have to make a choice between democracy and development. We deserve both.'[14]

'Democracy is not a good thing for Africa. We were all happy to see democracy come to Africa, but it destroyed the human sensibility. To have a democracy, people have to understand democracy, and how can people understand when 85% of the people in the country cannot read or write? They need a benevolent dictator like China has; someone who loves his country and acts for his country.' Salif Keita, Malian musician (Interview in The Guardian 2019)

---

[13] http://www.mo.ibrahim.foundation/news/2018/ellen-johnson-sirleaf-wins-2017-ibrahim-prize-achievement-african-leadership/ (Accessed 7 February 2019).

[14] See Hendricks and Kiven (2018) writing on Africa's 'slippery slope' to authoritarianism and the 'curse of third-termism'.

In their book on authoritarian Africa, professor of democracy Nic Cheeseman and reader in African politics Jonathan Fisher maintain that Africa's 'Big Men' are a legacy of colonial rule: 'The unstable authoritarian pathways that so many African states followed after colonial rule was no accident.' The colonial era strengthened the power of political leaders over their communities, which undermined pre-existing checks and balances in African societies and so helped institutionalise repressive forms of governance. At the same time, they note, colonial rule also ensured that the new leaders would face a major struggle to assert their authority. It did this by creating states with limited capacity to provide services and police their territories (Cheeseman and Fisher 2019a, 2019b).

Africa's longest-ruling leaders have come from across the continent (Fig. 7.6). In 2016, 15 leaders of 48 African countries that hold regular elections had served more than two terms or had indicated their intention to do so. Africa's 'Big Men', who personalise power, often have poor human rights records and use repression to hang on to power (Cohen and Doya 2016). They chiefly gain their support through Africa's widespread patronage system. There are numerous reports of clientelism, cronyism, nepotism and rent-seeking practices that have kept Africa's leaders in power and retarded economic growth and advances in democracy.[15] A number of Africa's authoritarian regimes have survived because they have provided political stability or support for the 'war on terror', thus attracting the foreign aid and investment needed for development.[16] The West was the main source of aid in Africa until China arrived as 'a no-strings' economic player at the end of the 1990s (Somerville 2017, p. 213).

While the Ibrahim Prize sets the standard for African leadership, there are concerns that Russian and Chinese examples of extending or abolishing term limits might set a different example, given their countries' growing influence on the continent. In 2018, the Chinese National People's Congress removed term limits for their president and vice president, which will allow President Xi Jinping to remain in power for life.[17] China's example might be regarded as a gratuitous 'gift to African despots' (Kiwuwa

---

[15]Many Africa scholars have written about the clientelism, cronyism, nepotism, and rent-seeking practices that have kept Africa's leaders in power and retarded economic growth and advances in democracy. See among others, Cheeseman (2015), Meredith (2011, 2014), Mills (2014), Mills and Herbst (2012), Ndulu and O'Connell (1999), van de Walle (2003), and Wrong's (2010) account of Kenya's whistle-blowers.

[16]In the case of Chad, President Idriss Déby became president of this resource rich nation in 1990, after leading a rebellion against former president Hissène Habré. Although regular multi-party elections are conducted, no leadership change has been forthcoming and this authoritarian leader is in effect a president for life. In 2018, parliament amended the constitution to allow him to remain in office until 2033, when he will be 81 years old, and in August 2020, to commemorate the country's 60th anniversary he declared himself "Maréchal du Tchad" (Marshall of Chad). He has been a leading partner in the subregional coalition to fight the Boko Haram terrorist group, and has cultivated the idea that he personally is instrumental in Chad's stability and security in the anti-jihadist fight in the Sahel. This, and the backing of France, has diminished the prospects of a likely peaceful transition to a political successor (Tampa 2020).

[17]Deng Xiaoping's reforms that guided China towards a market economy mandated retirement age for leaders at 70 (Mills et al. 2019, p. 48).

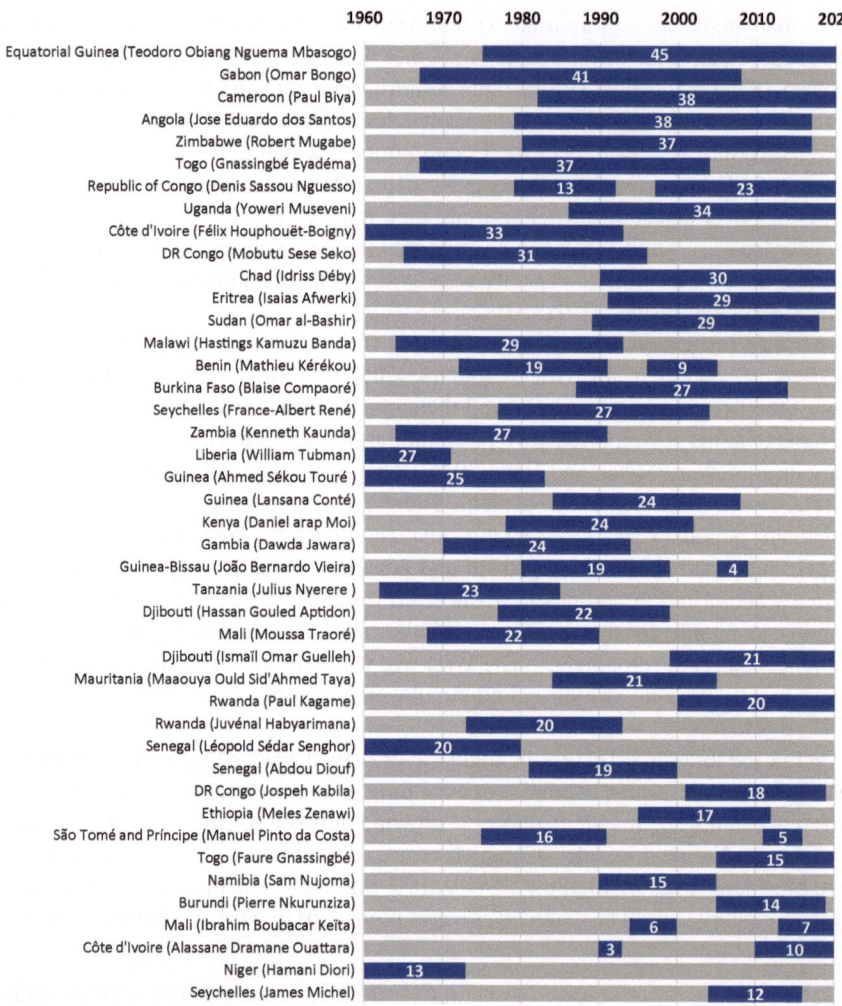

Fig. 7.6 Length of time heads of state were in office in sub-Saharan Africa, 1960–2020. The blue-shaded bars and numbers in the graph above represent the length of time (in years) that specific heads of state in sub-Saharan African nations spent in office. The figures are ranked in descending order from longest time in office to shortest

2018). Similarly, Russia's President Vladimir Putin set a further example to long-term African leaders when he effectively won a fourth term in 2018, after changes to the Russian constitution. In 2020, Russia's constitutional referendum confirmed amendments that allow Putin to run for further terms. He can potentially lead the country until 2036—effectively Putin could be Russia's president for the rest of his life.

The African Union's Charter for Democracy, Elections and Governance, ratified in 2012, does not state anything specifically about abolishing term limits. Political scientists Hendricks and Kevin (2018) draw attention to the fact that some of the men holding African Union leadership positions have themselves amended or abandoned presidential term limits, or come from countries that have done so, which may account for this omission.

An example of a country valued for its political stability and economic development after years of conflict is business-friendly Rwanda. The country was chosen to host the 2016 World Economic Forum on Africa in its capital city Kigali, in recognition of its role as a model for regional development. Rwanda's President Paul Kagame, a leader in Rwanda's post-genocide government since 1994, gained approval by referendum in 2015 to stand for an unprecedented third term in 2017. The controversial vote on the country's constitution means that Kagame could be in power until 2034, in a country with unusually low life evaluations in the Gallup World Poll[18] relative to its economic success. President Kagame is said to have remarked that African countries that change their leaders too often have not fared as well as his country has. He may not be alone in claiming that authoritarian rule is a more efficient form of democracy in less developed parts of the world.[19]

Citizens in a number of African countries appear to share President Kagame's view that strong leadership is in the interest of political stability and economic development. An influential exponent is Salif Keita, Mali's iconic musician, who favours strong leadership over democracy for Africa (see quotation above). Afrobarometer Round 7 shows that views across sub-Saharan Africa are divided on certain governance issues, such as one-man rule and term limits (see Table 7.2, top). On average across countries, one-man rule is rejected by four out of five citizens, while only 11% are in favour, and three-quarters support two-term limits for their president. However, the differences between highest and lowest values of support and rejection of two-term limits are striking. At least 85% in Gabon, Tanzania, Togo, Gambia and Benin were in favour of constitutional two-term limits. In Mozambique, a country still suffering from the effects of a 16-year civil war that ended in 1994, the difference in the proportional shares that were against (41%) and in favour (30%) of one-man rule were not especially large, and only 54% supported a term limit. Noteworthy is that all of these countries have experience of longer-term leadership.[20]

---

[18] In the World Happiness Report 2019, Rwanda's life evaluation ranked 152 out of the 156 countries included in the Gallup World Poll in the 2016–2018 period (Helliwell et al. 2019, p. 26) and 150 out of 153 countries in the 2017–2019 period (Helliwell et al. 2020, p. 26).

[19] See Schmemann's (2016) overview of the challenges facing democratic principles in an unstable world, which include authoritarian rule and the attraction of the 'Big Man'.

[20] Gabon's current President Ali Ben Bongo, sworn in for a second seven-year term in 2016 in a contested election followed by public protests, called a national dialogue that resulted in changes to the constitution in 2018 that left his power virtually untouched. Bongo took over from his late father who had ruled the country for 41 years until his death in 2009.

Anti-colonial activist Julius Kambarage Nyerere governed Tanganyika as Prime Minister from 1961 to 1962 and then as President from 1963 to 1964, after which he led its successor state, Tanzania, as President from 1964 to 1985.

Longer-term presidencies and authoritarian rule offer greater opportunities over time for rent-seeking and corruption. Longer-term presidencies also tend to produce autocratic rule that may lead to suppression of freedoms in society. Referring to Kagame's Rwanda, the influential *The Economist* notes that 'a land ruled by fear can never be happy or secure' (Mills et al. 2019, p. 57).

7.6   Conclusion

In this chapter we report that African democracy, as elsewhere on the globe, is still a work in progress. The majority of people living in the sub-Saharan countries consider democracy to be preferable to any other form of government. However, supply of democracy does not meet demand in many cases and sub-Saharan Africa's 'dissatisfied democrats' may provide a positive force for change in the region.

We highlight the role played by good governance in producing the material benefits of democracy. For many African citizens, freedom from poverty is as important as political freedom. Infrastructure and services matter for quality of everyday life in Africa. We also review the possible threat to the continent's democracy project by African leaders who are reluctant to relinquish power.

In the next chapter we look at the life chances for future generations of young people living in sub-Saharan Africa. Will the continent's vast youth population fare better under democracy or authoritarian rule? Can Africa's demographic dividend be realised in the longer term?

References

Africa Wikipedia (2019). List of elections in 2019. https://en.wikipedia.org/wiki/List_of_elections_in_2019. Accessed February 22, 2019.
Afrobarometer (2002). *What do Africans think about democracy and development?* Afrobarometer Briefing Paper No. 1. www.afrobarometer.org.

Togolese President Faure Gnassingbé has been in office since 2005, winning his fourth term in February 2020. Prior to coming to power, his father, Gnassingbé Eyadéma, served as president from 1967 until his death in 2005.

In Gambia, Yahya Jammeh was a military leader who became president of the country in 1996 following a coup d'état in mid-1994, overthrowing the country's first president, Sir Dawda Jawara, who ruled from 1970 to 1994 (after being prime minister from 1962 to 1970). Jammeh was in office for four consecutive terms until his defeat by Adama Barrow in the 2016 election.

Benin's Mathieu Kérékou, in and out of power over a thirty-year period since 1972, was barred from running for a third term as president in 2016 on constitutional and age grounds.

Mozambique's Joachim Chissano, installed as the country's second president in 1986 after President Samora Machel was killed in a plane crash, stepped down in 2005 after 18 years in office. He is credited with transforming the war-torn country into one of the most successful African democracies. He was awarded the first Mo Ibrahim prize for good governance in 2007.

Afrobarometer (2015). *Summary of results, Afrobarometer round 6 survey in South Africa, 2015.* Compiled by: Plus 94 Research. http://afrobarometer.org/sites/default/files/publications/Summary%20of%20results/saf-r6-sor.pdf#page=1&zoom=auto,-13,653. Accessed November 4, 2016.

Afrobarometer (2016). *Highlights of round 6 survey findings from 36 African countries.* http://afrobarometer.org/sites/default/files/summary_results/ab_R6_afrobarometer_global_release_highlights3.pdf. Accessed May 20, 2020.

Afrobarometer (2019). *Merged round 7 data (34 countries) (2019).* http://www.afrobarometer.org/data/merged-round-7-data-34-countries-2019. Accessed July 9, 2020.

Akokpari, J. K. (2004). The AU, NEPAD and the promotion of good governance in Africa. *Nordic Journal of African Studies, 13*(3), 243–263.

Aucoin, D., & Donnenfeld. (2016). *Unlocking Africa's potential: The relationship between effective governance and poverty.* Institute for Security Studies, African Futures Paper 21. https://issafrica.s3.amazonaws.com/site/uploads/af21.pdf.

Awami, S. (2020). Tanzania's John Magufuli—the man vowing to defeat coronavirus and imperialism. *BBC News,* 18 June. https://www.bbc.com/news/world-africa-52983563. Accessed June 19, 2020.

Berhe, M.G. (2020). Ethiopia's poll has been pushed out by COVID-19. But there's much more at play. *The Conversation,* 18 May. https://theconversation.com/ethiopias-poll-has-been-pushed-out-by-covid-19-but-theres-much-more-at-play-138322. Accessed June 19, 2020.

Bookwalter, J. T. (2012). Living the good life: An economic view of happiness in South Africa. In H. Selin & G. Davey (Eds.), *Happiness across cultures* (pp. 329–344). Dordrecht: Springer.

Bratton, M. (2006). Poor people and democratic citizenship in Africa, Afrobarometer Working Paper, no. 56. Afrobarometer: East Lansing, MI/Accra, Cape Town.

Cantril, H. (1965). *The pattern of human concerns.* New Brunswick, NJ: Rutgers University Press.

Chaligha, A., Mattes, R., Bratton, M., & Davids, Y.D. (2002). Uncritical citizens or patient trustees? Tanzanians' views of political and economic reform. Afrobarometer Working Paper No. 18. http://afrobarometer.org/sites/default/files/publications/Working%20paper/AfropaperNo18.pdf.

Charron, N., & Bågenholm, A. (2016). Ideology, party systems and corruption voting in European democracies. *Electoral Studies, 41,* 35–49.

Cheeseman, N. (2015). *Democracy in Africa: Successes, failures, and the struggle for political reform.* Cambridge: Cambridge University Press.

Cheeseman, N., & Fisher, J. (2019a). How colonial rule predisposed Africa to fragile authoritarianism. *The Conversation,* 4 November. https://theconversation.com/how-colonial-rule-predisposed-africa-to-fragile-authoritarianism-126114.

Cheeseman, N., & Fisher, J. (2019b). *Authoritarian Africa: Repression, resistance, and the power of ideas.* (African World Histories). Oxford: Oxford University Press.

Cheeseman, N. (2020). *A changing of the guards or a change of systems?* BTI Regional Report Sub-Saharan Africa. Gütersloh: Bertelsmann Stiftung. https://dx.doi.org/10.11586/2020048.

Cohen, M., & Doya, D.M. (2016). Power-drunk leaders block Africa's dawn. *Business Day,* Johannesburg, 8 February, p. 13.

Dahlberg, S., & Solevid, M. (2016). Does corruption suppress voter turnout? *Journal of Elections, Public Opinion and Parties, 26*(4), 489–510.

Diamond, L. J. (2008). *The spirit of democracy: The struggle to build free societies throughout the world.* New York: Times Books.

Diamond, L. J., & Plattner, M. F. (2010). *Democratization in Africa: Progress and retreat.* Baltimore, Maryland: Johns Hopkins University Press.

Diatta, M.M. (2018). With a busy election schedule, Africa needs a reversal of the old order, *The Conversation,* 15 February. https://theconversation.com/with-a-busy-election-schedule-africa-needs-a-reversal-of-the-old-order-91690.

Diener, E., Lucas, R. E., Schimmack, U., & Helliwell, J. F. (2009). *Well-being for public policy.* Oxford: Oxford University Press.

Ducharme, J. (2020). World Health Organization declares COVID-19 a 'pandemic'. Here's what that means. *TIME*, 11 March. https://time.com/5791661/who-coronavirus-pandemic-dec laration/. Accessed July 4, 2020.

Foa, R. S., & Mounk, Y. (2017). The signs of deconsolidation. *Journal of Democracy, 28*(1), 5–16.

Freedom House (2014). *Freedom in the world 2014*. Washington DC: Freedom House. https://fre edomhouse.org/sites/default/files/2020-02/Freedom_in_the_World_2014_complete_book.pdf. Accessed July 9, 2020.

Freedom House (2020). *Freedom in the world 2020: A leaderless struggle for democracy*. Wash ington DC: Freedom House. https://freedomhouse.org/report/freedom-world/2020/leaderless-str uggle-democracy. Accessed July 9, 2020.

Friedman, S. (2020). Unravelling why some democracies—but not all—are better at fighting pandemics. *The Conversation*, 14 April. https://theconversation.com/unravelling-why-some-dem ocracies-but-not-all-are-better-at-fighting-pandemics-136267.

Fukuyama, F. (2020). The pandemic and political order: It takes a state. *Foreign Affairs, 99*(4), 26–32.

Gernetzky, K. (2016). SA manufacturers urged to take on African rail projects. *Business Day*, Johannesburg, 10 October, p. 2.

Gqubule, D. (2020). Now is the time for better basic income grants. *New Frame news*, 14 June 2020. https://www.newframe.com/now-is-the-time-for-better-basic-income-grants/. Accessed June 11, 2020.

Hamilton, L. (2020). What sets good and bad leaders apart in the coronavirus era. *The Conver sation*, 7 June. https://theconversation.com/what-sets-good-and-bad-leaders-apart-in-the-corona virus-era-140013.

Helliwell, J. F., & Huang, H. (2008). How's your government? International evidence linking good government and well-being. *British Journal of Political Science, 38*, 595–619.

Helliwell, J., Huang, H., Grover, S., & Wang, S. (2014). Good governance and national well-being: What are the linkages? *OECD Working Papers on Public Governance*, No. 25, OECD Publishing, Paris. http://dx.doi.org/10.1787/5jxv9f651hvj-en.

Helliwell, J. F., Huang, H., & Wang, S. (2019). Changing world happiness. In J. Helliwell, R. Layard, & J. Sachs (Eds.), *World happiness report 2019 (chapter 2* (pp. 11–45). New York: Sustainable Development Solutions Network.

Helliwell, J. F., Huang, H., Wang, S., & Norton, M. (2020). Social environments for world happiness. In J. F. Helliwell, R. Layard, J. Sachs, & J.-E. De Neve (Eds.), *World happiness report 2020 (chapter 2* (pp. 12–45). New York: Sustainable Development Solutions Network.

Hendricks, C., & Kiven, G.N. (2018). Presidential term limits: slippery slope back to authoritar ianism in Africa. *The Conversation*, 17 May. https://theconversation.com/presidential-term-lim its-slippery-slope-back-to-authoritarianism-in-africa-96796.

Huntington, S. P. (1991). *The third wave: Democratization in the late twentieth century*. Norman, Oklahoma: University of Oklahoma Press.

Keulder, C., & Wiese, T. (2005). Democracy without democrats: Results from the 2003 Afrobarom eter survey in Namibia. Afrobarometer Working Paper No. 47. http://afrobarometer.org/sites/def ault/files/publications/Working%20paper/AfropaperNo47.pdf.

Kiwuwa, D.E. (2018). Why China's removal of term limits is a gift to African despots. *The Conver sation*, March 8. https://theconversation.com/why-chinas-removal-of-term-limits-is-a-gift-to-afr ican-despots-92746.

Kaufmann, D. & Kraay, A. (2020). The worldwide governance indicators. http://info.worldbank. org/governance/wgi/index.aspx#home. Accessed Jul 22, 2020.

Kwayu, A.C. (2020). Tanzania's COVID-19 response puts Magufuli's leadership style in sharp relief. *The Conversation*, 31 May. https://theconversation.com/tanzanias-covid-19-res ponse-puts-magufulis-leadership-style-in-sharp-relief-139417.

Lekalake, R. (2016). Support for democracy in South Africa declines amid rising discontent with implementation. *Afrobarometer Dispatch* No. 71. http://afrobarometer.org/sites/default/files/pub lications/Dispatches/ab_r6_dispatchno71_south_africa_perceptions_of_democracy.pdf.

Logan, S. (2017). Why elections matter for democracy in Africa. The cases of Kenya and Rwanda. *The Conversation*, August 4. https://theconversation.com/why-elections-matter-for-democracy-in-africa-the-cases-of-kenya-and-rwanda-82013.

Mattes, R. (2008). The material and political bases of lived poverty in Africa: Insights from the Afrobarometer. In V. Møller, D. Huschka, & A. C. Michalos (Eds.), *Barometers of quality of life around the globe: How are we doing?* (pp. 161–185). Social Indicators Research Series 33, Dordrecht: Springer.

Mattes, R. (2019). *Democracy in Africa: Demand, supply, and the 'dissatisfied democrat'*. Afrobarometer Policy Paper No. 54, February. https://www.africaportal.org/documents/18863/ab_r7_policypaperno54_africans_views_of_democracy.pdf.

Mattes, R., & Bratton, M. (2016). *Do Africans still want democracy?* Afrobarometer Policy Paper No. 36, November.

Mattes, R., Dulani, B., & Gyimah-Boadi, E. (2016). *Africa's growth dividend? Lived poverty drops across much of the continent*. Afrobarometer Policy Paper No. 29. https://www.afrobarometer.org/publications/pp29-africas-growth-dividend-lived-poverty-drops-across-the-continent.

Mattes, R., & Shenga, C. (2013). Uncritical citizenship in a low-information society: Mozambicans in comparative perspective. In M. Bratton (Ed.), *Voting and democratic citizenship in Africa (chapter 9* (pp. 159–178). Boulder, CO: Lynne Rienner Publishers.

Meredith, M. (2011). *The state of Africa: A history of the continent since independence*. London: Simon & Schuster.

Meredith, M. (2014). *The fortunes of Africa: A 5,000-year history of wealth, greed and endeavour*. London: Simon & Schuster with Johannesburg/Cape Town: Jonathan Ball Publishers.

Mills, G. (2014). *Why states recover: Changing walking societies into winning nations, from Afghanistan to Zimbabwe*. Johannesburg: Picador Africa.

Mills, G., & Herbst, J. I. (2012). *Africa's third liberation: The new search for prosperity and jobs*. London: Penguin.

Mills, G., Obasanjo, O., Herbst, J., & Biti, T. (2019). *Democracy works: Rewiring politics to Africa's advantage*. Johannesburg, South Africa: Picador Africa.

Møller, V., Roberts, B.J., Tiliouine, H., & Loschky, J. (2017). 'Waiting for happiness' in Africa. In: J. Helliwell, R. Layard & J. Sachs (Eds.), *World happiness report 2017* (chapter 4, pp. 84–120). New York: Sustainable Development Solutions Network. http://worldhappiness.report/ed/2017/, http://worldhappiness.report/wp-content/uploads/sites/2/2017/03/HR17-Ch4_w-oAppendix.pdf. ISBN 978-0-9968513-5-0.

Mitullah, W.V., Samson, R., Wambua, P.M., & Balongo, S. (2016). *Building on progress: Infrastructure development still a major challenge in Africa*. Afrobarometer Dispatch No. 69: http://afrobarometer.org/publications/ad69-building-progress-infrastructure-development-still-major-challenge-africa.

Mtimkulu, P. (2015). Democracy in Africa: The ebbs and flows over six decades. *The Conversation*, 12 June. https://theconversation.com/democracy-in-africa-the-ebbs-and-flows-over-six-decades-42011.

Mwai, P., & Giles, C. (2020). Coronavirus in Tanzania: What do we know? *BBC Reality Check*, 19 June. https://www.bbc.com/news/world-africa-52723594. Accessed June 19, 2020.

Ndulu, B., & O'Connell, S. (1999). Governance and growth in sub-Saharan Africa. *The Journal of Economic Perspectives, 13*(3), 41–66.

Njoh, A. J., Ananga, E. O., Ngyah-Etchutambe, I. B., Deba, L. D., Asah, F. J., Ayuk-Etang, E. N. M., et al. (2018). Electricity supply and access to water and improved sanitation as determinants of gender-based inequality in educational attainment in Africa. *Social Indicators Research, 135*, 533–548. https://doi.org/10.1007/s11205-016-1512-1.

Rahman, K. (2019). Mauritius: Overview of corruption and anti-corruption. Transparency International. https://knowledgehub.transparency.org/helpdesk/overview-of-corruption-and-anti-corruption-in-mauritius-1. Accessed June 9, 2020.

Riley, L., & Chilanga, E. (2018). 'Things are not working now': Poverty, food insecurity and perceptions of corruption in urban Malawi. *Journal of Contemporary African Studies, 36*(4), 484–498.

Roberts, B., Bekker, M., Rule, S,. Orkin, M., Bohler-Muller, N., & Alexander, K. (2020a). The calculus of trust: Diminished public confidence in the president's performance. *Daily Maverick*, 11 August. https://www.dailymaverick.co.za/article/2020-08-11-the-calculus-of-trust-diminished-public-confidence-in-the-presidents-performance/. Accessed August 19, 2020.

Roberts, B., Gordon, S. L., Mchunu, N., & Struwig, J. (2020b). Diminishing the power of the X? The electoral effect of corruption perceptions. In N. Bohler-Muller, V. Reddy, C. Soudien, & Y. D. D. Davids (Eds.), *State of the nation 2020: Ethics and politics of South Africa's struggle against poverty and inequality*. Cape Town: HSRC Press, in press.

Rose, R., & Peiffer, C. (2019). *Bad governance and corruption*. Cham, Switzerland: Springer.

Sachs, J. D. (2005). *The end of poverty: Economic possibilities for our time*. New York: Penguin.

Schmemann, S. (2016). Rough sailing for liberal values: Democratic principles face critical challenges in an unstable world. *International New York Times* supplement: Democracy 2016, a perfect storm of international crises, 14 September, p. S1.

Shanahan, G., & Smith, M. (2020). Could covid-19 be the push that Europe needs for unconditional basic income? *The Conversation*, 11 May. https://theconversation.com/could-covid-19-be-the-push-that-europe-needs-for-unconditional-basic-income-137843.

Somerville, K. (2017). *Africa's long road since independence: The many histories of a continent*. London: Penguin Books.

Stremlau, J.J. (2016). The US election: What's at stake for Africa's quest to deepen democracy? *The Conversation*, 17 August. https://theconversation.com/the-us-election-whats-at-stake-for-afr icas-quest-to-deepen-democracy-63777.

Sunday Times (2020). The BIG question we cannot afford to ignore. Johannesburg, 19 July, p. 20. https://www.timeslive.co.za/sunday-times/opinion-and-analysis/2020-07-19-the-big-que stion-we-cannot-afford-to-ignore/.

Tampa, V. (2020). With total control, President Déby is Chad's greatest threat to stability. *The Guardian*, 14 August. https://www.theguardian.com/global-development/2020/aug/14/pre sident-deby-chad-greatest-threat-to-stability.

The Guardian (2019). Interview with Salif Keita—Democracy is not a good thing for Africa. 6 February. https://www.theguardian.com/music/2019/feb/06/salif-keita-interview-democracy-is-a-not-a-good-thing-for-africa.

Van de Walle, N. (2003). Presidentialism and clientelism in Africa's emerging party systems. *The Journal of Modern African Studies, 41*(2), 297–321.

Wrong, M. (2010). *It's our turn to eat*. London: Fourth Estate.

Chapter 8
Future African Generations and Well-Being

Abstract Africa is the world's most youthful continent. Africa's future rests in the energy and creativity of its young people. In this chapter we examine the role of sub-Saharan youth in holding their leaders to account following the so-called the Arab Spring. We reflect on the push and pull factors that propel African youth to seek their life chances elsewhere, if they cannot realise their ambitions at home. Creating jobs for a growing population is a major concern for African leaders, who must find ways to turn the continent's youth bulge into an advantage. We give examples of initiatives that seek to invest in empowering Africa's youth and creating employment opportunities in the region. Lastly, we report on reasons why sub-Saharan Africa's population may continue to increase in the near future, and why leaders should act now rather than later to support women's needs for family planning, in order to enhance community well-being.

Keywords Sub-Saharan Africa · Demographic dividend · Youth protests · Youth unemployment · Youth migration · Reproductive health rights · Contraceptive use

8.1 'Africa Uprising'[1]

In the previous chapter, we outlined some of the ebbs and flows of democracies in Africa and presented some evidence that democracy goes hand in hand with prosperity. In countries where the supply of democracy has increased, citizen evaluations of life have improved over time. However, we also noted that recent years have seen a rise in authoritarian rule globally. With China's President Xi's extended tenure for life, international studies scholar Kiwuwa (2018) thinks African presidents now have a 'political godfather' to emulate, or at least to validate their continued stays in office.

The question is how long African citizens will support their 'Big Men' and long-serving leaders. Nine years ago, the so-called Arab Spring of 2011 saw regime change in North African countries that may have caused a ripple effect on the continent. When Burkina Faso's dictator of 27 years, Blaise Compaoré, was toppled in November

---

[1] The title is taken from a book by Branch and Mampilly (2015) on the new wave of popular protest in Africa.

© Springer Nature Switzerland AG 2021
V. Møller and B. J. Roberts, *Quality of Life and Human Well-Being in Sub-Saharan Africa*,
Human Well-Being Research and Policy Making,
https://doi.org/10.1007/978-3-030-65788-8_8

2014, Africa watcher Adebajo (2014) foresaw that a season of protest might have
hitched a ride on the Sahara's Harmattan, the wind that blows south every November.
Interestingly, the Gallup World Poll conducted a year prior to the coup in Burkina
Faso[2] found awareness of the Arab Spring was greater in Burkina Faso than in other
sub-Saharan countries (Loschky 2013).

In December 2016, Gambia's long-term president Yahya Jammeh's 22-year
authoritarian rule was set to end by a shock election result. Jammeh had boasted
he would rule The Gambia for a billion years.[3] The event was initially heralded
as a triumph for African democracy when Jammeh quickly accepted defeat, only
to dispute the election outcome a few weeks later. Mr Jammeh finally left office
in January 2017 after mediation by West African countries and the threat of armed
intervention.[4] Jammeh's successor, democratically elected President Adama Barrow,
has initiated reforms to transform Gambia into a democracy. One of Barrow's first
promises to his country was to establish a truth commission to chronicle atrocities
perpetrated against citizens in the past. This type of search for truth, conciliation and
closure has become an integral part of rebuilding societies after the fall of authoritarian regimes, or at the end of armed conflicts (Ateku 2019). Other countries in
West Africa have also followed this route to come to terms with their pasts.[5]

8.1.1 Clash of the Generations: Youth in the Forefront of Protest for Change

African democracies badly need a new generation of leaders, but 'where are they?'
asks professor of world politics, Chan (2018). Youth have always been in the forefront
of protest. Since the Arab Spring, youth and student protests have swept through many
countries south of the Sahara.

In 2016, South African students rallied under the banner of #FeesMustFall to
claim their rights to free tertiary education. Their protest action was successful in
that funds have been allocated to support students from poor households to attend
universities. It may be significant that these protests, following the Arab Spring, have
been interpreted as a clash between generations. For example, professor of sustainable
development Swilling (2016) saw the protests in South Africa and Ethiopia in 2016 as
part of a wave of protests sweeping through the continent known as 'Africa Uprising'.
Writing on Ethiopia's protests during the state of emergency in 2016, Gettleman

---

[2]Burkino Faso means 'land of honest men'. See BBC's Burkino Faso country profile. https://www.
bbc.com/news/world-africa-13072774 (Accessed 12 August 2020).

[3]See BBC's The Gambia country profile. http://www.bbc.com/news/world-africa-13376517
(Accessed 2 December 2016).

[4]See Kiwuwa's (2016) report on Jammeh's quick acceptance of defeat that astounded the world
until it was withdrawn. Pilling (2017) discusses the significance of the turn of events in The Gambia
for democracy in Africa.

[5]Ateku (2019) lists other West African countries that have taken this route in the past: Nigeria in
1999, Sierra Leone in 2000, Ghana in 2002, Liberia in 2005, and Côte d'Ivoire in 2012.

(2016) cites a university lecturer in central Ethiopia as saying, 'If you suffocate people and they don't have any other options but to protest, it breaks out. ...the whole youth... a whole generation is protesting.' In Kenya, Cooper (2014, 2016) has interpreted high school students' torching of boarding schools as political protest action. African studies professor Steinberg (2016) described South Africa's student protests as 'a war against the fathers' and 'inter-generational loathing'.

In 2016, Afrobarometer reported that their latest round of surveys found 11% of youth having been involved in at least one protest action in the preceding year.[6]

Since 2016, youth have been active in calling for change in several sub-Saharan countries:

In southern Africa, Zimbabwe's President Robert Mugabe, who was 93 years old and had ruled since 1987, was forced to resign in late 2017.

Angola's President José Eduardo dos Santos, who had ruled his country since 1979, handed over to João Lourenço in 2017 following elections that were declared free and fair.

Countrywide protests in Ethiopia led to a successful change of government when Hailemariam Desalegn stepped down voluntarily in early 2018 in order to hasten the country's return to democratic order. His successor, Abiy Ahmed Ali, Ethiopia's first prime minister from a minority ethnic group, quickly introduced bold reforms including offering amnesty to prisoners held during the state of emergency, and settling a long-standing border dispute with Eritrea that promises to bring peace and greater prosperity to the Horn of Africa. Abiy also deserves recognition for his role brokering the first historical meetings between Somalia and Somaliland (Gedamu 2020). For Ethiopia's Olympic silver-medalist marathoner, Lilesa (2019), Abiy represented new hope for democracy in Ethiopia. Endorsing Dr. Abiy as one of *TIME*'s influential leaders, Lilesa writes that Abiy made it possible for him to come home: 'Yes people are still protesting. But now, when thy protest, they aren't going to jail. To me, that's *democracy*. That is *hope*' (emphasis added).

In 2018, President Joseph Kabila of the Democratic Republic of Congo (DRC), who had postponed his country's presidential elections after his second full term of office ended in 2016, was finally voted out after 17 years in office when Felix Tshisekedi was announced the winner in 2019.

In a 'second wave'[7] of the Arab Spring in 2019, the youth of Algeria were the first to take to the streets, followed by their parents, to protest President Abdelaziz Bouteflika's seeking a fifth term in office. The youth invoked the memory of the war of independence in their allusions to slogans and songs from that time, calling for 'Algeria's liberation' (see Mahlouly 2019). By 2 April 2019, the countrywide protests over several months finally forced the ailing 82 year-old Bouteflika, a veteran of the country's war of independence, to step down after 20 years in power.[8]

---

[6]Afrobarometer (2016, p. 11).

[7]Our thanks go to our Algerian colleague and co-researcher, Habib Tiliouine, a professor at the University of Oran, for providing this concise label and interpretation for the protests taking place some eight years after the uprising in Tunisia in 2011.

[8]See https://www.bbc.com/news/world-africa-47795108 (Accessed 10 April 2019).

Emboldened by the success of the Algerian youth, Sudanese youth, in turn, risked their lives by demonstrating against President Omar Al-Bashir's 30-year rule. Al-Bashir is wanted by the International Criminal Court in The Hague for alleged war crimes and genocide in the conflict region of Darfur. *'Tasqut bas!*—just fall, that's all'—was the protest slogan that circulated on social media platforms to a global audience including the Sudanese diaspora, despite the government's media blackout (Satti 2019). Al-Bashir was finally forced to step down on 11 April 2019.

On 28 June 2020, Malawi's opposition leader, Lazarus Chakwera won the country's re-run presidential vote. Malawi's constitutional court had annulled incumbant President Mutharika's victory in the previous May 2019 election, citing vote tampering. Malawi is only the second African nation to annul a presidential election over irregularities, after Kenya in 2017. Chakwera's victory in the polls was hailed as a victory for democracy in Africa. Chakwera's victory means that three of the country's six competitive presidential elections have been won by opposition candidates (Abebe 2020).

Malawi's historic election campaign had gone ahead without any regard to the advancing coronavirus pandemic. Chakwera had held mass rallies dismissing concerns about Covid-19, saying the majority of Malawi's cases were imported. In a complete about-turn, in his first address to the nation a week after being sworn in as Malawi's new president, Chakwere now announced: 'Malawi, we have a situation'. Coronavirus is spreading 'all over Malawi' and 'faster than before' (BBC World Service Africa 2020a). The country's July 6 Independence Day celebrations, which would have been held in the capital's football stadium, were cancelled and his inauguration was limited to specially invited guests. The cancellation and scaling down of these events due to Covid-19 will have put a damper on the euphoria generated by Malawi's historic election triumph (BBC World Service Africa 2020b).

Football-loving Pierre Nkurunziza was Burundi's president for 15 years. He was elected president in 2005, in the first democratic elections to be held since the start of Burundi's civil war in 1994. A decade later, Burundi's Constitutional Court ruled in favour of his decision to stand for a controversial third term, which plunged the country into civil unrest 'of near civil war proportions' in 2015. Under pressure from his own political party, Nkurunziza decided not to seek a fourth term of office. Like other strong men in the region, he handpicked his successor, who won the presidential election of 20 May 2020, which went ahead despite the risk from the coronavirus pandemic (Kiwuwa 2020). Evariste Ndayishmiye was due only to take office in August, but was inaugurated as Burundi's new president a week after Nkurunziza suddenly died in hospital of a cardiac arrest on 8 June. His wife had tested positive for the coronavirus, so the first lady's status fuelled speculation that Nkurunziza also had Covid-19, but this was not verified (Allison 2020). Nkurunziza's administration had been unwilling to let the coronavirus interfere with the political transition. Political rallies went ahead with no form of social distancing and his government expelled the World Health Organisation's team backing the country's response to the coronavirus pandemic just days before the country's elections (The Guardian 2020).

Mali's President Ibrahim Boubacar Keïta resigned on 18 August 2020 after being seized by mutinying soldiers. He had been elected for a second term in 2018. The coup followed on weeks of demonstrations calling for the president to resign over economic mismanagement and failure to tackle jihadist insurgence. The soldiers who ousted Mali's president said they plan to set up a civilian transitional government and hold new elections (BBC World News Africa 2020).

8.1.2 Drought as a Risk Factor for 'Africa Uprising'

It might be worth considering that economic recessions following periods of drought have played a critical role in fueling the continent's discontent, as in the case of the 2011 Arab Spring and the 2019 protests in Sudan. 'What started as a fight against the tripling of the bread prices led to a challenge to the entire regime and the downfall of the dictatorship ... Finally it was something as simple and essential as bread that led to his [Al-Bashir's] downfall' (Plaut 2019).

Drought may well continue to spark further uprisings. Africa has a long history of extreme weather patterns,[9] conditions which are likely to be aggravated by climate change in the twenty-first century. Since 2016, countries in east and southern Africa have experienced severe drought conditions that negatively affected food production and increased food prices. The drought also caused tensions between herders and farmers when the former crossed country borders to find grazing for their animals. Predictably, severe flooding followed the drought.

On the nights of 14 and 15 March 2019, tropical cyclone Idai caused catastrophic rains and flooding and left more than 1,000 people dead in Mozambique, Malawi and Zimbabwe. Thousands of people were trapped for more than a week in submerged villages without clean water and food. Mozambique and neighbouring South Africa were plunged into darkness for hours.[10]

The United Nations estimates that US$2 billion worth of infrastructure will have been damaged by the most powerful cyclone to strike the region in decades (Weekend Post 2019). Rural villages affected by the flooding could only be reached by air. Among the first on the scene was The Gift of the Givers, a home-grown African charitable organisation that assists in the aftermath of natural and manmade disasters worldwide.[11] The organisation provided disaster response and humanitarian assistance in all three countries affected by Idai. It was not the first time it had helped victims of flooding in Mozambique and Malawi. First relief efforts in Mozambique

---

[9]See Reader's (1997) biography of the African continent, discussed in the introductory chapters.

[10]South Africa imports electricity from Mozambique.

[11]The Gift of the Givers is the largest disaster response NGO of African origin on the African continent. A South African trained medical doctor, Imtiaz Sooliman, first established the organisation on the instruction of a spiritual teacher in 1992. Gift of the Givers provides disaster response and relief as well as humanitarian aid. It has brought life-saving medical aid and humanitarian assistance to millions of people in 43 countries around the world, South Africa included. The Gift of the Givers actively seeks to build bridges between people of different cultures and religions engendering goodwill, harmonious co-existence, tolerance and mutual respect. See http://giftofthegivers.org/index.php?option=com_content&view=category&id=1198 (Accessed 4 April 2019).

focused on containing outbreaks of waterborne and infectious diseases. As cholera is endemic in the country, the World Health Organisation launched a vaccination campaign to contain an outbreak as soon as possible.

Barely a month following cyclone Idai, cyclone Kenneth left a wake of chaos in Mozambique, where many communities were still recovering from the earlier devastation (Weekend Post 2019).

On 30 January 2020, the World Health Organisation (WHO) declared the COVID-19 outbreak as a public health emergency of international concern that would also have economic effects. By February, the worst desert locust plague in 70 years had spread across seven east African countries down from Somalia to Tanzania, following on exceptionally wet weather in the region, including the rare cyclones that had struck eastern Africa. The locusts presented 'an extremely alarming and unprecedented threat' to food security and livelihoods according to the United Nations. In Kenya, coronavirus restrictions slowed efforts to fight the infestation, as crossing borders became more difficult and pesticide deliveries were held up. People in Uganda's Kumi district reportedly were filled with despair as their district had already endured flooding and an earlier swarm of locusts. They had been hopeful of receiving some food relief as the locust invasion and the Covid-19 lockdown had devastated the local economy—otherwise they would starve (Okiror 2020).

Responding to calls for assistance during the Covid-19 pandemic in mid-2020, the Gift of the Givers started a new disaster relief intervention in South Africa's Eastern Cape Province. The non-profit organisation provided food parcels, winter blankets and clothing to needy households; personal protective and other equipment and sanitisers to hospitals; and non-medical supplies, such as water tanks, to communities that had insufficient water for personal hygiene to protect against the virus (Nano 2020).

8.1.3   Commodity Prices as a Risk Factor for Discontent

A further risk factor for discontent and unrest in the sub-Saharan region is the combination of lower demand for commodities and lower commodity prices, which has required belt-tightening in Africa's oil-producing countries. A number of sub-Saharan countries had already had to turn to the IMF and the World Bank for bailouts in the past years (Khor 2016; Business Times 2019). By the time the Covid-19 pandemic arrived in Africa, many African countries had not fully recovered from the 2008–9 economic recession. Africa's unemployed youth and informal sector workers were among the worst affected by restrictions on 'business as usual' during lockdowns imposed on society to slow infections from overwhelming public health services. The economic downturn resulting from restrictions on livelihoods during Covid-19 lockdowns may push sub-Saharan countries further into debt. The World Bank (2020) took fast action to provide support to developing countries to strengthen their pandemic response. Some 26 sub-Saharan countries[12] stood to benefit from the World Bank Group's Operational Response to Covid-19 as of 17 June 2020. Sudan, which still featured on the US terrorism list was excluded at the time (Logan and Gali 2020), but United Nations Secretary-General António Gutteres pleaded for it to be included.

8.2 The Disconnect: Africa's 'Youth Bulge' and Ageing Leaders

A problem for Africans who yearn for change and greater life chances is that there is a dramatic disconnect between Africa's longest serving leaders and the continent's youth.[13] The age difference between leaders and the youth is striking. The average age of African leaders is 62 years, which is more than three times the average age of young people on the continent (Mills et al. 2019, p. 112). Some of Africa's leaders will have been born before the age of television and mobile phones and before the end of the colonial era. Uganda's President Museveni, campaigning virtually in 2020 during the coronavirus pandemic for his sixth term in office in 2021, is nicknamed *Katala*, a Luganda slang for someone 'out of touch and unsophisticated' (Mwine-Mugaju 2020). Given this generation gap, there is likely to be a mismatch between youth's expectations of democracy, and the reality that confronts them.[14]

8.2.1 *Africa's Mobile Phone Revolution*

The legacy of sub-Saharan Africa's oral tradition may have spurred enthusiasm for cellular phone connectivity. Most households in sub-Saharan Africa may never have had access to a landline telephone. Only 1.2% of people in the region had a telephone line in 2013[15] (World Bank 2014), but the first mobile phone has become a rite of passage for many teenagers. Figures 8.1 and 8.2 show that mobile phones have captured the imagination of the people on the continent. Africa's mobile cellular

---

[12]Beneficiaries included Benin, Burkino Faso, Burundi, Cabo Verde, Central African Republic, Chad, Côte d'Ivoire, Democratic Republic of Congo, eSwatini, Ethiopia, Gabon, Ghana, Kenya, Liberia, Lesotho, Mali, Malawi, Mauritania, Niger, Republic of the Congo, São Tomé e Príncipe, Senegal, Sierre Leone, Somalia, The Gambia, Togo. https://www.worldbank.org/en/about/what-we-do/brief/world-bank-group-operational-response-covid-19-coronavirus-projects-list (Accessed 17 June 2020).

[13]See Mills (2014, p. 571) on the disconnect between the expectations of youth and their ruling parties in authoritarian regimes in sub-Saharan Africa.

[14]See also Gopaldas (2015) and Population Reference Bureau (2016) on the age gap.

[15]Only three countries had figures exceeding 10%, namely Mauritius (29%), Seychelles (23%), and Cabo Verde (13%).

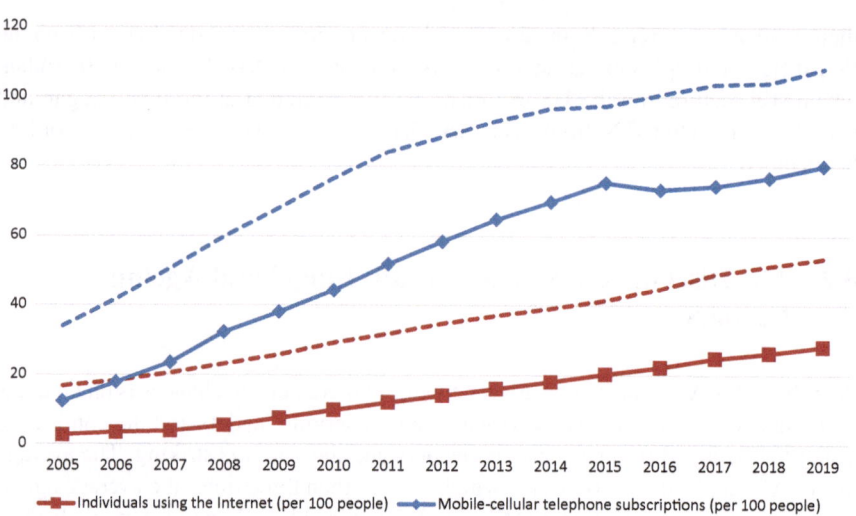

Fig. 8.1 Trends in mobile cellular telephone subscriptions and individual Internet usage per 100 inhabitants in Africa, 2005–19. The dashed lines represent the World average on the two ICT indicators. Data are from ITU World Telecommunications/ICT Indicators database

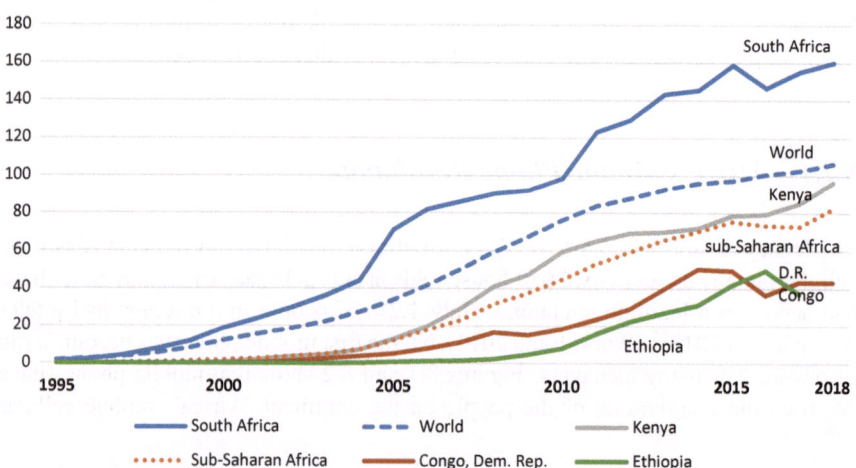

Fig. 8.2 Mobile cellular phone subscriptions, 1995–2018 (per 100 people). Data are from World Bank World Development Indicators 2020, based on ITU World Telecommunications/ICT Indicators database

telephone and internet usage is fast catching up with the rest of the world. Telecommunications may be one of the most readily adopted innovations in twenty-first century Africa, which has leapfrogged earlier stages of technological advances.

According to a recent report on world internet usage (Business Insider SA 2019), almost 40% of Africans went online in June 2019 compared to the world average of

60%. In terms of sheer numbers, more people were online in Africa than in South America. A new mammoth project to lay a subsea cable around Africa, the longest in the world, is set to boost internet access to Africa. The system is expected to go live by 2023/4, delivering more than the total combined capacity of all subsea cables serving Africa today (News24 2020).

Mobile phone technology has been used in innovative ways to improve quality of life in many domains, including health, finance, education, and family and social relations. In Kenya, for example, mobile phones are used for cash transfers. By 2011, some 40% of the population, or approximately 17 million people, were subscribers to M-Pesa, a digital banking system. This innovation has spread to other African countries, including Somalia. In South Africa, people living with HIV are reminded to take their ART medicine by text messaging. Health messages that inform of updates in malaria prevention and the Covid-19 virus are communicated rapidly by mobile phones to rural areas. We shall return to innovations produced by and adopted in African societies in a later chapter.

8.2.2 The Cellular Phone Divide Between Generations

Social media played an important role in the Arab Spring and has continued to do so in more recent youth protests across Africa. However, there are limitations to digital power. The hope that social media 'would be a boon to democrats and the enemy of authoritarians' has proved to be wishful thinking in some cases. African governments have learnt to use social media to their advantage, and at critical moments, turn it off to promote their own ends. According to the National Intelligence Council, social media is 'a double-edged sword' in that it 'will enable publics to press governments more effectively while also improving regimes' capacity to crack down on opponents' (Mills et al. 2019, p. 112). In 2016 alone, the internet was shut down 54 times in 27 African countries (Bauer 2019).

Both freedom of the mainstream press and social media have suffered under authoritarian rule. Maggie Dwyer and Thomas Molony, editors of *Social Media and Politics*, report that Chadians suffered the longest social media blockage seen in any African country. The 16-month ban was only lifted in mid-July 2019.[16] The Chadian case highlights the way that social media is framed as a threat to authoritarian leaders. The government of President Idriss Déby, who has been in power since 1990, claimed the shutdown was necessary because the internet was used by some for 'malicious purposes' (Conroy-Krutz 2019). At least nine other African countries have also experienced government ordered internet shutdowns, particularly during election periods and times of political instability (see Dwyer and Molony 2019a, b).

---

[16]See https://edition.cnn.com/2019/07/17/africa/chad-restores-internet-intl/index.html (Accessed 15 August 2019).

8.3   Youth Voting with Their Feet

At the heart of the Arab Spring were disgruntled youth seeking democratic representation and economic participation. Political analysts have warned that responses to Africa's current youth revolts may not necessarily meet protestors' demands for greater access to education and to skills that will lead to employment.[17] An important question, therefore, is what will happen to Africa's youth who do not find jobs in their countries of birth by their mid- to late twenties. Will they despair, join extremist groups, or emigrate?

Africa's increasingly IT-connected youth will have expectations of a higher standard of living than their parents. Not all rural youth are content to till the soil as past generations have done, and will try to find greener pastures in urban areas or, in some cases, even overseas. African people have always been on the move; there has been migration across the continent and beyond for millions of years.[18]

8.3.1   'Asinamali'[19]—We Have No Money!

Consider that South Africa's migrant labour system, introduced during the colonial era, forced rural men to work on faraway mines to earn the cash to pay a hut tax back in their home villages. In the twentieth century, labour circulation became a way of life and working on the mines became a rite of passage for young Xhosa men. Working underground, they earned both prestige and the money to pay bride wealth in order to get married.[20]

Fast forward to 2016. Young men in a rural village in The Gambia, where President Jammeh's authoritarian rule was challenged that year, see the need to risk a perilous 4800 km journey across the Sahara and the Mediterranean in search of work in Europe. They hope to earn money in order to be able to marry local young women and gain respect in their community. As many as 600 of the approximately 4000 people in this particular Gambian village have risked this so-called 'Back Way'.[21]

---

[17] Already in 2002, a special issue of the *African Studies Review* 45(2) was devoted to the role of Africa's universities in promoting a democratic culture in Africa. Amutabi (2002) examines the case of Kenya's universities. Nshimbi (2016) reviews the Nigerian experience of clashes between students and government in the past that led to repressive measures.

[18] See Reader's (1997) biography of the African continent referred to in our introduction to Africa's history of human well-being.

[19] Zulu for 'we have no money', the title of a play by Mbongeni Ngema in the Athol Fugard tradition, that expresses the rage of young black men in South Africa during the apartheid era.

[20] See Wilson (1972) on South Africa's migrant labour system.

[21] See The Daily Telegraph's (2015) report on the 'Back Way'. See Idemudia and Boenhnke (2020, Chapter 2, pp. 33–49) for an overview of African migration routes to Europe.

8.3.2 Africa on the Move

The latest Afrobarometer Round 7 conducted with 34 countries in 2016–2018 found that a third of Africans surveyed have considered emigrating. Potential emigrants who want to move abroad confirm the common notion that they will find greener pastures overseas. Chief motivations for considering emigration are first, to find work, and second, to escape poverty and economic hardship at home. On average across 34 countries, three-fourths of potential emigrants say the most important reason they would consider leaving is to search for work (44%) or to escape poverty or economic hardship (29%). Interestingly, the experience of 'lived poverty'[22] seems to have little impact on the motivation to emigrate. However, respondents from poorer countries with a low Human Development Index were more likely to say they wished to escape poverty as their reason for wanting to emigrate, while those from better-off countries stated they wished to search for work (Sanny et al. 2019).

Youth in the 18–25 cohort are most likely to consider going abroad, as are the most educated—24% of younger respondents have thought 'a lot' about emigrating, compared to 18% of other adults. Young, educated, and male respondents were more likely to say that they had taken steps to prepare for emigration than their older, less educated, and female counterparts (Sanny et al. 2019). This profile of the determined young emigrant suggests that countries in Africa stand to lose their most educated and productive citizens, whose scarce skills are crucial for growing their economies—a brain drain the continent cannot afford.

8.3.3 Intra-regional Migration in Pursuit of Opportunities

Contrary to the common idea that all African immigrants have their eyes set on Europe or North America, Afrobarometer's Round 7 reports that the most sought-after destinations for emigrants is often a neighbouring country in the region. In fact, more than 80% of Africa's migration is intra-regional. Among Afrobarometer Round 7's potential emigrants, more than one-third would like to move either to another country within their region (29%) or elsewhere in Africa (7%). In both Central and East Africa, an average of four in ten (41% each) say they would stay within the region or the continent. Southern Africans are most likely to want to stay within the region (51%) or somewhere on the continent (7%) (Sanny et al. 2019).

In line with this high interest in intra-regional migration and the pursuit of economic opportunity, a majority of sub-Saharan Africans favour free cross-border movement within their region. However, they also say that crossing borders is difficult. In Afrobarometer's Round 6 survey, 56% of respondents across 36 African

---

[22]On other continents, barometers typically apply subjective indicators, such as life satisfaction, to measure human well-being (Møller et al. 2008). In contrast, Afrobarometer uses an objective proxy indicator to assess well-being: the absence of 'lived poverty', that is, going without basic necessities (see Mattes 2008).

countries say they 'agree' or 'agree very strongly' that people should be able to move freely across borders in order to work or trade in other countries in the region, while the same proportion (56%) say that in fact it is 'difficult' or 'very difficult' to cross international borders in their region. In the Round 7 survey, only two in ten (22%) say cross-border movement is 'easy' or 'very easy' (Sanny et al. 2019).

A recommendation to policy makers based on these Afrobarometer findings, would be to keep borders open and to welcome the motivated young educated migrants who can contribute to economic growth and prosperity on the continent.

8.3.4 Moving Abroad for Greater Opportunities

Unlike their counterparts in other regions, potential emigrants in West Africa do look beyond the continent to search for greener pastures, by a margin of nearly 3 to 1 (72% vs. 25%). Their preferred destination would be Europe (31%) and North America (30%) rather than a country within the region (19%) or elsewhere in Africa (6%) (Sanny et al. 2019).

The Gambian village youth who risk the 'Back Way' to search for work in Europe described earlier fit this Afrobarometer profile (see Sanny et al. 2019). Gambia ranks third among 34 sub-Saharan countries[23] where respondents consider emigration. Over half of Gambian respondents (56%) have considered emigrating a 'little bit' or 'a lot'. Nine out of ten (94%) potential migrants would leave the continent, with Europe as preferred destination for 47%. Among the youth, almost four in ten (39%) have given 'a lot' of thought to emigration. A tradition of emigration may have become a way of life in Gambia. Over a third of Gambians have family members living abroad (37%) and almost half (47%) say they depend at least 'a little bit' on remittances.

Youth working overseas earn, not only to benefit themselves but also to support their families back in Africa. The remittances sent home by nearly 140 million Africans living abroad currently surpass Western foreign aid to the continent.[24] Africans fleeing conflict in their countries or seeking a better life have overwhelmed Europe in the past years (Idemudia and Boenhnke 2020). At least a million sub-Saharan Africans have moved to Europe since 2010 (Pew Research Centre 2018). Many families in Africa have come to rely, at least in part, on remittances for their livelihoods.

Afrobarometer's Round 7 asked their respondents if they 'depend on receiving remittances from relatives or friends living in other countries.' Across 33 countries, about one-fifth (21%) of respondents say they rely 'a little bit' (10%), 'somewhat'

---

[23] Only the two island states of Cabo Verde and São Tomé and Príncipe, off the West African coast, rank higher than Gambia in considering emigration.

[24] Bodomo (2013) reports that money sent home by Africans had surpassed foreign aid by 2013. Remittances benefit households directly, as they go towards paying school fees, building new homes, and growing businesses.

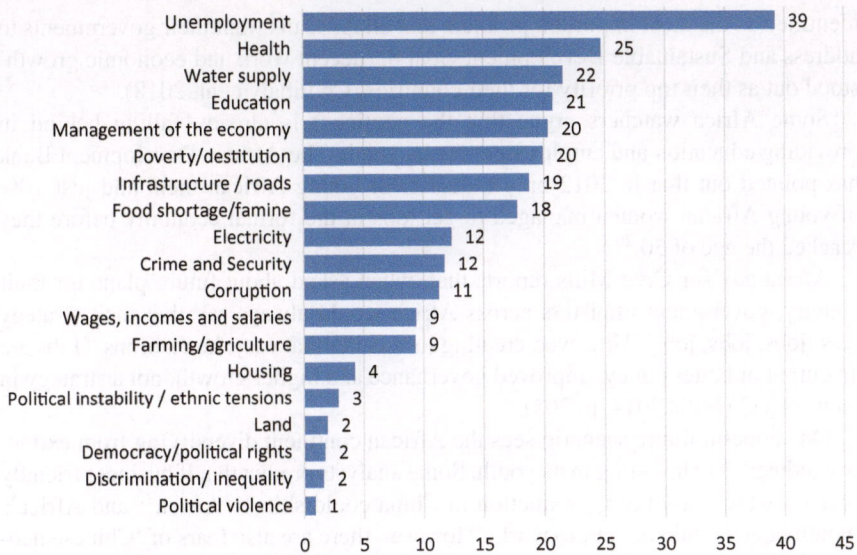

Fig. 8.3 The most important problems facing African countries, 2016–18 (%). Respondents were asked: In your opinion, what are the most important problems facing this country that government should address? Respondents were allowed to provide up to three responses. The bars in the figure show the percentage of respondents who mentioned each problem in their top three challenges. Data are from Afrobarometer Round 7 (2019)

(7%), or 'a lot' (4%) on such monies from abroad. As noted above, among Gambians, where Europe is the top destination for potential migrants, almost half say their families depend on remittances from abroad (Sanny et al. 2019).

8.4 Jobs for Africa

Africa will need to provide jobs for its youth if it is to meet their aspirations for the good life—or even just a better life. In 2010 there were roughly 200 million Africans between 15 and 24 years of age and this number could rise to over 450 million by 2050. According to an African Development Bank (2011, p. 2) report, young people aged 15 to 24 constitute only 37% of Africa's labour force but make up 60% of the continent's total. It is estimated that 18 million jobs will need to be created every year just to accommodate Africa's current jobseekers.[25]

Providing jobs for a growing population is a common concern across the African continent (World Economic Forum 2017). The latest Round 7 Afrobarometer identified unemployment as a top concern in African countries (see Fig. 8.3). In line with Afrobarometer's findings on motivations for emigration, unemployment was

_____
[25] See OECD (2016) for a report on youth unemployment in Africa.

identified as the most important problem that all Africans want their governments to address and Sustainable Development Goal 8, 'decent work and economic growth' stood out as their top priority for their countries (Coulibaly et al. 2018).

Some Africa watchers argue that the continent is already falling behind in providing education and employment for its youth. The African Development Bank has pointed out that in 2012 only a quarter of young African men, and just 10% of young African women managed to get jobs in the formal economy before they reached the age of 30.[26]

Africa advisor Greg Mills reports that, when asked about future plans for their country, government ministers across Africa would always say that their strategy was 'jobs, jobs, jobs'. However, creating jobs is not that easy, he cautions. 'Jobs are an output of better policy, improved governance and higher growth, not a strategy in themselves' (Mills 2014, p. 305).

One hopeful future scenario sees the African continent diversifying from extractive industries to investing in its youth. Some analysts predict that if business friendly policies were introduced, production in China could shift to Africa[27] and Africa's 'youth bulge' could be 'put to work'. However, there are also fears of 'Chinese neo-colonialism' if investments were to turn out not to be mutually beneficial to African people.[28]

The two countries with the largest populations in the region, Nigeria and Ethiopia, serve as examples of concerted efforts to create jobs in the region in order to stall emigration.

Nigeria's richest business person, Aliko Dangote, has hopes to transform his country's stagnant economy. He has succeeded where others have failed. Dangote's break-through came when business-friendly President Olusegun Obasanjo gave preferential treatment to domestic producers like himself. The billionaire wants to see other business people follow his lead by investing in job-generating industries throughout the continent. He notes that Africa's population will double by 2050 and more than a billion young people will be looking for jobs. Dangote has already invested towards initiatives that focus on education, health and youth empowerment, and aims to become a philanthropist like Bill Gates, his role model, with a foundation worth billions of dollars within the next five to seven years (see Baker 2018).

Ethiopia has ambitions to gain middle-income status by creating 16 modern industrial parks. It aims to revitalise its traditional textile industry in order to create thousands of new jobs. The country's low labour costs may be advantageous for attracting foreign investment (Fischer 2018, p. 49; Mills et al. 2020, pp. 255–8).

Africa's agricultural potential has not been fully exploited. Several sub-Saharan countries are about to change this situation. For example, to diversify its economy, Zambia has launched an agribusiness project that aims to assist 4000 subsistence

---

[26] See The Economist (2014), the Population Reference Bureau (2016), and Baker (2015).

[27] See Davies (2015).

[28] See Harding (2020), Khodor et al. (2020), and Qobo and Mzyece (2020) on how Africa might benefit from Chinese investments in Africa during the Covid-19 crisis.

farmers and some 300 to 400 small agribusinesses to boost their productivity, improve access to markets, and create more profitable supply chains (Fischer 2018, p. 395).

8.4.1 Skills Training for Youth

Throughout sub-Saharan Africa, programmes to promote teaching and learning are underway to equip youth with the skills they will need to enter the modern economy. An example is a development project conducted in Tanzania, which became known as *"hisabati ni maisha"*—mathematics is living/life. The goal of the project is to build capacity for mathematics teaching and learning in rural and remote communities. The enthusiasm with which local teachers responded was a major factor contributing to the success of the project, that also promised to ensure its longer-term continuity. One of the teachers enthused about the collective action that drove the project's success: suddenly it 'took on a life of its own!' (Simmt et al. 2019).

SciFest Africa,[29] a science festival held annually in South Africa, aims to promote a better understanding of science, technology and innovation among young learners and to awaken their interest in so-called STEM subjects, science, technology, engineering and mathematics, which are key to meeting Africa's development needs. In 2018, SciFest attracted more than 60,000 visitors.

8.4.2 Youth Leaders of Tomorrow

Opportunities are opening up for the next generation of African leaders. Ghanaian Fred Swaniker,[30] nominated one of *TIME*'s hundred most influential people in 2019, believes that Africa's young people are the continent's greatest asset. As founder of the African Leadership Academy, the African Leadership Network and the African Leadership University, he hopes his initiatives will groom 3 million young leaders of tomorrow (Ibrahim 2019).

Entrepreneurs have a pivotal role to play in creating jobs for African youth; a third of the 15–35 year-old workforce are unemployed (Hruby 2019). The annual, year-long Hult Prize Challenge[31] invites innovative students across the globe to present smart ideas that will change the world for the better and create thousands of meaningful jobs. The team with the best business idea will be awarded one million US dollars as a start-up injection. The top position in the 2019 regional summit, held in Nairobi, Kenya, went to four South African Ph.D. chemistry students. Their 'Esmart' business idea is to collect and recycle or repurpose electronic waste. According to the Esmart team, South Africa annually produces about 316 thousand tons of electronic

---

[29] See https://www.scifest.org.za/ and https://en.wikipedia.org/wiki/SciFest_Africa.

[30] See https://en.wikipedia.org/wiki/Fred_Swaniker.

[31] See https://en.wikipedia.org/wiki/Hult_Prize.

waste, of which only 12% is collected and recycled, and it is exported to other countries. Esmart team member, Lindekuhle Nene, says that her team decided 'to be the youth that is going to stand up and create things for themselves. We are the driving force and agents of change and improvement in our country. We want to lay a platform for generations to come after us. They must know that as a human being, you can do anything you put your mind to.' (Grocott's Mail 2019).

8.4.3   Covid-19 Youth Initiatives

Africa is not waiting to be saved from the coronavirus[32]

Young people across sub-Saharan Africa have shown agency during the coronavirus pandemic. Their initiatives assist communities to cope in uncertain times.

Sudanese youth, who had been at the forefront of protests since the Arab Spring, are now taking initiatives to fight the coronavirus that arrived in Africa in 2020. Weston (2020) based in Khartoum, reports that neighbourhood resistance committees who see themselves as the guardians of the revolution and were instrumental in ousting dictator Omar al-Bashir in 2019, are now helping to keep the new democracy on track during the Covid-19 pandemic. Committees are involved in distributing hand sanitiser, sterilising public spaces such as markets, enforcing social distance in queues and educating people on how to prevent infection. Others are assisting those confined in their homes with supplies and identifying the poorest people in the neighbourhood in need of government assistance. Resistance volunteers say they would prefer to get back to more traditional revolutionary activities, but know their work is making a difference as long as the new government is not able to carry out their duties at the local level.

In one of South Africa's sprawling informal settlements outside Cape Town, rival gang leaders have held an unprecedented truce during the country's strict lockdown. Instead of fighting each other, they have joined forces to distribute donations of food parcels across turf boundaries to poor households who would otherwise have starved. The community hopes the gang leaders will keep the peace once lockdown is over, but that outcome is uncertain.

In Ghana, a network of young educated women, who want to bring the benefits of education to the people, have taken to the airwaves to replace fears about the virus with knowledge. One of the anchors interviewed by the BBC on 12 June 2020 said their local radio programmes broadcast health workers' talks in the local dialects to assist their listeners to better understand the nature of the virus and how to stay safe from infection (BBC World News 2020).

---

[32]See Cheeseman (2020) citing Kenyan writer and political analyst Nanjala Nyabola's article with that title in The Nation (see https://www.thenation.com/article/world/coronavirus-colonialism-afr ica/. (Accessed 11 July 2020).

Spokesperson Tariro Bure for the African Youth Networks Movement, writing for the Mo Ibrahim newsletter, said their members want to do their part in fighting the virus and think their work will go a long way to 'flatten the curve'. For example, the Tshanduko Innovation Youth Network aims to dispel misinformation and superstitions about the virus by informing people about how to protect themselves and others. In Uganda, a team of young innovators are working on recycling plastic material to 3D-print personal protective equipment for rural health care providers. Senegalese entrepreneurs are developing inexpensive test kits and 3D-printed ventilators, which cost $60 as against the $16,000 market price (Bure 2020).

8.5 Summary

Since independence, Africa's youth have been instrumental in shaping the future of their country and their lives. As reported here, they have taken principled stands against leaders who are suppressing democratic freedoms and holding back development in their countries. The youth are prepared to take risks to escape poverty and find jobs to support themselves and their families. If they cannot find work at home, the majority of potential emigrant job seekers would prefer to seek 'greener pastures' in neighbouring counties rather than overseas. At present, many African youth lack the education and skills to follow through on their ambitions in life. Jobs for Africa are the most urgent problem that citizens wish their governments to address. We have drawn attention to a number of initiatives that seek to stem a 'brain drain' out of Africa. Such initiatives will need to be multiplied in future, to meet the demands for a growing youth population. During the Covid-19 pandemic, youth volunteers have taken the initiative themselves to assist their local communities to fight the virus.

In the section that follows, we turn to the new challenges related to realising Africa's so-called 'youth dividend,' and providing quality of life for a rapidly growing sub-Saharan population.

8.6 Africa's Population Success Story and Population Well-Being

If the rate of population growth slows down, … there will be more resources to invest in each African's health, education, and opportunity – in other words, in a good life.

Alex Ezeh, Visiting Fellow, Centre for Global Development (2018, p. 14)

For centuries, Africa was underpopulated. As detailed in the introduction to the history of well-being in sub-Saharan Africa, population survival was often precarious owing to famine, pestilence and disease, and the continent was deprived of many hands needed for food production during the centuries of conquest and the slave trade. The continent only started to reach its potential for population growth toward

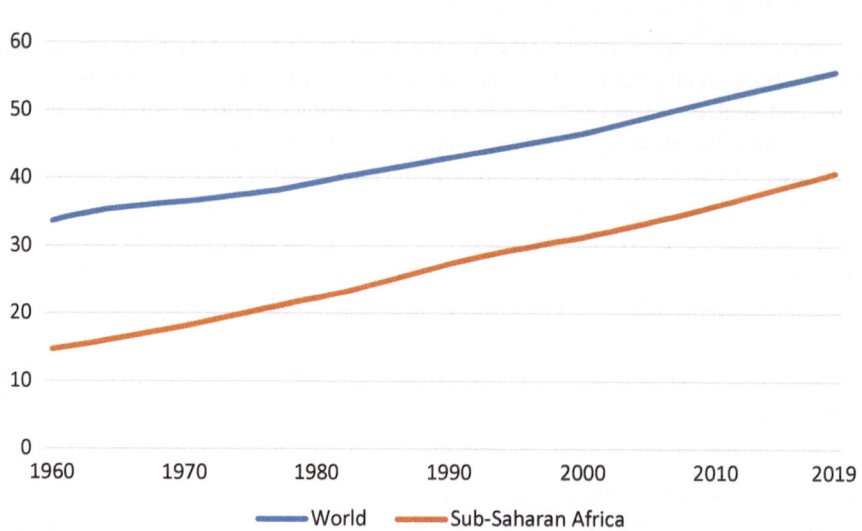

Fig. 8.4 Urbanisation in sub-Saharan Africa and the world, 1960–2019 (%). Data are from World Bank World Development Indicators 2020 database

the end of the twentieth century (Reader 1997). Now Africa's exploding population is expected to double by 2050.

Population growth, together with migration to Africa's urban areas, has put severe pressure on the sub-Saharan region's capacity to provide education, health services and infrastructure. Further population growth may undermine progress in human development achieved so far. One of the most populous sub-Saharan African countries, Nigeria, experienced a fourfold increase in population since independence in 1960, and its population is expected to increase to 500 million by 2050 and to more than 900 million by 2100 (Mills 2014, p. 108). It is predicted that by 2050, Africa could have 35 cities with over 5 million inhabitants each, with Kinshasa in the DRC and Lagos in Nigeria each exceeding 30 million.[33]

8.6.1   Africa's Population Growth and Urbanisation

At the time of independence, sub-Saharan Africa was populated mainly by rural subsistence agriculturalists. Only approximately 15% of the population were city dwellers. Since the 1960s, urbanisation has increased rapidly in line with world trends. More than twice as many people lived in cities by 2012—some 40% of the population (see Fig. 8.4). However, urbanisation rates vary widely over the region. Between 50% and 70% of the population is urbanised in Botswana, South Africa,

---

[33] See Guengant and May (2013), and a report referring to their work in The Economist (2014), and Baker (2015).

Angola, Ghana, and Nigeria. In contrast, Ethiopia's rate of urbanisation increased from 6% in 1960 to only 21% in 2012. However, Ethiopia may start catching up under the new leadership of Prime Minister Abiy, who has introduced reforms since taking office in 2018.

People have moved to cities in search of economic opportunities, health services and a better quality of life. The question is whether greater concentrations of people in cities will improve access to economic opportunities and delivery of infrastructure and services. Demographers Guengant and May (2013) predict that Africa's overall population will rise sharply, its big cities will grow alarmingly, and although its labour force will also expand, its 'youth bulge' will be 'hard to manage'.

In Kenya, for example, over 60% of the urban population live in slums and are deprived of central and local government services owing to antiquated town planning laws. The majority of slum dwellers are underemployed in the informal sector (see Mills 2014, pp. 38ff).

8.7 Africa's Population 'Time Bomb'

Today, Africa is the world's youngest continent. Some 60% of the population is under 25, and by 2100, almost half of the world's youth are expected to be in Africa. Africa's youth 'dividend' can only be realised if the next generation is equipped with the education and skills to become the drivers of economic growth and development on the continent. Although major investment in Africa's youth is needed to address barriers to youth employment, there may not be time to make sufficient investment to avert a population 'time bomb'.

Jean-Pierre Guengant and John May describe the scale of the continent's new population challenge (Guengant and May 2013; The Economist 2014). The ten countries with the top fertility rates in the world are all found in sub-Saharan Africa. Currently, some 78% of Africa's people live in countries that have not passed the demographic transition to low fertility and low mortality; only the countries in the far north and south of the continent are exceptions, with lower fertility rates. Fertility rates are particularly high among Africa's land-locked countries and ones with low rates of urbanisation. Niger, a land-locked country in the Sahel is a case in point. In 2016, Niger had the world's highest fertility rate of 7.2.

8.7.1 Demographic Trends in Africa

Demographic trends are cause for concern in Africa. Fertility in sub-Saharan Africa stood at 5.1 births per woman in 2005–10, more than double the replacement level (United Nations 2011). This high fertility combined with declining mortality, has resulted in rapid population growth.

Demographic transition occurs when both fertility and mortality pass from high rates to lower rates. According to conventional demographic theory, in less developed societies, high fertility in the early stages of the demographic transition is the consequence of high desired family size (Bongaarts and Casterline 2012). Many children make lighter work of farming and family businesses, and provide old-age security for their parents. With rising levels of urbanisation and education, economic growth, and declining mortality, parents wish for a smaller number of births. As Africa is still characterised by relatively low levels of social and economic development, it still has high fertility.

In Latin America, fertility decline began in the mid-1960s, and slightly later in Asia. In both regions decline proceeded steadily and rapidly. In contrast, Africa's fertility transition only began in the late 1980s and has proceeded less rapidly.[34] There may be several reasons for Africa's slower demographic transition.

8.7.2   Africa's 'Ideal Family Size' (IFS)

Bongaarts and Casterline (2012) examined trends in Africa's fertility preferences and the demand and use of contraceptives, which are important indicators related to demographic transitions. A standard straight-forward question on the 'Ideal Family Size' (IFS) asks women: 'If you could go back to the time you did not have any children and could choose exactly the number of children to have in your whole life, how many would that be?' Bongaarts' and Casterline's study found that the Ideal Family Size is higher in Africa than in other regions. Yet, despite its high Ideal Family Size, Africa also has a higher unmet need for contraception than other regions of the world.

8.7.3   Demand for Contraception

When examining the historical trends in demand and use of contraceptives among women of child-bearing age in 16 sub-Saharan countries between 1990 and 2010, Bongaarts and Casterline (2012) found notable differences between sub-regions in sub-Saharan Africa. There was generally higher demand for and use of contraceptives in East and southern Africa compared to Central and West Africa, which is consistent with the generally lower levels of fertility and smaller Ideal Family Size in the East and Southern regions. In addition, in most countries in East and southern Africa, use of contraceptives was increasing, and unmet need falling. In contrast, in the countries of West and Central Africa, unmet need generally exceeded use.

---

[34]In the early 1960s, African countries had fertility rates of between 5.5 and 7.5, comparable with other developing economies at that time (Guengant and May 2013).

Interestingly, Rwanda showed the most unusual pattern of change. Between 2005 and 2010 demand for contraception rose, contraceptive use more than doubled, and unmet need declined by nearly half. The plausible explanation for the rapid increase in use of contraception, according to Bongaarts and Casterline, is the reinvigoration of the country's family planning programme since the mid-2000s. Contributing factors will have been rapid socio-economic change since the early 2000s, accompanied by rising school enrolment and declining infant and child mortality, following on a period of political instability and civil war in the 1990s (Bongaarts and Casterline 2012).

Table 8.1 Fertility rates in select sub-Saharan countries in 2018

Fertility rate	1960	1990	2000	2018	Change 1990–2000	Change 2000–18	Change 1990–2018
West African region							
Niger	7.5	7.8	7.7	6.9	−0.1	−0.8	−0.9
Mali	7.0	7.2	6.9	5.9	−0.3	−1.0	−1.3
Nigeria	6.4	6.5	6.1	5.4	−0.4	−0.7	−1.1
Burkina Faso	6.3	7.0	6.6	5.2	−0.4	−1.4	−1.8
Senegal	7.0	6.4	5.4	4.6	−1.0	−0.8	−1.8
Ghana	6.7	5.6	4.8	3.9	−0.8	−1.0	−1.7
Central and Eastern African region							
Uganda	7.0	7.1	6.9	5.0	−0.2	−1.9	−2.1
Tanzania	6.8	6.2	5.7	4.9	−0.5	−0.8	−1.3
Zambia	7.1	6.4	6.0	4.6	−0.4	−1.4	−1.8
Ethiopia	6.9	7.2	6.5	4.2	−0.7	−2.3	−3.0
Malawi	6.9	6.9	6.1	4.2	−0.8	−1.9	−2.7
Madagascar	7.3	6.2	5.6	4.1	−0.6	−1.5	−2.1
Rwanda	8.2	7.2	5.6	4.0	−1.5	−1.6	−3.1
Kenya	7.9	6.1	5.2	3.5	−0.9	−1.7	−2.6
Southern African region							
Zimbabwe	7.2	4.9	3.7	3.6	−1.1	−0.1	−1.2
Namibia	6.1	5.2	3.9	3.4	−1.3	−0.5	−1.8

Average number of live births for a woman in line with age-specific fertility rates throughout the life course (Fischer 2018, p. 535). Data from World Development Indicators, World Bank
Source World Development Indicators, World Bank

8.7.4   Demographic Challenges and Well-Being

Table 8.1 shows the latest available fertility rates for the 16 sub-Saharan countries that were included in Bongaarts and Casterline's (2012) examination of historical change in fertility between 2005 and 2010. In line with their observations, West Africa's Niger still has the highest fertility rate in the world, of 6.9 children per woman in 2018. Fertility rates of five children are common in the other West African countries and in Central Africa. The lowest fertility rates are found in southern Africa, represented by Namibia and Zimbabwe in Table 8.1.[35]

Our examination of demographic challenges in the sub-Saharan region suggest that countries with higher fertility rates and a large youth population may find it harder to provide quality of life for their citizens.

8.8   Women's Rights to Control Their Reproductive Health

In a recent interview with philanthropists Bill and Melinda Gates, Melinda Gates was asked what might bring about the most important change to the lives of people in Africa. She named women's access to contraceptives as her choice: 'Giving women access to contraceptives, so she can choose which one she wants to use at what time, so that she can space the births of her children. … It changes everything in the family dynamic, and it changes the community, and ultimately you get country-level effects where it's good for everyone' (Gates and Gates 2018b).

The rate of contraception use among child-bearing age women in sub-Saharan Africa is lower than in other regions of the world (Guengant and May 2013). Their high unmet need for contraception evidenced in the study by Bongaarts and Casterline (2012) is indicative of frustrated demand, which has implications for policy. Bongaarts and Casterline are hopeful the demand can be met: 'Fortunately, family planning programmes can also bring about changes in preferences through information campaigns that present evidence on the health and socio-economic benefits of

---

[35]Beyond the selection of countries' fertility rates shown in Table 8.1: The fertility rates of 6.9 for Niger and 6.1 for Somalia are the highest in the world according to the latest World Bank records for 2018. Nine further sub-Saharan countries have fertility rates over 5: Angola, Burkina Faso, Burundi, Chad, DRC, Gambia, Mali, Nigeria, and Uganda. The majority of countries (26) have fertility rates between 4 and 5: Benin, Cameroon, Central African Republic, Comoros, Republic of Congo, Côte d'Ivoire, Equatorial Guinea, Eritrea, Ethiopia, Gabon, Guinea, Guinea-Bissau, Liberia, Madagascar, Malawi, Mauritania, Mozambique, Rwanda, São Tomé and Príncipe, Senegal, Sierra Leone, South Sudan, Sudan, Tanzania, Togo, and Zambia. Eleven countries, including island, landlocked and southern African ones, have fertility rates below 4: Botswana, Cabo Verde, Djibouti, eSwatini, Ghana, Kenya, Lesotho, Namibia, South Africa, Seychelles, and Zimbabwe. The island state of Mauritius has the lowest fertility rate in the region of 1.4. In 2018, the average sub-Saharan fertility rate of 4.7 is almost twice as high as the world average of 2.4. Only 3 sub-Saharan countries other than Mauritius have fertility rates on par or lower than the world average: Cabo Verde (2.3), Seychelles (2.4) and South Africa 2.4). See https://data.worldbank.org/indicator/SP.DYN.TFRT.IN (Accessed 2 August 2020).

contraception and smaller families.' They note that such messages are particularly effective when they have the support of political leaders. Commitments to family planning in several sub-Saharan countries have already had the expected result of rising use of contraception and declining unmet need (Bongaarts and Casterline 2012, pp. 166–7).

8.9 Need for Action Now: Better Sooner Than Later

… 'The time to act is now. Investing in health and education is especially urgent at this precise time in the history of sub-Saharan Africa because of the region's youth boom. The children who can transform the continent have already been – or are about to be born. It will be up to them to lead the innovations their societies need: to transform subsistence farms into profitable small business, to provide a bank account for every adult on their mobile phones, to eradicate malaria and other neglected diseases'. (Gates and Gates 2018a)

Even if the unmet need for contraception could be eliminated, it is unlikely that Africa's fertility rates will decline as rapidly as elsewhere given Africa's high Ideal Family Size. Rapid population growth is expected to continue for some time even if social and economic development reduces preferences for large families in Africa (Bongaarts and Casterline 2012). Therefore, policy makers will need to act now to address the needs of a growing population, before the challenge is insurmountable.

8.10 Conclusion

African policy makers need to recognise that the current demographic trajectory is a major obstacle to their countries' development. Sub-Saharan Africa needs to feed and educate its youth, and develop its infrastructure to 'make Africa work' (Mills et al. 2017). The time to act is urgent, in order to keep up with the demands of a growing population. Demographers foresee that Africa's fertility rates will not decrease overnight as sub-Saharan women have a high Ideal Family Size and their supply of contraception falls short of their demand. Around the world, parents hope their children will have an easier life than they did and children expect to live better than their parents do. Africa needs to act now to make this vision come true.

In the next chapter, we describe advances in providing a better quality of life for minorities and marginal groups in society, whose needs have been neglected in the past or whose human rights and dignity have been violated.

Malawi as case study of Africa's rapid population growth
Central Africa's landlocked Malawi presents a case study of the twin challenges of population growth and the youth 'time bomb'.

Profile. Malawi is a small country comprising 118 km². Currently, the population density is 157 per square kilometre, and only 17 percent live in urban areas. Life expectancy stands at 63 years. As is the case for most sub-Saharan countries, Malawi is a youthful country: 44% of the population is younger than 15 years and only 3% older than 65 years. The country's fertility rate stood at 4.6 in 2016; in the same year, infant and child mortality stood at 39 and 55 per thousand live births respectively. In 2015, only 44% of the population had access to sanitation, 67% to drinking water. Some 30% of men and 45% of women are still illiterate. (Fischer 2018, pp. 526–537)

History. Half a century after its independence from British rule in 1964, Malawi is one of the poorest countries on earth, even though, unlike many other African countries, it has never experienced a civil war. Hastings Kamuzu Banda was installed as the post-colonial president of a one-party state with his Malawi Congress Party. He hoped to be president 'for life'. Under his autocratic rule, Malawi prospered in spite of its landlocked and resource-poor status. The country achieved notable progress in both agriculture and industrialisation. Banda was adept in using his foreign ties in the Cold War context to secure development funding and foreign investment, and to gain security advice and intelligence from outside. The army was Western trained and the police and paramilitary Young Pioneers had support from the East. Parastatals ran large parts of the economy. During the 1960s, Malawi diversified from agriculture into other areas, including tourism. The land-locked country was known as the smiling face in the warm heart of Africa. There was corruption, but 'at the highest levels only' according to a senior government official, and Banda kept dishonesty in check (see Mills 2014, pp. 295–305).

Population explosion. What is important in this story is that President Banda's task of ruling the country with an iron fist in the 1960s was an easier one than it will be for his successors. When Banda was in power, the demand for Malawi's tobacco, its chief export item, was still relatively high and he had fewer mouths to feed. In 1966, the population stood at some 5 million. Malawi's population passed the 10 million mark after 1998 and thereafter the population increase rose steadily to reach more than 19 million in 2020. Malawi's population is expected to reach 50 million by mid-century in 2050.

The challenge—act sooner than later. Malawi's changing demographic picture should be regarded as a crisis, which calls for reformers to institute necessary changes. According to Africa advisor Mills (2014, p. 305) reformers are more likely to be successful 'when they act fast, tough and do not spare their own people in the process, that they share the pain.' The Arab Spring is a reminder of the consequences of inaction, he cautions.

Malawi needs to improve the country's living standards and grow the economy, in anticipation of reaching the country's ten-fold population explosion mark by 2050. The population is increasing faster than opportunities. It will be easier to carry out reforms sooner than later, to prepare for its youth 'time bomb'.

A first step—banning Malawi's child marriages. One of the factors that contributes to Malawi's high fertility rate is the wide-spread practice of child marriages. Malawi is one of the countries in the world with the highest rate of girls married under the age of 18 years. Although violence against women and girls is punishable, abuse suffered by women within and outside the family, and repression of women in everyday life is a major problem. In 2015, marriages of under-age youth was prohibited by law, a measure intended to reduce child marriages (Fischer 2015, p. 292).

The ban on child marriages has the potential not only to lower fertility rates, but it might also protect against the spread of HIV/AIDS. Age differences between partners and early sexual debuts are among known factors that contribute to HIV infections. Relative to its current population size of some 19 million, Malawi has a high number of new HIV infections (38,000 in 2018) (Fischer 2018, p. 537).

References

Abebe, A. K. (2020). Malawi's victory for democracy: After the euphoria, long, hard work. International Institute for Democracy and Electoral Assistance, IDEA news, 30 June. https://www.idea.int/news-media/news/malawi-victory-democracy-after-euphoria-long-hard-work. Accessed June 1, 2020.

Adebajo, A. (2014). From 'Arab Spring' to 'African Harmattan', *Business Day*, Johannesburg, 17 November, p. 9.

African Development Bank (2011). Enhancing capacity of youth employment in Africa. *Africa Capacity Development, 2*(1), 1–5. http://www.afdb.org/fileadmin/uploads/afdb/Documents/Publications/Africa%20Capacity%20Dev%20Brief_Africa%20Capacity%20Dev%20Brief.pdf. Accessed July 4, 2020.

Afrobarometer (2016). *Highlights of Round 6 survey findings from 36 African countries.* http://afrobarometer.org/sites/default/files/summary_results/ab_R6_afrobarometer_global_release_highlights3.pdf. Accessed July 4, 2020.

Allison, S. (2020). Burundi's president put politics before the pandemic. Now he's dead. *Mail&Guardian*, 9 June. https://mg.co.za/africa/2020-06-09-burundis-president-put-politics-before-the-pandemic-now-hes-dead/. Accessed July 4, 2020.

Amutabi, M.N. (2002). Crisis and student protest in universities in Kenya: Examining the role of students in national leadership and the democratization process. *African Studies Review, 45*(2), 157–177. Special Issue: African universities in crisis and the promotion of a democratic culture.

Ateku, A.-J. (2019). How The Gambia is going about its search for truth and reconciliation. *The Conversation*, March 27. https://theconversation.com/how-the-gambia-is-going-about-its-search-for-truth-and-reconciliation-114203.

Baker, A. (2015). Let's prepare for Africa's population surge now—or face the consequences. *TIME*, 11 June. http://time.com/3918006/lets-prepare-for-africas-population-surge-now-or-face-the-consequences/.

Baker, A. (2018). Lifting Nigeria up: Africa's richest man is determined to bring jobs to the continent. *TIME*, 5 November, pp. 44–47.

Bauer, G. K. (2019). The Congo finally witnesses political change, but how meaningful will it be? https://africasacountry.com/2019/01/the-congo-finally-witnesses-political-change-but-how-meaningful-will-it-be. Accessed April 29, 2019.

BBC World News. (2020). 'We want to bring the benefits of education to the people'. https://www.bbc.com/news/world. Accessed June 12, 2020.

BBC World News Africa (2020). Mali coup: Military promises elections after ousting president. 19 August. https://www.bbc.com/news/world-africa-53833925. Accessed August 19, 2020.

BBC World Service Africa (2020a). Coronavirus: 'Malawi, we have a situation'. 4 July. https://www.bbc.com/news/topics/clm1wxp5pert/malawi. Accessed July 6, 2020.

BBC World Service Africa (2020b). Malawi cancels independence day celebrations, 6 July. http://www.channelafrica.co.za/sabc/home/channelafrica/news/details?id=42e2c0c8-eeb9-43c5-9708-6242f07fc890&title=Malawi%20cancels%20Independence%20Day%20celebrations. Accessed July 6, 2020.

Bodomo, A. (2013). Sending money back home beats foreign aid. *Africa in Fact* 10, April, 33–35. www.gga.org.

Bongaarts, J., & Casterline, J. (2012). Fertility transition: Is sub-Saharan Africa different? *Population and Development Review, 38*(Supplement), 153–168.

Branch, A., & Mampilly, Z. C. (2015). *Africa uprising: Popular protest and political change.* Chicago: University of Chicago Press.

Bure, T. (2020). COVID-19 in Africa: Youth Perspectives—Tariro Bure. *Mo Ibrahim Foundation News,* 2 June. https://mo.ibrahim.foundation/news/2020/covid-19-africa-youth-perspectives-tariro-bure. Accessed June 30, 2020.

Business Insider SA (2019). *This startling graph shows how many Africans are now using the internet—far more than in North America, and on track to beat Europe.* https://www.businessinsider.co.za/internet-users-in-africa-2019-7. Accessed August 19, 2019.

Business Times (2019). World Bank warns 17 African countries near debt distress. *Sunday Times*, South Africa, 14 April, p. 6.

Chan, S. (2018). African democracies badly need a new generation of leaders—where are they? *The Conversation*, 31 January. https://theconversation.com/african-democracies-badly-need-a-new-generation-of-leaders-where-are-they-90887.

Cheeseman, N. (2020). Compendium of new research celebrates African solutions to national and global problems. *The Conversation*, 24 May. https://theconversation.com/compendium-of-new-research-celebrates-african-solutions-to-national-and-global-problems-139238.

Conroy-Krutz, J. (2019). Fresh vigilance is needed to protect media freedom across Africa. *The Conversation,* 4 August.

Cooper, E. (2014). Students, arson, and protest politics in Kenya: School fires as political action. *African Affairs, 113*(453), 583–600. https://doi.org/10.1093/afraf/adu059.

Cooper, E. (2016). A burning question: why are Kenyan students setting fire to their schools? *The Conversation*, 25 November. https://theconversation.com/a-burning-question-why-are-kenyan-students-setting-fire-to-their-schools-69153.

Coulibaly, M., Silwé, K. S., & Logan, C. (2018). Taking stock: Citizen priorities and assessments three years into the SDGs. *Afrobarometer Policy Paper* No. 51. http://afrobarometer.org/publications/pp51-taking-stock-citizen-priorities-and-assessments-three-years-sdgs.

Davies, M. (2015). Why Africa must adapt or die—sustained investment in people key for continent's development. *Business Times*, Johannesburg, 18 January, p. 8.

Dwyer, M., & Molony, T. (2019a). *Social media and politics in Africa: Democracy, censorship and security.* London: Zed Books.

Dwyer, M., & Molony, T. (2019b). Analysis across Africa shows how social media is changing politics. *The Conversation,* 15 August. https://theconversation.com/analysis-across-africa-shows-how-social-media-is-changing-politics-121577.

Ezeh, A. (2018). Family planning: Human capital and population growth. In Bill & Melinda Gates (Eds.), *2018 Goalkeepers Data Report,* pp. 13–14.

Fischer, (2015). *Der neue Fischer Weltalmanach 2016: Zahlen, Daten, Fakten, Schwerpunkt Flüchtlinge.* Frankfurt am Main, Germany: Fischer Verlag.

Fischer, (2018). *Der neue Fischer Weltalmanach 2019: Zahlen, Daten, Fakten, Schwerpunkt Arbeit.* Frankfurt am Main, Germany: Fischer Verlag.

Gates, B., & Gates, M. (2018a). Progress on poverty, precariously. *The New York Times International Edition,* 26 September, pp. 1 & 14.

Gates, B., & Gates, M. (2018b). Keeping goals in sight. National Geographic interview, November, pp. 7–11.

Gedamu, Y. (2020). Abiy put Ethiopia on the road to democracy: but major obstacles still stand in the way. *The Conversation,* 16 June. https://theconversation.com/abiy-put-ethiopia-on-the-road-to-democracy-but-major-obstacles-still-stand-in-the-way-140750.

Gettleman, J. (2016). Protests destabilize Ethiopia, a steady U.S. ally. *International New York Times,* 13-14 August, p. 3.

Gopaldas, R. (2015). Ageing leaders need to bridge generation chasm. *Business Day,* Johannesburg, 4 February, p. 7.

Grocott's Mail (2019). E-Waste startup prize for students. 26 April, Makhanda (Grahamstown), South Africa, p. 5.

Guengant, J.-P., & May, J. F. (2013). African demography. *Global Journal of Emerging Market Economies, 5*(3), 215–267.

Harding, A. (2020). China-US rivalry in Africa fuelled by coronavirus. *BBC World Service Africa,* 9 June. https://www.bbc.com/news/world-africa-52966148. Accessed June 21, 2020.

Hruby, A. (2019). Entrepreneurship funds in Africa: distinguishing the good from the bad. *The Conversation,* 29 April. https://theconversation.com/entrepreneurship-funds-in-africa-distingui shing-the-good-from-the-bad-115927.

Ibrahim, M. (2019). *Fred Swaniker—Building opportunity. TIME,* Vol. 193, No. 16–17, 29 April/ 6 May, p. 19.

Idemudia, E. & Boenhnke, K. (2020). *Social Indicators Research Book Series 81. Psychosocial Experiences of African Migrants in Six European Countries.* Cham, Switzerland: Springer Nature. https://link.springer.com/content/pdf/10.1007%2F978-3-030-48347-0.pdf.

Khodor, C., Ware, C., & Lieurade (2020). Coronavirus weekly: where next for globalisation after the crisis? *The Conversation,* 27 May. https://theconversation.com/coronavirus-weekly-where-next-for-globalisation-after-the-crisis-139495.

Khor, M. (2016). New debt crises threaten global stability. *Southviews* No. 133, 19 October. www. southcentre.int.

Kiwuwa, D. E. (2016). The Gambia keeps dream of deepening democracy in Africa alive. *The Conversation,* 6 December. https://theconversation.com/the-gambia-keeps-dream-of-deepening-democracy-in-africa-alive-69899.

Kiwuwa, D. E. (2018). Why China's removal of term limits is a gift to African despots. *The Conversation,* March 8. https://theconversation.com/why-chinas-removal-of-term-limits-is-a-gift-to-afr ican-despots-92746.

Kiwuwa. D. E. (2020). Why history will judge Burundi's Pierre Nkurunziza harshly, *The Conversation,* 11 June 2020. https://theconversation.com/why-history-will-judge-burundis-pierre-nkurun ziza-harshly-140492.

Lilesa, F. (2019). Abiy Ahmed—A new hope. *TIME,* Vol. 193, No. 16–17, 29 April/ 6 May, p. 64.

Logan, S., & Gali, H. (2020). Sudan's transitional government must be supported through COVID-19. Here's why. *The Conversation*, 17 June. https://theconversation.com/sudans-transitional-government-must-be-supported-through-covid-19-heres-why-14018.

Loschky, J. (2013). *Arab Spring largely ignored in Sub-Saharan Africa.* Gallup World Poll. http://www.gallup.com/poll/172079/arab-spring-largely-ignored-sub-saharan-africa.aspx. Accessed January 9, 2017.

Mahlouly, D. (2019). Bouteflika steps aside as Algerians push to reclaim and own their history. *The Conversation*, April 5. https://theconversation.com/bouteflika-steps-aside-as-algerians-push-to-reclaim-and-own-their-history-114380.

Mattes, R. (2008). The material and political bases of lived poverty in Africa: Insights from the Afrobarometer. In V. Møller, D. Huschka, & A. C. Michalos (Eds.), *Social Indicators Research Series 33. Barometers of quality of life around the globe: How are we doing?* Dordrecht: Springer.

Mills, G. (2014). *Why states recover: Changing walking societies into winning nations, from Afghanistan to Zimbabwe.* Johannesburg, South Africa: Picador Africa.

Mills, G., Obasanjo, O., Desalegn, H., & van der Merwe, E. (2020). *The Asian aspiration—Why and how Africa should emulate Asia.* Johannesburg, South Africa: Pan Macmillan.

Mills, G., Obasanjo, O., Herbst, J., & Biti, T. (2019). *Democracy works: Rewiring politics to Africa's advantage.* Johannesburg, South Africa: Picador Africa.

Mills, G., Obasanjo, O., Herbst, J., & Davis, D. (2017). *Making Africa work: A handbook for economic success.* Cape Town, South Africa: Tafelberg.

Møller, V., Huschka, D., & Michalos, A. C. (Eds.). (2008). *Social indicators research series 33. Barometers of quality of life around the globe: How are we doing?.* Dordrecht: Springer. ISBN 978-1-4020-8685-4.

Mwine-Mugaju, E. (2020). Meet Katoto, Museveni's big fan. *Mail & Guardian*, June 26 to July 2, p. 12.

Nano, A. (2020). Gift of the Givers brings help to the Eastern Cape. *Daily Dispatch* (East London, South Africa), 7 July, p. 2.

News24 (2020). Massive undersea cable project set to give Africa internet boost. 14 May. https://www.news24.com/news24/africa/news/massive-undersea-cable-project-set-to-give-africa-internet-boost-20200514. Accessed July 5, 2020.

Nshimbi, C. C. (2016). When politics and academia collide, quality suffers. Just ask Nigeria. *The Conversation*, 25 October. https://theconversation.com/when-politics-and-academia-collide-quality-suffers-just-ask-nigeria-67313?utm.

OECD (2016). *Youth in the MENA Region: How to bring them in.* Paris: OECD Publishing. http://www.keepeek.com/Digital-Asset-Management/oecd/governance/youth-in-the-mena-region_9789264265721-en#page1.

Okiror, S. (2020). Second wave of locusts in east Africa said to be 20 times worse. *The Guardian*, 13 April. https://www.theguardian.com/global-development/2020/apr/13/second-wave-of-locusts-in-east-africa-said-to-be-20-times-worse. Accessed June 1, 2020.

Pew Research Center. (2018). *At least a million sub-Saharan Africans moved to Europe since 2010.* http://www.pewglobal.org/2018/03/22/at-least-a-million-sub-saharan-africans-moved-to-europe-since-2010/.

Pilling, D. (2017). Democrats in Africa take fight to its dictators. *Business Day*, Johannesburg, 26 January, p. 4.

Plaut, M. (2019). Bread led to al-Bashir's end. *Weekend Post*, South Africa, 13 April, p. 12.

Population Reference Bureau (2016). *World Population Data Sheet 2016.* http://www.prb.org/pdf16/prb-wpds2016-web-2016.pdf. Accessed November 1, 2016.

Qobo, M. & Mzyece, M. (2020). African countries need to seize opportunities created by US-China tensions. *The Conversation*, 15 June. https://theconversation.com/african-countries-need-to-seize-opportunities-created-by-us-china-tensions-140448.

Reader, J. (1997). *Africa: A biography of the continent*. London: Hamish Hamilton.

Sanny, J. A.-N., Logan, C., & Gyimah-Boadi, E. (2019). In search of opportunity: Young and educated Africans most likely to consider moving abroad. *Afrobarometer Dispatch* No. 288. http://afrobarometer.org/publications/ad288-search-opportunity-young-and-educated-africans-most-likely-consider-moving-abroad.

Satti, M.A. (2019). Songs of freedom: the soundtracks of political change in Sudan. *The Conversation*, 12 April. https://theconversation.com/songs-of-freedom-the-soundtracks-of-political-change-in-sudan-115383.

Simmt, E., Binde, A., Glanfield, F., & Mgombelo, J. (2019). Developing capacity for teacher in-service education in rural Tanzania: Embracing emergent phenomena. In I. Eloff (Ed.), *Quality of life in African societies* (pp. 327–344). Dordrecht: Springer.

Steinberg, J. (2016). The war against the fathers of freedom. *Business Day*, Johannesburg, 28 October, p. 9.

Swilling, M. (2016). The death knell of Zuma's rule echoes transitions elsewhere in Africa. *The Conversation,* 3 November. https://theconversation.com/the-death-knell-of-zumas-rule-echoes-transitions-elsewhere-in-africa-68084.

The Daily Telegraph (2015). Gambia loses its youth to 'Back Way'. 11 November. http://www.timeslive.co.za/thetimes/2015/11/11/Gambia-loses-its-youth-to-Back-Way.

The Economist (2014). The dividend is delayed – hopes that Africa's dramatic population bulge may create prosperity seem to have been overdone. 8 March. http://www.economist.com/news/middle-east-and-africa/21598646-hopes-africas-dramatic-population-bulge-may-create-prosperity-seem-have. Accessed January 26, 2016.

The Guardian (2020). Burundi expels WHO coronavirus team as election approaches. 14 May. https://www.theguardian.com/world/2020/may/14/burundi-expels-who-coronavirus-team-as-election-approaches. Accessed July 4, 2020.

United Nations (UN). (2011). *World population prospects: The 2010 REVISION*. New York: Department of Social Affairs, Population Division, United Nations.

Weekend Post (2019). Kenneth leaves wake of chaos. Port Elizabeth, South Africa, 27 April, p. 6.

Weston, M. (2020). Revolutionaries turn to healthcare. *Mail & Guardian*, 11 June. https://mg.co.za/africa/2020-06-11-revolutionaries-turn-to-healthcare/. Accessed June 24, 2020.

Wilson, F. (1972). *Labour in the South African Gold Mines, 1911–1969*. Cambridge University Press.

World Bank. (2014). *World development indicators 2014*. Washington, DC: World Bank. https://doi.org/10.1596/978-1-4648-0163-1.

World Bank (2020). World Bank Group's operational response to COVID-19 (coronavirus)—projects list. 17 June. https://www.worldbank.org/en/about/what-we-do/brief/world-bank-group-operational-response-covid-19-coronavirus-projects-list.

World Economic Forum (2017). In 2050, Africa will be home to 1 billion young people. And they'll need educating. https://www.weforum.org/agenda/2017/04/in-2050-africa-will-be-home-to-1-billion-young-people-and-theyll-need-educating.

Chapter 9
Human Rights and Well-Being Among Sub-Saharan Minorities

Abstract Since independence, the majority of citizens living in sub-Saharan African countries have enjoyed greater freedom from poverty, oppression, and neglect. However, there are still a number of minority groups whose needs have been overlooked or whose dignity has been compromised. In this chapter we have identified a select number of minority groups and we review the challenges they face in different states of sub-Saharan Africa. There are plenty of positive stories to tell. We provide examples of agency on the part of courageous and resilient individuals and minority groups who have succeeded in improving their lot in life and claiming their unique identities. We also report initiatives to address minority concerns and reforms aimed at bringing marginal citizens back into mainstream society.

Keywords Sub-Saharan Africa · Human rights · Minorities · Identities · Women's empowerment · Indigenous people · LGBTI · Refugees · Decolonisation

9.1 Human Rights and Dignity for Africa

A right to dignity is an acknowledgement of the intrinsic worth of human beings. …

Everyone has inherent dignity and the right to have their dignity respected and protected.

Fukuyama (2018, p. 51) citing the South African Constitution

Until fairly recently, the majority of people living in sub-Saharan Africa might have been regarded as disadvantaged minorities, despite being majorities in terms of their numbers. Although many sub-Saharan Africans have seen positive changes in their life chances since the 1960s, a number of groups in society still fare worse than others. Nonetheless, there are also prospects for the worth of Africa's minorities to be recognised and their contributions to society to be valued in future. In this chapter we outline some of the disadvantages and problems experienced by minorities, and report efforts underway to improve their life chances in future.

© Springer Nature Switzerland AG 2021

V. Møller and B. J. Roberts, *Quality of Life and Human Well-Being in Sub-Saharan Africa*,
Human Well-Being Research and Policy Making,
https://doi.org/10.1007/978-3-030-65788-8_9

9.2 Urban Slum Dwellers

The depressed quality of life of the growing proportion of slum dwellers among the urban poor presents a challenge for Africa. According to the African Development Bank, sub-Saharan Africa has the lowest proportion of urban dwellers worldwide, yet it has the highest proportion of slum dwellers, at 65% (Mills et al. 2017, p. 80). Slum dwellers are overrepresented among the informally and marginally employed, if they can find sources of income at all. They have become the new second-class citizens in their own countries with less access to services and to a political voice.

Tanzania's largest city of Dar es Salaam is one of Africa's fastest growing cities. It is home to about 5 million people and urbanisation continues rapidly. An estimated 70% of its residents live in informal settlements, without clean water and decent sanitation. The government has recently overturned a nationwide programme, announced in 2017, to demolish homes in informal settlements. In an about-turn, a new directive by President John Magufuli has been introduced which will instead provide land tenure for Dar es Salaam's urban poor. With a formal land title to her home, a beneficiary of the new policy said she was now confident that her family had a bright future. Proof of ownership will allow her to access a loan to grow her business of selling fried fish from a street stall. This policy shift on urban land tenure follows on an earlier 2016 programme to return land left undeveloped by investors to poor farmers in a bid to quell conflicts between farmers, herders and developers (Makoye 2019).

9.3 Africa's Women

There is a saying in Africa: 'When you strike a woman, you strike a rock,' alluding to African women as the backbone of society. Nevertheless, the World Happiness Report 2013 (Helliwell et al. 2013) reported that well-being among the women of sub-Saharan Africa is lower than that of men. Customary tribal law, codified during the colonial period and still recognised today, has in some instances halted the emancipation of women in many regions of sub-Saharan Africa. At the same time, though, women in most African societies have enjoyed equal access to education since independence, and a number of countries have introduced quotas for women to serve in public office, where they can exert influence on creating better opportunities and protection for women's rights. Land rights for women are regarded as vital for food production to feed Africa's growing population.

9.3.1 Role Models for African Women

In the new millennium there are new role models for women in many domains of life. For example, Ellen Johnson Sirleaf, the former President of Liberia, was the latest recipient of the Ibrahim Prize for Achievement in African Leadership. She received the award in recognition of her exceptional and transformative leadership in the face of unprecedented and renewed challenges, to lead Liberia's recovery following many years of devastating civil war. It was during her two terms of office (2006–2017) that the Ebola epidemic broke out in West Africa. In 2020, The World Health Organization (WHO) has appointed two women with experience of pandemics, Liberia's former president Ellen Johnson Sirleaf and New Zealand's former prime minister to head a panel to review the global response to the Covid-19 pandemic.

Kenya's Nobel laureate Wangari Maathai[1] serves as role model for African women of all ages. Born in 1940, Maathai is the first African woman to receive the Nobel Peace Prize in 2004. She was also the first female scholar from East and Central Africa to earn a doctorate and the first female professor in her home country of Kenya. Maathai played an active part in the struggle for democracy in Kenya. In 1977, Maathai started a grass-roots movement to halt deforestation that was threatening the means of subsistence of Kenya's agricultural population. The main focus of the campaign was the planting of trees with womens' groups in order to conserve the environment and improve their quality of life. The so-called Green Belt Movement rapidly spread to other African countries and globally. Maathai saw tree planting in a broader perspective, which included democracy, women's rights, and international solidarity. In the words of the Nobel Committee: 'She thinks globally and acts locally'. More recently, Wangari Maathai's campaign against land grabbing and the rapacious allocation of forest land has received renewed attention in Africa.

Sub-Saharan countries that have introduced quotas for women to serve in parliament do not necessarily feature as free or partly free, according to the Freedom House index. Some Africa observers note there may be a perverse incentive for authoritarian leaders to introduce quotas to present their countries as progressive, in order to gain international recognition and to attract foreign direct investment. For example, business-friendly Rwanda, a country with a poor human rights record, reserves at least 24 seats for women among the 53 elected members of parliament. Women in Africa are increasingly aware of the problem of quotas and are beginning to deal with male chauvinism.

9.3.2 Women Victims of Violence

The Democratic Republic of Congo has been called the worst place in the world to be a woman. Sexual violence and rape are considered defining features of the civil war in

---

[1] Wangari Maathai—Biographical. NobelPrize.org. Nobel Media AB (2020) https://www.nobelprize.org/prizes/peace/2004/maathai/biographical/ (Accessed 10 July 2020).

the eastern part of the country. In 2018, the Nobel Peace Prize was awarded to Nadia Murad and Denis Mukwege for their work in trying to end sexual violence during war and armed conflict. UN Goodwill Ambassador Murad was herself a victim at the hands of the Islamic State and has campaigned for the protection of survivors of human trafficking. Mukwege is a Congolese physician who heals broken bodies and restores dignity to survivors of sexualised violence at Panzi Hospital in the eastern DRC. According to hospital records, he has personally treated over 20,000 women, girls, men and boys who have suffered the physical and psychological wounds of traumatic rape (De Reus 2015). Mukwege has also, at much risk to himself, spoken out against those who shield military rapists (Brewer 2018).

Although women in the DRC have been victims of tremendous abuse and violence, they have wanted their voices to be heard. Victims of abuse, including some women who have been treated by Mukwege and his staff, have spoken out in documentaries[2] to bring the abuse to the attention of the world. One of the rape survivors who had experienced unspeakable horrors said she wanted her story to be told, 'because so many people don't know' (De Reus 2015).

Women victims of violence are often portrayed as citizens without political agency. Maria Martin De Almagro wishes to counter this image by presenting an alternative one, of DRC women as innovative activists willing to fight for their rights. She describes how a movement, aptly titled 'Nothing Without the Women',—*Rien sans les Femmes*—kicked off in March 2015 as a hybrid coalition of international NGOs and local women's groups in eastern Congo. It successfully petitioned for the DRC's electoral laws to include women candidates on all electoral lists. The movement collected more than 200,000 signatures from across the country, and over 6000 people joined one of its marches in eastern Congo. Thanks to these concerted efforts, the Parity Law was passed in August 2015 (De Almagro 2018a, b).

9.3.3   Child Marriages

Globally, some 650 million women and girls were married before they turned 18. In Niger, this is the case for three out of four women (77%) in the age group 18–22 years. Child marriages accelerate population growth, support patriarchal structures, entrench poverty, increase the risk of sexual violence and HIV/AIDS, and prevent women and girls from gaining access to education and income-earning work.

The good news is that the average age at time of marriage is increasing throughout the world. This can be observed in Ethiopia and Uganda. A recent Demographic and Health Survey provides comparative data on two cohorts of sub-Saharan women, aged 23–30 and 18–22, and their age at marriage. The share of women who were under age 18 at the time of marriage had dropped over only a decade in both Ethiopia and Uganda. Among the older 23–30 age cohort at the time of the survey, over half or close on half of the women were under-age when they married: 55% of women

---

[2]See the documentaries *The Greatest Silence: Rape in the Congo*, and *The Man Who Mends Women*.

in Ethiopia and 46% in Uganda. Among their younger counterparts, women aged between 18 and 22 at the time of the survey, only 36% in Ethiopia and 37% in Uganda were under-age (Der Spiegel 2018). Ethiopia has now launched a plan to end both child marriage and Female Genital Mutilation in 2024.[3]

The Children's Act of Ghana specifically prohibits the betrothal or marriage of a child. It gives the child the right to refuse either. Ghana's Ministry of Gender, Children and Social Protection has set up a unit to end child marriages. Sarfo Fordjour (2020) was interested in learning more about why young Ghanaian girls entered into child marriages, their lived experience of marriage, and its impact on their psychological well-being. She found that girls who were satisfied with married life were often ones who had found relief from previous mistreatment in the parental home. These girls found married life less psychologically distressing and their marital home gave them a feeling of safety and relief.

Sarfo Fordjour notes the experience of positive psychological well-being in child marriages is novel in the literature and may explain why some young girls agree to marriage in Ghana. However, most of her study participants regretted marrying early or were disappointed in their marriages. Girls who had considered marriage as an only means to come out of difficult family situations and poverty reported regretting the decision when these expectations were not realised. The decision to marry early also prevented girls from completing their education or training, so they expressed concern about their own and their childrens' future and livelihoods (Sarfo Fordjour 2020; Sarfo et al. 2020).

As reported in an earlier chapter, in Malawi, child marriages and domestic and other abuse of women are widespread, even though under-age marriages were banned by law in 2015 and abuse is also punishable by law. In September 2017, a country-wide march was organised to protest gender violence following the death of seven women in just the two months of August and September of that year, as reported by Amnesty International (Fischer 2018, p. 304).

There are important lessons to be learnt from Sierra Leone's Ebola pandemic of the impact of school closures for girls. A team of researchers studied how the closure of all primary and secondary schools through the 2014–2015 academic year affected the lives of young women during the West African Ebola outbreak. Originally designed as an empowerment programme for girls, the study provided clubs where young women were offered vocational skills training, financial literacy, and information on health and reproductive issues. Most importantly, the clubs offered women a safe space to meet. The researchers compared how the Ebola shock affected club participants compared to controls by tracking over four thousand girls to assess the lasting impacts on the girls' lives post-epidemic, when lockdown policies had ended and markets and schools had reopened. They found club members were more likely than controls to spend less time with men and were able to retain more of their social ties to others post-epidemic. In contrast, girls in control villages with no access to the clubs were more likely to get pregnant during the Ebola school closures and

---

[3]See 'Ethiopia vows to root out child marriage and female genital mutilation' https://www.bbc.co.uk/programmes/p07kt173 (Accessed 16 August 2019).

thus not able to return to school when schools reopened. The findings from Sierra Leone point to the importance of protecting vulnerable young women and their future during health crises that call for prolonged lockdown periods, such as the Covid-19 pandemic (Rasul et al. 2020).

Sierra Leone's Sexual Offenses Act, which raises the age of consent to 18 years, also aims to protect women, particularly girls, from abuse. However, while conducting her research in the capital city of Freetown and observing court cases stemming from the law, Schneider (2019) found the act's rigidity often undercuts the agency of young Sierra Leoneans and threatens their futures. She repeatedly witnessed court cases that resulted in boys from economically weak families being imprisoned if their consensual sexual relationships led to the young woman falling pregnant. The girls' family fear they will be left in a position where the boy will not be capable of supporting his partner and their child.

Under Sierra Leone's Sexual Offenses Act, men can receive a prison sentence of up to 15 years for having sex with a minor. Since consent is no longer considered, sexual acts with the consent of minor parties now fall into the same category as rape. For example, during her year-long fieldwork, Schneider (2019) witnessed court cases where the alleged victims, 17-year-old girls, and the accused, 19-year-old boys, told the court they were in love. In such cases, she reports, the 19-year-old youth almost always goes to prison, while his 17-year-old girlfriend loses her partner and cannot rely on his help to raise their child. The young woman may also be prevented from continuing her education. When schools re-opened after the Ebola pandemic in 2015, Sierra Leone's minister of education introduced a ban on pregnant girls attending school, as they are seen as negative influences. Alternative, separate classes for pregnant girls are limited and associated with stigma. Many girls do not return to school after giving birth.

Based on her research, Schneider contends that Sierra Leone's Sexual Offenses Act, as it is applied, along with the country's ban on pregnant girls attending school, actually harms young women rather than protecting them. The policing of a young couple's relationship puts both partners' futures at risk. She recommends that the law refocus on criminalising rape rather than on sending boyfriends who are barely over 18 years to prison.

An alternative to punishing teenage offenders, a project underway in Kenya's capital, Nairobi, invites teenage girls and young women to learn more about safe sex and family planning options. The youth-friendly centres 'speak the same language' as young people. They can compete with other attractive meeting places and recreational centres where young women like to spend their leisure time (Arunga 2018). In Zimbabwe, 'sisters' clinics that specialise in catering for sex workers have opened; here sex workers are both the professional consultants and the first-served clients (Bafana 2018).

9.3.4   A 'Republic' for Independent Women

In rural Kenya, a small group of 26 women live in what *Le Monde's* special correspondent Douet (2018a) calls an independent women's 'republic' that has been operating for 25 years. Interviewed by Douet, the women say they are happy to live peacefully with their children in a village where women are in charge and free of any restrictions imposed by others. The fathers of their children may visit, but the women decide if a man is allowed to stay overnight, often to assist them with patrolling at night. Protecting a village and its animals, typically a role assigned to men, is one the women are proud to carry out by themselves. The women's village is also financially independent, as the women raise livestock. When their herd was reduced to only four goats during the recent drought, they also supplemented their income by selling traditional bead necklaces to the tourists who visit the nearby game parks.

9.3.5   New Coming-of-Age Ceremonies

Some of the Kenyan women who live in the 'republic' have fled domestic abuse or poverty. Others may have wished to avoid undergoing genital cutting before marriage, which until recently has been a traditional custom among some of Kenya's ethnic groups, including the Samburu, visited by Douet. Kenya outlawed female genital mutilation (FGM) in 2011 and the rite is seldom practised except in remoter rural areas where people have not heard of the new law. Douet (2018a) notes that increasingly, the custom has been replaced by symbolic coming-of-age ceremonies in Kenya.

New coming-of-age ceremonies are trending in other countries across sub-Saharan Africa. For example, in Sierra Leone, a country which still has high rates of child marriages and where female genital cutting is still practised, *National Geographic* contributors visited a village where girls take part in alternative ceremonies to initiate them into womanhood without resort to FGM. Reporter Okeowo (2017, pp. 136–137) and photographer Stephanie Sinclair report that since 2010, more than 600 girls have participated in alternative ceremonies in a programme that also provides education for the young women.

In post-Al-Bashir Sudan, the country's new Sovereign Council, in power since August 2019, has outlawed female genital mutilation. Women played a key role in ousting the country's former long-term president. Support for FGM in Sudan has decreased from 79% in 1990 to 43% in 2014. It is not expected that FGM will disappear overnight in Sudan as it is deeply engrained in the local culture, but its abolishment is seen as a welcome start.[4]

---

[4]See Bradley (2020) and https://www.bbc.com/news/world-middle-east-52922079 (Accessed 5 June 2020).

9.4 Indigenous People

The descendants of Africa's first people, the hunter-gathers, who prefer to be known as the San or Bushmen, were gradually dispersed by the Bantu who migrated to southern Africa, and later also by white settlers. Bushmen could be shot like vermin until 1937 in Namibia and until 1926 in South Africa (Grant-Marshall 2013). Hunters could apply for a licence to shoot a number of bucks and a wildebeest, along with a male and a female Bushman. More recently, the extraordinary skills of San trackers have been appreciated but also exploited by regional defence forces and commercial organisations. Today, a dwindling number of Bushmen continue to preserve their way of life in the areas reserved for them in Botswana and Namibia; others have chosen to integrate into modern society where they may occupy the lowest social stratum. Similarly, the well-being and survival of other indigenous peoples, including the pygmy of central Africa, the Hadza of East Africa, and the Cimba (also Tjimba) of southern Africa, are at stake in the twenty-first century.

Bushmen's superb tracking skills and intimate knowledge of the bush may once again become fully recognised if a project to introduce walking trails for tourists visiting South Africa's famed Kruger National Park succeeds. The proposed pioneering trail project will engage Namibia's top two recognised master trackers, members of the Ju/'hoansi from the remote Jyae Nyae Nyae Conservancy, the last group in southern Africa allowed to hunt in the traditional way. The Ju/'hoansi are poor but they get by using their peerless command of animal tracking, the most ancient art of human survival. The two renowned Bushmen trackers will take tourists, who wish for a deeper wilderness experience, on guided walks using their intimate reading of the bush. 'History will be made … when Bushmen again walk the savannah of the [South African] lowveld hundreds of years after their presence was eclipsed by incoming forces', enthuses a *Business Day's* staff writer. If the pioneering trails work and are followed up, it is anticipated that 'the Kruger National Park experience will be enriched and the fragile cause of the Ju/'hoansi trackers and their communities will receive a powerful boost' (Business Day 2018).

9.5 Lesbian, Gay, Bisexual, Transgender, and Intersex People (LGBTI)

Identity and gender politics are beginning to gain ground in sub-Saharan Africa, a region that has a history of patriarchy at all levels of society.

South Africa's post-apartheid Constitution guarantees the rights of people regardless of gender, race, religious or sexual persuasion, and recognises marriage between same-sex partners. In many other sub-Saharan countries, homosexuals are still threatened with imprisonment or even death.[5] Prejudice also keeps LGBTI people from

---

[5]While British and Portuguese colonies inherited laws that penalised same-sex conduct, Viljoen (2019a, b) reports that two countries in the SADC region, the former Belgian Democratic Republic

seeking health care and treatment for HIV. In total, 32 African states still criminalise same-sex acts (Viljoen 2019a).

Former British colonies around the world are among the countries that still have laws on their statute books penalising same-sex conduct. Writing in 2018, Enze Han and Joseph O'Mahoney note that while laws on same-sex relations inherited from British colonial rule may be superficially similar among African nations, they were drafted very differently and specify penalties of varying severity. For example, colonial Ghana, then the Gold Coast, received a completely different colonial-era code from British administrators than other British colonies in Africa. Ghana's criminal code classifies 'unnatural carnal knowledge' with a potential prison sentence of up to three years. By contrast, Kenya, Nigeria and Gambia treat gay sex as a felony, with a penalty of up to 14 years' imprisonment. In Uganda and Zambia, the maximum penalty is life (Han and O'Mahoney 2018).

Han and O'Mahoney (2018) found little evidence that former British colonies have decriminalised homosexual conduct any more slowly than colonies of other European states. The 'stickiness' of repressive institutions appears to be 'relatively consistent across different countries and histories, and not specific to a particular type of colonialism'.[6]

9.5.1 Changes to Colonial Penal Codes

Several sub-Saharan countries that inherited penal laws from colonial times are reconsidering these laws in the light of their constitutions and of international law. Among them are two former British colonies, Kenya and Botswana, and Angola, formerly a Portuguese colony, and most recently, Gabon, a former French colony.

Kenya. In Kenya, the recent banning of a cinema film caused outrage in art circles. According to the classification board, the film contained 'homosexual scenes that are against the law, the culture and moral values of the Kenyan people' (Ndanyi 2019). In Kenya, both men and women involved in same-sex relationships face the possibility of legal prosecution based on colonial era laws. The British Empire first introduced laws against 'unnatural offences' and 'indecent practices among males' in India in 1860, which were subsequently copied into penal codes in Africa (Van Klinken 2019a). Sections of these anti-sodomy laws were inspired by England's King Henry VIII's Anti-Buggery Act of 1533 (Novak 2019).

While other former British colonies, such as Uganda and Nigeria, have sought to introduce even more wide-ranging laws targeting LGBTI people in recent years,

---

of Congo and the former French Madagascar never criminalised same-sex conduct. In Tanzania, 13 activists were arrested in 2018 when they called for debate on restricted access to health care for LGBTI people (Fischer 2018, p. 461).

[6]In 2018, British prime minister Theresa May urged Commonwealth heads of government to overhaul outdated homosexuality laws held over from British colonial rule. 'Nobody should face discrimination or persecution because of who they are or who they love', she stated.

Kenya's new Constitution of 2010 allows its judges to look to international and foreign law to resolve the issue of the recognition of the rights of LGBTI people (Van Klinken 2019a).

In 2019, Kenyans were awaiting a court ruling on a petition before the High Court seeking to decriminalise homosexuality due for a decision in May (Novak 2019). Churchgoers in Nairobi who support gay rights were lighting candles ahead of the court ruling. The petition argued that the law contravenes several rights enshrined in the Constitution, and denies lesbian, gay and bisexual people the right to privacy (Van Klinken 2019a). The Nairobi High Court ruled against the petition, but did grant the petitioners the right to appeal to the decision (Van Klinken 2019b).

Botswana. Meanwhile, Botswana's High Court has ruled that private consensual sex between adults of the same sex is no longer criminal. Botswana's constitution is the oldest surviving constitution in Africa, dating back to the country's independence in 1960. It offers less leeway than in Kenya for judges to look to treaties or other sources of international law to aid in their decision-making and international law is not binding in their courts (Novak 2019).

Botswana's anti-sodomy laws have come under review before. Responding to a similar challenge in 2003, the High Court invoked public morality to justify keeping penal codes inspired by Victorian-age morality. This decision was confirmed by the Court of Appeal based on no evidence of attitudes in society that called for decriminalisation of homosexual practices. Viljoen (2019a) argues that the latest High Court decision of June 2019, which places less emphasis on public opinion and questions public morality as the basis of its decision, shows that times have indeed changed.

The landmark Botswana High Court decision sets a precedent, on which other African courts can rely, including the Kenyan Court of Appeal. However, Viljoen (2019a) notes the situation in Kenya differs in important respects. Its political elite has not taken a public stance that accepts LGBT people. Also, an 2014/15 Afrobarometer survey on public acceptance of LGBT people found only 14% of respondents showed tolerance towards homosexuals in Kenya compared to 43% in Botswana.

Angola. The former Portuguese colony inherited a colonial statute dating back to 1886, that criminalised 'indecent acts' and persons habitually engaging in 'acts against nature', that were widely interpreted as a ban on homosexual conduct. Punishment upon conviction included confinement in an asylum for the mentally insane, jail time with hard labour, or disqualification from practising a profession (Viljoen 2019b). However, the recent change in government may see improvements to the quality of life of members of Angola's LGBTI community. Since Angola's new President João Lourenço took over power in September 2017, an openly LGBTI organisation was for the first time officially registered and in January 2019, the Angolan National Assembly voted 155 to 1 to abolish the provision criminalising homosexual relationships. In fact, the Assembly went a step further. In future, it will be homophobia, not homosexual acts, that will be punished (Viljoen 2019b).

Gabon. In June 2020, the lower house of Parliament in Gabon voted to decriminalise homosexuality. Although same-sex marriage is still prohibited, the 'act', which could lead to a jail term of up to six months, will now not be punishable by law.

9.6   Refugees and Displaced People

Five of the world's top refugee-producing countries (Somalia, Sudan, the Democratic Republic of Congo, Eritrea and most recently South Sudan) are in Africa. Of the estimated 16.7 million refugees worldwide, 2.3 million or close to 14% are from Africa. Of the 33.3 million internally displaced persons in the world, half or 16.8 million are displaced in African countries. Although various United Nations conventions provide for the rights of refugees, such people are often placed in conflict with members of host societies and may become targets of xenophobia. Displaced individuals, though they are within the borders of their own country, are often disadvantaged both economically as well as socially.

Thankfully, not all refugees and refugee camps in Africa fit this picture of depressed well-being.

9.6.1   Uganda's Bididi

Uganda is considered a model host country for refugees from neighbouring countries. Refugees are offered land to till, and are allowed to seek work and to choose where to settle in the country. In late 2017, Uganda offered refuge to some 1,4 million individuals in Bididi.[7] This settlement hosts the largest number of displaced individuals on the continent (Fischer 2018, p. 484).

9.6.2   Kenya's Kukuma

Kukuma, another one of the largest refugee camps in the world, may not be worst place on earth to live, according to a recent report (Douet 2018b). Kukuma was initially set up in 1992 to receive victims of the war in Sudan. Over time it has welcomed waves of refugees from Ethiopia, Somalia, the DRC, Burundi, and most recently from South Sudan. Located in the north of Kenya and some 456 km from Juba, the capital of South Sudan, the camp today provides shelter for 185,000 persons.

---

[7]See the illustrated report on the Bididi refugee settlement by Nina Strochlic, with photographs by Nora Lorek (Strochlic and Lorek 2019), 'Can Uganda turn Africa's largest refugee settlement into an urban hub?', published in a special issue of the *National Geographic* on 'Cities, ideas for a brighter future'.

Contrary to the stereotypical view of refugee camps, there is a spirit of entrepreneurship and a thriving economy. Shopkeepers and artisans have set up over 2000 small businesses in its bustling market.

Esperance Tabisha, whose first name means 'Hope' in English, embodies this image of positive agency among residents of Kukuma. Esperance had studied fashion design and dress-making at the University of Goma in the DRC, before she fled the violence there to find refuge in Kukuma. Within a week of arriving in the camp, she unpacked her sewing machine and started to work. Eight years later and on to her third machine, she now runs a successful business designing and producing garments in a workshop in the entrance to her home. Her clientele include refugees in the camp as well as Kenyans living in the next village, also called Kukuma. *Esperanza Fashion and Designs* advertises on Facebook and Instagram (Douet 2018b).

9.6.3 Nigeria's 'Flying Midwives'

Africa's efforts to achieve the Sustainable Development Goals for maternal health include supporting mothers during childbirth, even under difficult conditions in conflict zones. In Nigeria, which is one of the worst African countries in which to give birth, *TIME*'s Africa correspondent Baker (2019) reports that, amid a scarcity of doctors, volunteer midwives are saving the lives of mothers and their babies. In the northern Borno state, where Boko Haram has led a decade-long terrorist insurgency, some 6500 newborns die every year of preventable causes. That is twice the rate of the rest of the country, which ranks fourth in maternal mortality in spite of being the wealthiest country in Africa by GDP. In one of the camps for internally displaced people in Borno, some 50 midwives from across Nigeria have volunteered to support pregnant women, under an UNICEF programme. The programme has the support of the country's First Lady, Aisha Buhari, whose husband was re-elected for a second term in early 2019. President Buhari has made it one of his priorities to reduce maternal and infant deaths.

The volunteer midwives try to see the women in their care once a month. This is more often than the number of visits recommended by Nigeria's health ministry and more in line with the latest World Health Organisation's recommendations. The midwives know there may be no recourse to emergency medical assistance, so they try to foresee any potential problems in advance. 'Preparing is our prevention,' explains one of the midwives. Among other precautions, the midwives make sure that the women are taking their antimalarial medication and sleeping under impregnated mosquito nets to protect them from preterm labour and complications during delivery. Working in a remote clinic in a conflict zone calls for both dedication and ingenuity. There may be little worse than 'suturing a woman at night by the light of a cell phone because the clinic has no electricity', says a flying midwife, 'but there is nothing more rewarding than bringing a baby into the world' (Baker 2019, p. 51).

9.7 Decolonalisation

During colonial rule in Africa, people suffered indignities of many kinds which have left deep scars on the national psyche. Thousands of cultural artefacts were plundered from the continent by Western countries. Reparations are currently underway that may heal and restore a sense of worth and dignity to communities in sub-Saharan Africa. Promoting indigenous languages will also play an important role in restoring African identity. Here we report on select cases by way of example.

9.7.1 Returning Home

In 1810, Sarah Baartman, the first Khoisan woman to leave Africa, was taken to Europe where she was exhibited as the 'Hottentot Venus' in freak shows. She died in 1826 after serving as a specimen for French scientists. Following a request by President Mandela to the French, her remains were finally returned to South Africa, and laid to rest in dignity on Women's Day in 2002.[8] A district in her province of origin in the Eastern Cape is named in her honour. Her homecoming is commemorated in a tapestry embroidered by Elizabeth Malete under the motto 'to strike a woman is to strike a rock'[9] (See Fig. 9.1).

West African countries have for many years wished for their artwork to be returned, for display in their own local museums. At present, treasures from Benin and other ancient civilisations can be viewed in museums in Europe, where they have been preserved since colonial days. Although the restitution of Africa's art treasures is a controversial issue in France (Hugeux 2019), a report commissioned by President Emmanuel Macron has recommended that African art treasures in French museums be returned to their countries of origin.

The recent announcement that Britain's National Army Museum is to return two stolen locks of hair from a nineteenth century Ethiopian king, was hailed as an 'exemplary gesture of goodwill' by the Ethiopian Embassy in London (Girma 2019). The locks were cut from Emperor Tewodros II's head after he shot himself rather than be taken prisoner by invading British forces. His hair wasn't the only thing taken. After sacking his fortress at Maqdala during Easter in 1868, the British soldiers went on a looting spree. It is said that 15 elephants and 200 mules were needed to cart the booty away. According to Girma (2018), the return of Emperor Tewodros II's locks has a special meaning for the 'story-telling nation'. Tewodros represents a significant chapter in the history of Ethiopia, then known as Abyssinia. He is a symbol of the

---

[8] See https://en.wikipedia.org/wiki/Sarah_Baartman (Accessed 4 April 2019).

[9] Introducing the tapestry, art historian Schmahmann (2006, pp. 1–3) writes that the slogan has a specific historical reference. On 9 August 1956, hundreds of women marched against a South African law that black females, like black males, be obliged to carry so-called 'pass books'. 'The metaphor of a rock speaks of resilience that black women in South Africa have shown in the face of oppression, discrimination and economic disadvantage.'.

Fig. 9.1 When *you strike a women (sic), you strike a rock*. Elizabeth Malete, Mapula Embroidery Project, 2005. Collection of the Institute of Social and Economic Research, Rhodes University, South Africa

indomitable strength of the country that warded off attacks from powerful nations and still stands tall in its independence.

9.7.2 Language as Identity

In many sub-Saharan countries local indigenous languages are side-lined, while prestige is associated with a good command of the colonial language that serves as lingua franca in business and education. In South Africa, where mother-tongue instruction is a contentious issue, university lecturer Jantjies (2018) found that using multiple languages in learning platforms, such as apps and websites for maths and science subjects, enhanced the learning experience for students. Professor of Education Science Balfour (2016) argues that promoting local languages in teaching and learning in South Africa may open up new spaces for decolonisation and inter-culturalism, and become key to developing an authentic national identity.

Mose (2019) makes a case for the importance of mother-tongue education in multi-lingual Kenya, a country with over 42 different indigenous languages. Kiswahili, the national language, enjoys widespread acceptance and use as the lingua franca, while knowledge of English, another official language, is perceived as a true sign of a good education. Both languages enjoy greater prestige than the indigenous languages that the majority of Kenyans use in their homes, in open-air markets across the country, in worship services and to some extent in pre-primary and primary schools as co-languages of teaching and learning. Mose believes that such perceptions might gradually shift with the inclusion of indigenous languages in Kenya's new curriculum, which places the learners and their mother tongue at the centre of learning activities. For many lower primary school pupils, their mother tongue is the only resource they have to negotiate ideas. The rebirth of the use of indigenous languages in schools in Kenya could have a profound effect on children's educational outcomes, as well as much broader beneficial effects on Kenyan society.

In West Africa, Edosa Edionhon, a linguist who teaches at the University of Benin, applauds the BBC World's new English-based Pidgin radio service for West and Central Africa. Although Pidgin does not have the official status of a recognised language, it is widely spoken across West Africa. According to the broadcaster, BBC's News Pidgin reaches a weekly audience of 7.5 million people in Nigeria and around the world on radio, online, Facebook and Instagram (Edionhon 2018).

To celebrate the 50th anniversary of his country's independence from Great Britain, King Mswati III of Swaziland proclaimed on 19 April 2018 that his county would henceforth be renamed eSwatini, land of the Swazis. Swaziland was a British protectorate from 1871 until its independence on 6 September, 1968. The September jubilee celebrations, which saw the official name-change, also marked the king's 50th birthday.

9.8 Conclusion

In this chapter we have identified some minority populations in sub-Saharan Africa whose prospects of enjoying a 'life worth living' (Csikszentmihalyi and Csikszentmihalyi 2006) have been variously curtailed to date. We have also showcased instances when members of minority groups have nevertheless managed to improve their life chances in spite of restrictions on their freedoms. Their agency gives cause for celebration. We have told stories about citizens who have volunteered to assist members of minority groups. And we have presented cases where countries are in the process of recognising the worth of minority groups, which promise dignity to their members. Returning African artworks and other precious relics to their countries of origin on the continent is another way to boost national pride in Africa. Recognising the significance of local languages as cultural heritage and as inclusive means of communication in Africa, will further restore confidence in home-grown talent and creativity.

In the next chapter we turn to new ideas and innovations that promise to improve the lives of people in sub-Saharan Africa and earn recognition and standing for the region.

References

Arunga, A. (2018). Putting her in charge. Bill & Melinda Gates Foundation, *2018 Goalkeepers Data Report*, pp. 15–17.

Bafana, B. (2018). Stigma & the sisterhood. Bill & Melinda Gates Foundation, *2018 Goalkeepers Data Report*, pp. 21–23.

Baker, A. (2019). The Flying Midwives. To the rescue: with doctors scarce in Nigeria, midwives are saving thousands. *TIME*, Vol 193, No. 6–7, 18–25 February, pp. 46–51.

Balfour, R. J. (2016). How universities can use language as a force for fundamental change. *The Conversation*, 3 October. https://theconversation.com/how-universities-can-use-language-as-a-force-for-fundamental-change-65691.

Bradley, T. (2020). Sudan's political change gives hope for young women and girls. Here's why. *The Conversation*, 12 August. https://theconversation.com/sudans-political-change-gives-hope-for-young-women-and-girls-heres-why-144293.

Brewer, J. (2018). Nobel Peace Prize awarded to Nadia Murad and Denis Mukwege for campaigns against sexual violence. *The Conversation*, 5 October 2018. https://theconversation.com/nobel-peace-prize-awarded-to-nadia-murad-and-denis-mukwege-for-campaigns-against-sexual-vio lence-104494.

Business Day. (2018). *Walk trails with world's best trackers*. Johannesburg, 22 March, p. 8.

Csikszentmihalyi, M., & Csikszentmihalyi, I. S. (Eds.) (2006). *A life worth living: Contributions to positive psychology*. Oxford University Press.

De Almagro, M. M. (2018a). Women activists in the DRC show how effective alliances can be forged. *The Conversation*, 14 August. https://theconversation.com/women-activists-in-the-drc-show-how-effective-alliances-can-be-forged-101203.

De Almagro, M. M. (2018b). Hybrid clubs: A feminist approach to peace-building in the Democratic Republic of Congo. *Journal of Intervention and Statebuilding, 12*(3), 319–334. https://doi.org/10.1080/17502977.2018.1482125. https://www.tandfonline.com/doi/pdf/10.1080/17502977.2018.1482125?needAccess=true. Accessed March 25, 2019.

De Reus, L. A. (2015). Denis Mukwege deserves the Nobel peace prize for his work in Congo. *The Conversation*, 9 October.https://theconversation.com/denis-mukwege-deserves-the-nobel-peace-prize-for-his-work-in-congo-48489.

Der Spiegel (2018). Married Girls. No. 132 in the 'Früher war alles schlechter' series ('Things were worse back then'), Vol 72, No. 28, July, p. 46.

Douet, M. (2018a). Au Kenya, une petite "republique de femmes". *Le Monde*, 26 May, p. 4.

Douet, M. (2018b). A Kakuma, les réfugiés ont l'esprit d'entreprise. *Le Monde*, 30 June, p. 11.

Edionhon, E. J. (2018). Why West Africa's pidgins deserve full recognition as official languages. *The Conversation*, 23 August. https://theconversation.com/why-west-africas-pidgins-deserve-full-recognition-as-official-languages-101844.

Fischer, (2018). *Der neue Fischer Weltalmanach 2019: Zahlen, Daten, Fakten, Schwerpunkt Arbeit*. Frankfurt am Main, Germany: Fischer Verlag.

Fukuyama, F. (2018). *Identity: The demand for dignity and the politics of resentment*. London: Profile Books.

Girma, M. (2018). Ethiopia: A nation in need of a new story. *The Conversation*, April 18. http://africanarguments.org/2018/04/18/ethiopia-a-nation-in-need-of-a-new-story-abiy-ahmed-ethiopiawinet/.

Girma, M. (2019). Why it's significant that the UK has returned the locks of hair of an Ethiopian king. *The Conversation*, 17 March.https://theconversation.com/why-its-significant-that-the-uk-has-ret urned-the-locks-of-hair-of-an-ethiopian-king-113382.

Grant-Marshall, S. (2013). A journey into the heart of bleakness. *Business Day*, 25 June. http://www.bdlive.co.za/life/books/2013/06/25/a-journey-into-the-heart-of-bleakness. Accessed July 23, 2015.

Han, E., & O'Mahoney, J. (2018). How Britain's colonial legacy still affects LGBT politics around the world. *The Conversation*, 15 May. https://theconversation.com/how-britains-colonial-legacy-still-affects-lgbt-politics-around-the-world-95799.

Helliwell, J. F., Layard, R., & Sachs, J. (Eds.). (2013). *World happiness report 2013*. New York: UN Sustainable Development Solutions Network.

Hugeux, V. (2019). Retour au bercail pour l'art Africain? *L'Express*, 30 January, pp. 54–57.

Jantjies, M. (2018). Marrying technology and home language boosts maths and science learning. *The Conversation*, 14 October. https://theconversation.com/marrying-technology-and-home-lan guage-boosts-maths-and-science-learning-104587.

Makoye, K, (2019). Slum dwellers on solid ground: With formal land titles, Tanzania's urban poor about to tackle poverty. *The Star*, Johannesburg, 8 February, p. 9.

Mills, G., Obasanjo, O., Herbst, J., & Davis, D. (2017). *Making Africa work: A handbook for economic success*. Cape Town, South Africa: Tafelberg.

Mose, P. (2019). Why embracing indigenous languages could have major benefits for Kenya. *The Conversation*, 20 February. https://theconversation.com/why-embracing-indigenous-languages-could-have-major-benefits-for-kenya-111846.

Ndanyi, S. S. (2019). How young filmmakers are protecting artistic freedom in Kenya. *The Conversation*, 21 February.https://theconversation.com/how-young-filmmakers-are-protecting-artistic-freedom-in-kenya-111837.

Novak, A. (2019). Botswana joins list of African countries reviewing gay rights. *The Conversation*, 19 March. https://theconversation.com/botswana-joins-list-of-african-countries-reviewing-gay-rights-113586.

Okeowo, A. (2017). The dangerous lives of girls. *National Geographic, 231*(1), January, pp. 130–151.

Rasul, I., Smurra, A., & Bandiera, O. (2020). Lessons from Sierra Leone's Ebola pandemic on the impact of school closures on girls. *The Conversation*, 20 May. https://theconversation.com/les sons-from-sierra-leones-ebola-pandemic-on-the-impact-of-school-closures-on-girls-137837.

Sarfo, E. A., Yendork, J. S., & Naidoo, A. V. (2020). Understanding child marriage in Ghana: The constructions of gender and sexuality and implications for married girls. *Childcare in Practice*. https://doi.org/10.1080/13575279.2019.1701411.

Sarfo Fordjour, E. A. (2020). The psychological effects of early marriage: What I learnt from some Ghanaian girls. *The Conversation*, 3 June. https://theconversation.com/the-psychological-effects-of-early-marriage-what-i-learnt-from-some-ghanaian-girls-135069.

Schmahmann, B. (2006). *Mapula Embroidery and Empowerment in the Wintersveld*. Parkwood: South Africa, David Krut Publishing.

Schneider, L. T. (2019). Sierra Leone's laws to protect women have unintended consequences. *The Conversation*, 23 January. https://theconversation.com/sierra-leones-laws-to-pro tect-women-have-unintended-consequences-109815.

Strochlic, N., & Lorek, N. (2019). Can Africa's largest refugee settlement grow into an urban hub? *National Geographic, 235* (4), April, pp. 104–121.

Van Klinken, A. (2019a). Explainer: What's at stake in Kenyan court case on gay rights. *The Conversation*, 22 February. https://theconversation.com/explainer-whats-at-stake-in-kenyan-court-case-on-gay-rights-112317.

Van Klinken, A. (2019b). Homosexuality remains illegal in Kenya as court rejects LGBT petition. *The Conversation*, 24 May. https://theconversation.com/homosexuality-remains-illegal-in-kenya-as-court-rejects-lgbt-petition-112149.

Viljoen, F. (2019a). Botswana court ruling is a ray of hope for LGBT people across Africa. *The Conversation*, 12 June. https://theconversation.com/botswana-court-ruling-is-a-ray-of-hope-for-lgbt-people-across-africa-118713.

Viljoen, F. (2019b). Abolition of Angola's anti-gay laws may pave the way for regional reform. *The Conversation*. 15 February. https://theconversation.com/abolition-of-angolas-anti-gay-laws-may-pave-the-way-for-regional-reform-111432.

Chapter 10
Innovations for Enriched Quality of Life

Abstract For centuries the African continent was isolated from the rest of the globe. In pre-colonial times only the coastal regions were involved in trade and exchange of new ideas. The colonial era introduced new laws and regulations that were foreign to local people and indigenous customs. The era of structural adjustment, which called for new democracies to cut back on health services, infrastructure and education, are regarded by respected African scholars as decades lost to development. In the new millennium, a digitally connected Africa is embracing new ideas from around the globe and is producing its own innovations to enhance the well-being of the current generation and future generations. In this chapter we report on select ideas and innovations that have made everyday life in Africa more pleasant and productive. We also reflect on daring scientific enterprises, which have captured the imagination, and may foretell a future African century.

Keywords Sub-Saharan Africa · Innovations · Basic needs · African start-ups · Eco-friendly · Vaccines · Astronomy · Square Kilometre Array telescope

10.1 Innovations for Africa

Always something new out of Africa

There is a saying attributed to the Roman, Pliny the Elder, that there is always something new coming out of Africa. This may become particularly true in the new millennium. The youth of Africa have embraced social media and are keen to see change on the continent. While Africans living in sub-Saharan Africa may have been cautious to accept new ideas or change proven habits passed down for centuries, this is no longer the case. In this chapter we review a number of innovations and ideas that have potential to improve quality of life and people's outlook on the future.

In our introduction to African well-being in earlier times, we noted that innovations on the continent had often occurred to ensure survival during stressful times of drought and famine. Once such periods were over, people tended to revert to their former habitual and traditional ways of living (Reader 1997). We also noted that not

© Springer Nature Switzerland AG 2021

V. Møller and B. J. Roberts, *Quality of Life and Human Well-Being in Sub-Saharan Africa*,
Human Well-Being Research and Policy Making,
https://doi.org/10.1007/978-3-030-65788-8_10

all innovations were adaptable to the African climate and terrain. The first horses brought by ship to West Africa did not survive long enough to be of use. The wheel arrived late in Africa as it was less appropriate than head loaders for transporting goods over rough terrain.

In the new millennium, there appears to be a greater enthusiasm for embracing labour-saving devices and new technologies than in the past, provided they are afford-able and useful. In Africa, the incentive to innovate may still be more for reasons of necessity rather than curiosity or fashion. This may be why African innovations tend to service the actual needs of people[1] and are therefore more likely to make a real difference to lived quality of life on the continent.

Here we should like to detail a number of innovations that have contributed to a better life in sub-Saharan Africa in recent times, or at least have the potential to do so. The examples we have chosen are ordered under the headings of key quality-of-life domains, ranging from basic needs, such as water and food security, to higher order ones such as thought-provoking ideas and innovations that inspire awe and optimism for the future of Africa.

10.2 Basic Needs—Water, Electricity, Sanitation

10.2.1 A New Use for African Drums

For centuries African women have drawn water from streams and dams as part of their household chores. Water is carried home on their heads in water-tight vessels, such as calabashes, and more recently in metal and plastic buckets. Fetching water can be an onerous task, and it has been a common practice to send a young girl child in the extended family to live in the rural area to assist an older family member with this and other household chores. A new invention that makes water collection less taxing and more fun is the hippo water roller, a barrel drum that is filled with water and then rolled home instead of transported balanced on one's head. The hippo roller is particularly popular among the youth, who regard the invention as a toy.

By 2016, over 32,000 hippo water rollers had been sold or distributed in Africa, benefitting 225,000 people (Bruton 2018).

---

[1] We are grateful to Professor Mike Bruton of Mike Bruton Imaginengineering for making this point in his SciFest lecture on home-grown innovations in Africa. Bruton's (2018) book, 'What a Great Idea', covers South African inventions. A second book, in preparation, will present innovations from across the African continent (www.mikebruton.co.za). South Africa's national science festival, established in 1996 and held annually, aims to promote better understanding of science, technology and innovation (https://www.scifest.org.za/).

10.2.2 A No-Touch Hand-Washing Machine to Curb the Spread of Covid-19

Nine-year-old Stephen Wamukota received Kenya's presidential award for his wooden hand-washing machine. He was the youngest of 68 people to receive President Uhuru Kenyatta's award on 1 June 2020 for their contributions to contain the spread of the coronavirus in the country. Stephen created his machine with the wood, nails, and a small water tank he found at home. The hand washing machine has two foot pedals, one to release soap and the other to release water. It allows users to operate the pedals without touching surfaces with their hands, thereby reducing the possibility of contracting the coronavirus.

Stephen Wamukota came up with the idea for his machine after hearing about Covid-19 infection on a local television station and that everyone should wash their hands regularly to stay safe from the virus and prevent it from spreading. He wanted to help make hand washing easier. His father, who repairs electronics for a living, helped him to stabilise his semi-automatic machine. Stephen learnt how to assemble and construct things thanks to Kenya's school curriculum which includes practical subjects. He wants to be an engineer and has been promised a scholarship by the governor of his county in Western Kenya to continue his primary and secondary education once schools reopen after the country's lockdown (Salaudeen 2020).

The demonstration of the no-touch hand-washing machine (Photo of Stephen Wamukota with his invention; https://str8talkmagazine.com/wp-content/uploads/2020/06/boy2-pic-data.jpg)

10.2.3   Electricity for a Better Life

One of the expectations for a better life under democracy is to have electricity in the home. Simple innovations using the right approach and making use of Africa's abundant hours of daily sunshine may assist urban customers to finally get access to electricity.

Many households in Kenya cannot afford a grid connection and households in informal urban settlements without a formal address cannot be metered. 'Under-the-grid', decentralised electrification using renewable energy technologies solves such problems. The installation time is quick, and compared to the high upfront connection costs in Kenya, a 15-watt solar home system costs on average USD $9 per month for 36 months, after which point the household owns its system. Moreover, there is evidence that the willingness to pay for decentralised renewables is much higher than for a grid connection because they are seen as more reliable (Shirley 2018).

10.2.4   Smart Sanitation for Africa

More people in Africa have access to a cellular phone than to a decent toilet. Over half of the people in sub-Saharan Africa, about 507 million, make do without proper sanitation: Close to a quarter (about 23%) do not have access to any toilet, while a further 31% use toilets that are not connected to a formal sanitation system. Kenya's iconic 'flying toilets'[2] represent the extreme indignity associated with the lack of sanitation in African cities.

In the twenty-first century, access to safe toilet facilities is considered the most fundamental of dignities for many urban dwellers. Bucket toilets and pit latrines, let alone flying toilets, are no longer acceptable under democracy, especially if these toilets are not properly serviced or maintained. The flush toilet has become the standard to which Africa's urban dwellers aspire.

At the same time, water is precious in Africa and it does not make sense to flush it down toilets. Citizens in water-scarce urban areas are reminded that 'every drop counts' and one flush is equal to five days' supply of drinking water for one person.[3] Every flush sends between 6 to 16 l of fresh water to wastewater plants. The energy to source the fresh water for flushing and then to treat the resulting wastewater is hugely expensive—up to 15 kWh per flush, whereas only about 2 kWh is needed to charge a smart phone over a whole year (Han and Hashemi 2018).

During the recent drought that affected East and southern Africa, the city of Cape Town was the first in the developed world to anticipate running out of drinking water, let alone water for flushing. One solution to postpone 'Day Zero', when the city's taps would run dry, was to re-use 'grey' water to flush. Citizens were asked to collect

---

[2]The reference is to a plastic bag that is used to collect human waste where there is a lack of a formal sanitation system. https://www.en.wikipedia.org/wiki/Flying_toilet (Accessed 25 May 2019).

[3]A public service message on posters during South Africa's continuous drought.

and recycle their shower water for this purpose. This practice has now been adopted in cities and towns across South Africa.

Cape Town residents were encouraged to limit their showers to two minutes at most. A novel idea to assist in delaying the looming 'Day Zero' was to invite local musicians to record their two-minute water-saving songs for Capetonians to listen to—or sing along to—while showering.

The longer-term solution for Africa's urban sanitation problem may be the water-less toilet. Han and Hashemi (2018) claim that this innovation may be the first step in building 'smarter, greener' cities in Africa. The idea is that nutrients from human waste can be used as a resource. Using solar energy, waterless toilets collect waste into tanks, where microbes are added so that solid waste can be turned into fertiliser to grow crops. At the same time the process eliminates offensive smells.

The introduction of these new water-saving, eco-friendly toilets may be most cost-effective for community public facilities and institutions such as schools. A campaign for safe sanitation in South Africa's public schools was started following the tragic death of a pupil who fell into a school pit latrine in 2018[4] (Cleary 2018). A number of private and public schools have started to introduce the new smart and safe composting toilets.

10.3 Tech Solutions for Health, Food, and Financial Security

10.3.1 Health Messages by Phone

In an earlier chapter we reported that the cell phone revolution has captured the imagination of people living in Africa. For centuries people have relied on the oral tradition to pass on their family history and their society's customs. This modern mode of oral communication in everyday life is popular and venders of cell phones and air-time can be seen on African streets across the region.

Back in the 1970s, Zulu night watchmen would while away the hours deftly braiding colourful lengths of wire around a long walking stick. Today, most South African security guards can be seen consulting their cell phones while on duty.

Cell phone technology is also used to help manage health issues at both the personal and societal level. For example, individual TB patients and people living with HIV/AIDS, who must observe strict medication regimens, can receive reminders to do so on time, while outbreaks of disease can be monitored and pre-empted. People living in African communities are known to have fluid movement patterns, often travelling across borders to work or to visit family, or because they have been displaced by war or natural disaster. Such movement may criss-cross areas where

---

[4]https://www.news24.com/SouthAfrica/News/girl-5-dies-after-falling-into-pit-toilet-at-eastern-cape-school-20180315 (Accessed 25 May 2019).

malaria is endemic, thus inadvertently spread the disease. Mobile technology is now being harnessed to spread information about malaria outbreaks and high-risk areas to assist travellers to assess such dangers to health (De Jager et al. 2019).

10.3.2 'Serious Games'

Like youth in other parts of the world, young people in sub-Saharan Africa have become attached to their phones. Acquiring their first cell phone, was described as their best time in life by some South African youth responding to a survey question on their experiences of peak well-being over the life course (Møller and Roberts 2019). Given its popularity, the technology can play an important role in communicating health and life style messages to young people.

Initially videogames were played in arcades. Now that games have also been incorporated into handheld devices, there is a new use for gaming on the African continent. Pendergrass et al. (2019) report that a new genre of video games has evolved over the past 20 years, known as 'serious games', that are an effective entertainment-education hybrid. One example is the unique and serious 'Game for Health', which was developed to address eSwatini's high HIV/AIDS prevalence rate, the highest in sub-Saharan Africa. (eSwatini was known as Swaziland until 2018). The *SwaziYolo* game was designed for mobile phones, making it highly accessible in a country where almost everyone uses some form of smartphone. The game informs youth about HIV/AIDS and assists them to identify and navigate risky behaviour, so that they are able to make choices that will better protect them and their partners from harm. The designers are currently working on finding a solution to the limitations of affordable air-time available to Swazi gamers.

10.3.3 African Start-Ups—Tech Hubs and Mobile Money

Kenya is often referred to as Africa's own Silicon Valley. Nairobi is fast becoming a tech hub, creating solutions to everyday problems in the developing world. An example is a start-up that aims to create greater efficiency in food-supply chains to lower food prices for urban dwellers. Many Nairobians spend an average of 45% of their disposable income on food. Twiga Foods has created a platform that aggregates farm produce and distributes it to vendors at street corners. Twiga sources fruit and vegetables from 17,000 farmers and delivers to 180,000 informal retailers in Nairobi, creating a predictable market for growers and reducing transport costs for the vendors. The start-up hopes to extend its operations to other capital cities in sub-Saharan Africa (Sunday Times 2019a).

Kenyan social media platforms, such as Mkulima Young, encourages young people to get interested in farming (Mercy Corps 2016). They can exchange farming ideas and obtain information on the latest technology to improve their farming practices. Digital farming also assists farmers to market their produce more efficiently by cutting out middlemen. The logo on the Digital Farmers Kenya (2020) website says the platform aims to 'inform, educate, and market'.

The Mpesa mobile banking and money transfer system developed for Kenya is perhaps the best-known innovation to come out of Africa in modern times. Less well known is that Somalia has one of the most active mobile money markets in Africa, outpacing most other countries on the continent, according to a recent World Bank report (Owuor 2018). Initially mobile money started as a simple exchange of airtime credit between users, before the system was formalised. Mobile money services were quickly perceived as a convenient and safe way of making transactions and storing money, in view of the limited access to traditional banking services in Somalia. About nine out of ten Somalis over 16 years own a cell phone, and a large proportion of Somalia's population is nomadic or semi-nomadic, so mobile money suits their lifestyle.

Mobile money has become an effective substitute for cash in Somalia. A recent survey found that about 73% of Somalis above the age of 16 use mobile money services at least once a month. Mobile money is used for a wide range of purchases, including items such as water, electricity, charcoal, groceries, durable goods and livestock. It is also used to pay children's school fees and to send money to family and friends, and for putting aside savings. The business model used by Somalia's service providers is based on generating revenue from other services, such as the sale of airtime. This allows operators to offer mobile money transfers as a free service, without transaction charges or taxes, which is not the case in many other countries in the region.

Mobile money is an African success story. In 2017, an estimated 21% of adults in sub-Saharan Africa had mobile money accounts. First launched in Kenya in 2007, mobile money services are now active in some 90 countries around the world. As noted earlier, mobile money adoption has flourished in Africa out of necessity. It represents a convenient and affordable alternative for the unbanked, particularly for people living in rural areas. Hamden's (2019) recent literature review of economists' research on mobile money adoption in sub-Saharan Africa highlights the wide range of longer-term benefits afforded to users. To cite just a few select examples of results from Hamden's review: In Kenya, mobile money adoption has lifted an estimated 2% of households out of poverty; in Tanzania M-Pawa savings accounts have boosted the empowerment and subjective well-being of female small business owners. Benefits for Tanzanian users included not only affordability and convenience but also addressed their security concerns. Panel studies conducted in several of the countries[5] reviewed by Hamden showed that mobile money users were more likely to receive remittances, which assisted them to smooth over economic shocks, such as ones caused by heavy rainfalls.

---

[5] Hamden's (2019) economic literature review covers studies conducted in Kenya, Rwanda, Tanzania and Uganda.

10.4   Eco-friendly Innovations

10.4.1   Waste Management

In the absence of incinerators to process waste in African cities, enterprising Nairobi start-ups have taken on the challenge to transform waste into opportunity. Waste pickers who supply recycling facilities on garbage collection days are also to be seen on the streets of many of South Africa's cities. On the Eastern Cape coast of South Africa, an eco-friendly hotel located in a tourist resort has developed a model to sort all its waste at source. Food waste is composted on site while other waste is sorted for recycling. The model is cost-efficient as the hotel grows its own vegetables on site and saves on transport.

African people, who have only recently been introduced to consumerism, might be excused from feeling that their new habits might threaten the planet. After all, individuals living in sub-Saharan Africa, most of whom enjoy fewer material benefits than in more developed regions of the world, may think that people living elsewhere are chiefly responsible for global pollution, and therefore should shoulder most of the concern. Efforts underway to contain the proliferation of Africa's plastic litter suggests a different mindset.

Rwanda has taken the lead in banning plastic bags and Kenya followed suit in late 2017, by prohibiting both the use and the production of plastic bags. Exceptions are plastics for industrial packaging and refuse bags. The so-called 'African daisies' have become part of the landscape in many sub-Saharan countries, including in tourist hot spots. Plastic is also responsible for causing blockages and flooding of water-ways, and plastic particles present a danger to hippopotamus and other animals that feed close to rivers and lakes.

10.4.2   Mud Stoves to Fight Climate Change

Uganda has one of the world's highest rates of deforestation. The vast majority of the country's rural population is not connected to the electrical grid, so villagers in Mukono in central Uganda have no option but to burn wood for cooking. The scale of wood-cutting in the area inspired Mukono scout leader Badru Kyewalyanga to act. His home-produced energy-saving mud cooking stove uses less wood and allows Mukono's villagers to breathe cleaner air. Its simplicity is key: The materials cost nothing and are freely available in rural areas. 'The stoves are fast and easy to construct—they literally can be thrown together!' (Tyson 2020).

Fist-sized balls of mud are pelted into the ground to form the body of the stove. This technique forces out unwanted air, making the stoves one solid mass and preventing cracks. The stove's shape is moulded around the trunk of a matooke tree, a banana-like plant common across Uganda, which has been cut and arranged to form the ventilation chambers, combustion chamber and chimney. The trunk rots away once the mud hardens clearing the chambers for use. Working with his scout troop and other volunteers, Kyewalyanga has already built some 100 stoves over a three-year period. According to a Mukono volunteer, the 'stoves are really important because they slow the rate at which trees are used. In the long run, we're trying to combat climate change' (Tyson 2020).

10.4.3 Monitoring Weather Conditions in Real Time

South Africa has suffered a stubborn drought since 2015. Hundreds of livestock and thousands of people have gone for days and weeks without a consistent water supply. In the Eastern Cape, the government has installed weather stations throughout the province so that farmers can monitor conditions on their cell phones in real time and respond accordingly. Given the effects of climate change, things might get worse before they get better, is the motivation behind this innovation. Things might of course only get worse, but thinking 'out of the box' is essential if the war against the persistent drought is to be won, according to a provincial spokesperson (Department of Rural Development & Agrarian Reform 2019).

10.4.4 African Drones

Drones are used for a wide variety of purposes in Africa. Perhaps best known are the ones that deliver blood supplies to rural areas in Rwanda (Mills et al. 2019, p. 56). In other sub-Saharan countries, they are variously employed in the protection of livestock from theft, in game counts in national parks, and in the fight against rhino poaching. Drones are now also used to combat malaria in Africa.

Seeing is believing. In Zanzibar, an island off the Tanzanian coast, the newest malaria elimination campaign flies drones over known malaria hot spots to identify and map the bodies of water where mosquitoes breed, in order to eliminate larvae more efficiently. The drones sound a bit like mosquitoes themselves, notes Harvey (2017), a university lecturer in sensory images, when he explains the campaign to Zanzibari villagers of all ages. The demonstrations are aimed at persuading Zanzibaris that the drones—alongside the traditional interventions of bed nets and indoor spraying— can 'really help' make malaria elimination a reality in their communities.[6] Harvey's university in Wales plans to 'incorporate the drone imagery into smartphone technology to help guide larvicide-spraying teams to water bodies on the ground, and to track their progress and coverage.' He even foresees that the drones might take on the automatic spraying of larvicide in future!

---

[6]For more information on how the drones are used to map malaria vectors and the Zanzibari Malaria Elimination Programme, see https://www.theconversation.com/pasha-2-fighting-malaria-with-dro nes-109526 (Accessed 25 April 2019).

10.5   Optimistic Innovations

10.5.1   New Vaccines

Philanthropist Bill Gates, co-chair of the Bill & Melinda Gates Foundation and the guest editor of *TIME*'s 2018 Optimists issue, says he is optimistic when he meets with scientists to discuss inventing new vaccines. He sees in them a passion for turning their knowledge into big breakthroughs to improve our lives (Gates 2019). In 2019, a number of new Ebola vaccines were tested on infected volunteers, as part of the response to the outbreak in Democratic Republic of the Congo. The most advanced malaria vaccine developed to date will be pilot tested first in Malawi, and then in neighbouring countries in East Africa (Osier 2019).

The Bill and Melinda Gates Foundation has been instrumental in ensuring that people in sub-Saharan Africa are provided with impregnated mosquito nets as protection against malaria. However, in some areas, mosquitoes have started to change their behaviour and bite their victims earlier in the evenings while people are still outside their dwellings. An innovative project aims to deplete malaria-carrying mosquitos altogether.

10.5.2   'Mozzies that Fire Blanks'

Maureen Coetzee, a professor of medical entomology at the University of the Witwatersrand, Johannesburg, has a subgenus of the *Aedes* mosquito species named after her in honour of her contribution to science. She heads a project that plans to breed and release sterile male mosquitoes that will decrease the population of malaria-carrying mosquitoes. Most species of mosquito mate only once. When a female mosquito mates with a sterilised male, the chances are that she will never have offspring. The project aims to sterilise up to a million male mosquitoes with 'a zap of radiation' at a breeding centre in South Africa. Four species of mosquitoes are targeted (Child 2013).

10.6   Innovations that Inspire Awe

> Remember to look up to the stars and not down at your feet. Try to make sense of what you see and wonder about what makes the universe exist. Be curious. And however difficult life may seem, there is always something you can do and succeed at. It matters that you don't give up. Unleash your imagination. Shape the future.
>
> Hawking (2018, p. 211)

10.6.1 The World's Largest Radio Telescope in Africa

The Square Kilometre Array (SKA) project is an international enterprise to build the world's largest radio telescope. The scale of the SKA represents a huge leap forward in science and engineering, that will allow us to look back at the very first stars and galaxies formed just after the Big Bang.

The gigantic composite instrument, which will ultimately extend over most of the African continent, will break new ground in astronomical observations. South Africa's Karoo desert will host the core of the high and mid-frequency dishes of the SKA.[7]

Work on the SKA commenced in 2012. The earliest science observations were expected to start in 2020 with a partial array of the SKA.[8]

The MeerKAT. The South African MeerKAT radio telescope, a precursor to the SKA telescope, began operation in 2018.[9] For now, the MeerKAT is the largest and most sensitive radio telescope in the southern hemisphere until the SKA is completed. It will then be integrated into a component of the Phase 1 SKA.

The Karoo Meerkat, after which the MeerKAT project is named, is a little desert mongoose which rises up on its hind legs like a sentry to peer over the horizon, in the same manner as the antennae of the telescope.

Commenting on the MeerKAT's unveiling, astronomer Vanessa McBride says her discipline addresses development challenges in Africa. Astronomy has a unique ability to stimulate thoughts of 'what is possible' in the minds of people. For instance, astronomy has been used to improve middle school pupils' literacy in Sierra Leone. 'It worked because pupils loved what they were learning,' she says (McBride 2018; McBride et al. 2018).

10.6.2 'Watch This Space'—A Glimpse of the Elusive 'Black Hole'

World renowned cosmologist Stephen Hawking[10] was always fascinated by black holes and he passed on his enthusiasm to young people around the world. In his book

---

[7]South Africa's SKA partners are Botswana, Ghana, Kenya, Madagascar, Mauritius, Mozambique, Namibia, and Zambia. Western Australia will host additional low-frequency dishes at the *Murchison* Radio-Astronomy Observatory (MRO).

[8]https://www.ska.ac.za/ (Accessed 13 May 2019).

[9]https://www.ska.ac.za/gallery/meerkat/ (Accessed 13 May 2019).

[10]Cosmologist Stephen Hawking's (1942–14 March 2018) *The Brief History of Time*, published in 1988, became a bestseller. The book awakened interest in our universe among young people around the globe. The world-renowned British theoretical physicist, confined at an early age to a wheelchair and communicating with a flat electronic voice, is known for his contributions to the fields of cosmology, general relativity and quantum gravity, especially in the context of black holes. He was director of research at the Centre for Theoretical Cosmology at the University of Cambridge

on 'Brief Answers to the Big Questions' of our times, published posthumously in 2018, he explains to a curious lay audience 'what is inside a black hole' (pp. 99–122). Hawking (2018) tells us that 'from the outside, you can't tell what is inside a black hole.' A black hole 'has a boundary called the event horizon', where 'gravity is just strong enough to drag light back and prevent it from escaping' (underline added, p. 106).

Hawking (2018) was frequently asked the question: 'Is falling into a black hole bad news for a space traveller?' His answer is that it would be 'definitely bad news' (p. 114). However, he is positive that the unresolved questions about the characteristics of black holes will be solved. 'I am optimistic that we are moving towards a solution. Watch this space' (p. 122).

The Event Horizon Telescope (EHT) captures a black hole. Hawking would be delighted that in April 2019, the Event Horizon Telescope, a planet-wide array of radio telescopes, captured the image of a gargantuan black hole situated 55-million light years from Earth. The image gave humanity its first view of a 'one-way door out of our universe', according to the EHT project director. It has facilitated a giant leap forward in understanding one of the mysteries of the universe.[11]

The ETH, which links telescopes around the globe to form an 'earth-sized' virtual telescope, is the result of years of international collaboration, including partners in Africa.

Proof of the existence of the black hole made international headlines in April 2019. It was also cause for celebration in South Africa. South Africans were among the 200 scientists from 40 countries involved in capturing the data to produce the image, including a young Ph.D. student at Rhodes University, which is involved in the SKA,[12] and his University of Pretoria supervisor. Ph.D. student Tariq Blecher wrote the code used by his supervisor to create a simulation of what the EHT group might find as they scoured the skies for evidence of the black hole. 'Laid-back' 27-year-old Blecher told reporters that he conducts his doctoral research from the SKA head office in Cape Town, using a precursor telescope[13] to SKA (Sunday Times 2019b).

---

at the time of his death. See https://en.wikipedia.org/wiki/Stephen_Hawking (Accessed 29 April 2019).

[11] See https://www.ska.ac.za/media-releases/nrfsarao-congratulates-event-horizon-telescope-eht-consortium-on-first-image-of-black-hole/ (Accessed 12 April 2019).

[12] Rhodes University's Centre for Radio Astronomy Techniques and Technologies (RATT), established in 2012, has been crucial to the development of the MeerKAT and SKA in South Africa. The Centre has also made significant contributions to cutting-edge radio telescopes like the Event Horizon Telescope (Carlisle 2019).

[13] The Australian Pathfinder.

A Down-to-Earth 'Game-Changer' for Covid-19 Treatment. In 2020, the South African Radio Observatory was to turn its sights towards a more down-to-earth project. During the Covid-19 crisis, standard ventilators were in short supply worldwide, especially in Africa. Based on its stellar experience in developing the MeerKAT radio telescope—the precursor to the Square Kilometre Array—the Observatory was to oversee the production of less invasive and less expensive ventilators to treat Covid-19 patients battling to breathe. The National Ventilator Project would see the rollout of 20,000 locally made Continuous Positive Airway Pressure (CPAP) and High-Flow Nasal Oxygen (HFNO) devices. The CPAP mask ensures that the air sacs in the lungs remain inflated while the HFNO supplies air to the patient via a high-flow cannula inserted into the nostrils rather than via the mouth. Most patients requiring hospitalisation for Covid-19 treatment need only low-level oxygen therapy rather than treatment with invasive ventilators, which require specialised staff to administer them. So non-invasive therapy 'could be a game-changer' (Saba 2020).

10.7   Conclusion

The innovations described in this chapter constitute only a selection of the many new ideas circulating in Africa, that potentially could make everyday living either less onerous, healthier, less dangerous or more economically or ecologically sound. As was the case in earlier times in Africa, new technologies must be practical if they are to be adopted. Innovations that are affordable, match contemporary lifestyles, and meet aspirations, particularly those of the youth, have the greatest chance of contributing to welfare in the region.

Beyond everyday concerns, we have also included new inventions and projects that capture the imagination and inspire hope for the future. Such innovations should also be welcome in Africa. Humans have always looked to the heavens for inspiration. The continent that had only four universities at the time of independence is now capable of operating drones to protect humans and wildlife, and of participating in international scientific discoveries that inspire awe.

References

Bruton, M. (2018). *What a great idea: Awesome South African inventions*. Johannesburg, South Africa: Jacana Media.

Carlisle, A. (2019). Rhodes proud of black hole role. *Weekend Post*. Port Elizabeth, South Africa, p. 2.

Child, K. (2013). Plan to breed mozzies that fire blanks. *The Times*, Johannesburg, December 5, p. 2.

Cleary, K. (2018). More than just a toilet. *Grocott's Mail*, Makhanda (Grahamstown), South Africa, 23 November, p. 9.

De Jager, C., Kruger, T., & Tosh, C. (2019). Research, innovation and education towards malaria elimination: Improving quality of life in Africa. In I. Eloff (Ed.), *Quality of life in African societies* (pp. 179–200). Dordrecht: Springer.

Department of Rural & Agrarian Reform, Province of the Eastern Cape. (2019). Doing its bit about drought. *Daily Dispatch*, East London, South Africa, Special feature on Sustainable Rural Communities, p. 7.

Digital Farmers Kenya (2020). Kenyan farmers' online platform. https://www.facebook.com/gro ups/254019644745036/?ref=br_rs. Accessed July 4, 2020.

Gates, B. (2019). Because innovation is an art form. *TIME*, special issue on the art of optimism, feature: The optimists, Vol. 193, No. 6–7, 18–25 February, pp. 55–56.

Hamden, J. (2019). *The impact of mobile money in developing countries*. Department of International Economics at DIW Berlin. DIW Roundup 131. https://www.diw.de/documents/publikationen/73/ diw_01.c.669402.de/DIW_Roundup_131_en.pdf. Accessed July 19, 2019.

Han, M., & Hashemi, S. (2018). Some smart ideas to make toilets fit for purpose in Africa's cities. *The Conversation*, 18 November. https://theconversation.com/some-smart-ideas-to-make-toilets-fit-for-purpose-in-africas-cities-106756.

Harvey, A. (2017). How drones are being used in Zanzibar's fight against malaria. *The Conversation*, 22 November. https://theconversation.com/how-drones-are-being-used-in-zanzibars-fight-against-malaria-86355.

Hawking, S. (2018). *Brief answers to the big questions*. London: John Murray.

McBride, V. (2018). A big moment for Africa: Why the MeerKAT—and astronomy—matter. *The Conversation*, 12 July.https://theconversation.com/a-big-moment-for-africa-why-the-mee rkat-and-astronomy-matter-99714.

McBride, V., Venugopal, R., Hoosain, M., Chingozha, T., & Govender, K. (2018). The potential of astronomy for socioeconomic development in Africa. *Nature Astronomy, 2*, 511–514.

Mercy Corps (2016). Kenyan farmers go digital. https://www.mercycorpsagrifin.org/2016/02/03/ kenyan-farmers-go-digital/. Accessed July 4, 2020.

Mills, G., Obasanjo, O., Herbst, J., & Biti, T. (2019). *Democracy works: Rewiring politics to Africa's advantage*. Johannesburg: Picador Africa.

Møller, V., & Roberts, B. J. (2019). The best and worst times of life for South Africans: Evidence of universal reference standards in evaluations of personal well-being using Bernheim's ACSA. *Social Indicators Research, 143*(3), 1319–1347. https://doi.org/10.1007/s11205-018-2018-9. Online appendix, http://hdl.handle.net/10962/67024.

Osier, F. (2019). Malawi is testing a new malaria vaccine. But it's still early days. *The Conversation*, 30 April 2019. https://theconversation.com/malawi-is-testing-a-new-malaria-vaccine-but-its-still-early-days-116007.

Owuor, V. O. (2018). Mobile money transfers have taken off in Somalia. But there are risks. *The Conversation*, 12 October. https://theconversation.com/mobile-money-transfers-have-taken-off-in-somalia-but-there-are-risks-104162.

Pendergrass, T. M., Hieftje, K., & Fiellin, L. E. (2019). Improving health outcomes and quality of life for African adolescents: The role of digital and mobile games. In I. Eloff (Ed.), *Quality of life in African societies* (pp. 149–176). Dordrecht: Springer.

Reader, J. (1997). *Africa: A biography of the continent*. London: Hamish Hamilton.

Saba, A. (2020). Observatory's starring role in pandemic. *Mail & Guardian*, 26 June to 2 July, p. 3.

Salaudeen, A. (2020). 9-year-old Kenyan wins presidential award for building wooden handwashing machine. *CNN News*, 5 June. https://edition.cnn.com/2020/06/05/africa/kenyan-boy-presidential-award/index.html. Accessed July 5, 2020.

Shirley, R. (2018). Millions of urban Africans still don't have electricity: Here's what can be done. *The Conversation*, 19 April. https://theconversation.com/millions-of-urban-africans-still-dont-have-electricity-heres-what-can-be-done-92211.

Sunday Times (2019a). Tech targets vendors to lower prices. *Business Times*, Johannesburg, South Africa, 14 April, p. 6.

Sunday Times (2019b). Skygazer Tariq quite sane, really. Johannesburg, South Africa, 14 April, p. 5.

Tyson, J. (2020). Cooking up a solution to Uganda's deforestation crisis with mud stoves. *The Guardian*. 29 June. https://www.theguardian.com/global-development/2020/jun/29/cooking-up-a-solution-to-ugandas-deforestation-crisis-with-mud-stoves. Accessed August 17, 2020.

Part III
A New African Dawn?

Character with chin resting on his knee, artist unknown, c. 500 BCE. Nok sculpture, Nigeria (*Photo by* Marie-Lan Nguyen; public domain; https://en.wikipedia.org/wiki/African_art#/media/File:Nok_sculpture_Louvre_70-1998-11-1.jpg)

Chapter 11
The Unfinished Story: African Resilience, Religion, and Hope for the Future

Abstract We return to the values and strengths common to societies in sub-Saharan Africa. Resilience and resourcefulness are qualities that allow African people to cope with everyday trials and hardships. Religiosity plays an important role in nurturing community cohesiveness and empowering of individuals. Religious rituals that underscore African identity enhance both individual and collective well-being. Although countries in Africa score lower than elsewhere on the Gallup World Poll's measure of happiness, outlook on the future is far more positive than elsewhere. In particular, Africa's youth expect their lives to be better in the future.

Keywords Sub-Saharan Africa · Resilience · Religion · Religiosity · Customary rituals · Optimism · Future happiness

11.1 African Resilience

Patience has long been a virtue—almost a way of life—in Africa. For centuries, people have stoically waited for drought and pestilence to be gone, for the rains to come, for freedom from oppression to arrive, and for a better life since independence (Møller and Roberts 2017). When Nelson Mandela became South Africa's first democratically elected president in 1994, he asked citizens to be patient; it would take time to build the new foundations for an inclusive society. In 2020, citizens across sub-Saharan Africa were asked to patiently make sacrifices on their basic freedoms and democratic rights to fight the coronavirus until a vaccine became available. The hardships suffered at the time were buoyed by hopes of living to see a more just and equal world in future.

To date, African countries achieve lower scores on happiness and well-being than ones on other continents. Given the continent's turbulent history and its many development challenges since independence, it may take a while before people in sub-Saharan Africa join the happiest people on the globe. Meanwhile, people living in the region are buoyed by their remarkable resilience and resourcefulness.

West African scholars, writing on how improbable it was for their countries to achieve high happiness rankings in international studies of well-being, referred to

© Springer Nature Switzerland AG 2021
V. Møller and B. J. Roberts, *Quality of Life and Human Well-Being in Sub-Saharan Africa*,
Human Well-Being Research and Policy Making,
https://doi.org/10.1007/978-3-030-65788-8_11

African people's coping skills in everyday life. In the case of Nigeria, Aaron Agbo and his colleagues in their chapter included in a volume on culture and human well-being, reasoned that the country's happiness 'paradox' served as an 'adaptive mechanism' (Agbo et al. 2012, p. 303). In the same volume, Dzokoto (2012, p. 319) reproduced a typical 'emblematic' conversation between a foreign visitor and a local to illustrate how Ghanaians cope in everyday life. The visitor to Africa is perplexed to find there is no running water when turning on the tap, and asks successive questions to seek a plausible explanation. In response, the Ghanaian, who takes such things for granted, simply shrugs and says: 'My friend, this is Ghana. Sometimes, the water runs, sometimes, it doesn't. That is how it is. Here, take this bucket. There is water in the tank around the corner.'

11.2 Drying Tears[1]—African Religiosity

African people tend to turn to religion to find fellowship, comfort, and also a sense of hope in the future.[2] An examination of data collected by the Pew Research Center on religiosity[3] across multiple countries and world regions over the 2010 to 2019 period indicates that the importance of religion is higher, on average, in Africa than elsewhere (see Fig. 11.1). Similar patterns can be observed in relation to the role that God and prayer play in people's lives (Pew 2020).

The relationship between religiosity and happiness among these countries lends support to the idea that faith might assuage feelings of discontent and unhappiness in Africa (see Fig. 11.2). This idea underlies what political scientists Pippa Norris and Ronald Inglehart in their book *Sacred and Secular* (2011) termed 'the theory of existential security'. Using empirical data from the World Values Survey, they argue that 'existential *in*security' in poorer nations promotes a higher degree of religious commitment, and vice versa. In the face of risks and hazards that threaten safety, security and well-being, such as impoverishment, hunger, conflict and violence, disease and climatic shocks, feelings of vulnerability encourage a turn to religion as a way of promoting hope and overcoming anxieties.

This is a pattern that is likely to endure for some time to come. While many world regions show a tendency for younger generations to display a generally lower level of religious commitment than older generations, this does not appear to be true of sub-Saharan Africa. In 17 out of 21 countries from the region with available data,

---

[1]With reference to a South African evangelical church's promise of salvation and prosperity: 'We are open seven days a week and seven services a day. The God of the Bible will dry away your tears and you will have the result you need in your life' (See Van Wyk 2014, p. 160).

[2]For example, see Pokimica et al. (2012) on the relationship between religion and subjective well-being in Ghana. Dickow (2012) reports on religion, personal well-being, and attitudes to democracy among South Africans.

[3]See Pew Global Attitudes and Trends question database, https://www.pewresearch.org/global/. For a useful overview of global religiosity patterns, see the 2020 Pew publication 'The Global God Divide' by Christine Tamir, Connaughton and Salazar.

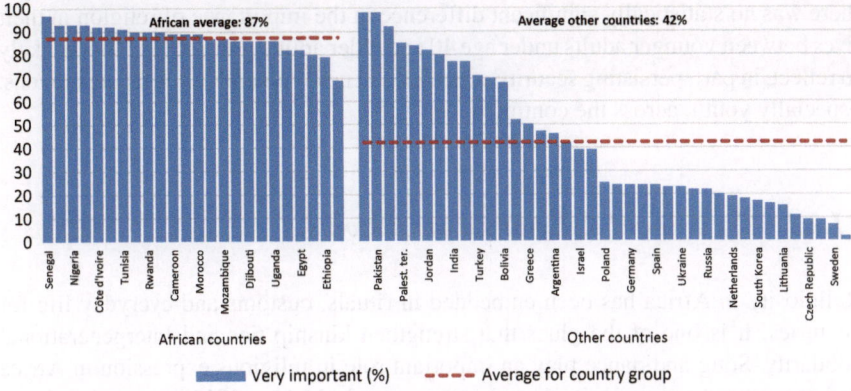

Fig. 11.1 Importance of religion in life, 24 African and 39 other countries, 2010–2019. The religious commitment data are based on the percentage saying that religion is 'very important' in life. Data are from the Pew Research Center. Data are from surveys conducted by Pew over the 2010 to 2019 period, with the only exceptions being non-probability samples from Angola (2002) and Côte d'Ivoire (2007)

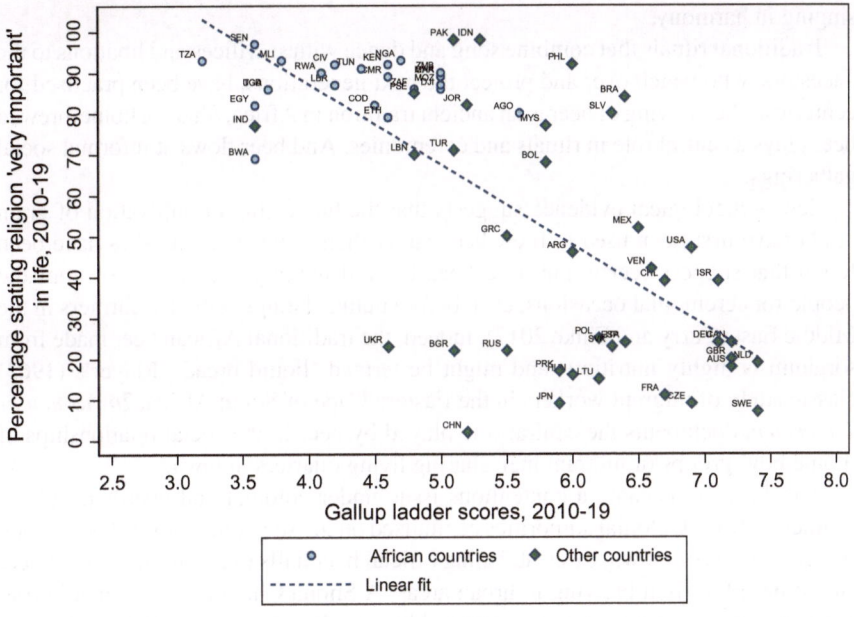

Fig. 11.2 Happiness and the importance of religion in life, 23 African and 39 other countries, 2010–19. The religious commitment data are based on the percentage saying that religion is 'very important' in life. Data are from the Pew Research Center, covering the period 2010 through 2019, with the exceptions being Angola (2002) and Côte d'Ivoire (2007). Average contentment with life today using the Cantril ladder question (0-10 scale) relies on Gallup World Poll ladder-of-life data. The ladder values refer to the closest possible year of surveying relative to the collection date of the Pew religion data. Guinea-Bissau was excluded due to lack of Gallup ladder-of-life data

there was no statistically significant difference in the importance of religion in their lives between younger adults under age 40 and older adults (Pew 2018). This is likely to reflect, in part, persisting security concerns and new vulnerabilities facing citizens, especially youth, across the continent.

11.2.1 Traditional Religions and Customs

Religiosity in Africa has been embedded in rituals, customs and everyday life for centuries. It is one of the glues that strengthen kinship ties and intergenerational solidarity. Song and dance play an important role in religious expression in Africa and accompany religious rituals and ceremonies. LaMothe (2019) argues that dance is essential to quality of life. In his study of ecstatic, transformative dances that have survived the colonial era, he reports that Kalahari Bushmen describe their healing dancing in religious terms. Benin's voodoo religious tradition has survived to the present day and its celebration is marked in the country's annual calendar.[4] Members of Christian church choirs in South Africa often tell us they experience 'flow'[5] when singing in harmony.

Traditional rituals that combine song and dance with sacrifices and libations to the ancestors, who watch over and protect the next generations, have been practised for centuries. The brewing of beer is an ancient tradition in Africa. Sharing home-brewed beer plays a central role in rituals and ceremonies. And beer flows at informal social gatherings.

New archeological evidence suggests that the harvesting or cultivation of grain might have first been used to brew beer rather than to bake bread. Sites have been found that suggest beer might have been brewed for large gatherings of nomadic people for ceremonial occasions, even before human beings settled as farmers in the Middle East (Curry and Finke 2017). Indeed, the traditional African beer made from sorghum is highly nutritious and might be termed 'liquid bread'. Mayer's (1963) classic study of migrant workers in the Eastern Cape of South Africa, *Townsmen or Tribesmen*, documents the central role played by beer in the social relationships of 'home boy' groups of migrant men sharing living quarters in town.

Beer brewing became a contentious issue under colonial and apartheid rule in southern Africa. Colonial authorities capitalised on the social function of beer among African workers in town, by establishing official beer halls to control the sale of beer and to prohibit illicit brewing in urban areas. A Shona Christian clergyman in pre-independence Zimbabwe was so outraged by the idea of 'Beer for Sale', which he regarded as an affront to the African tradition of hospitality, that he published a book

---

[4]Benin's diverse ethnic and religious mix includes 60 ethnic groups, Christians (49% including 26% Catholics), Muslims (28%), and indigenous religions (14%) including voodoo (Fischer 2018, p. 64).

[5]Csikszentmihalyi (1990) coined the peak experience of 'flow' in quality-of-life studies. Flow is a deeply rewarding experience characterised by an intense focus on activity to the point of becoming totally absorbed by it.

with that title. The book was among the first to be written in the English language by an African Rhodesian author.[6]

Drinking beer was one of the only forms of social recreation available to rural migrants working away from home.[7] A common complaint voiced by hostel dwellers was, 'How long do I have to drink beer before my children can drink water?' The 1959 uprising of Zulu women who brewed illicit beer made history in South Africa.[8]

The successors to the state-controlled beer halls of the colonial and apartheid era are the mammoth southern African breweries, which market their products globally. The beer halls of the former period are no longer landmarks in the cities. In South Africa, informal taverns known as *shebeens*[9] flourish in townships where they still function as neighbourhood meeting places.[10] *Shebeens* mostly sell commercial beer as well as other liquor. Attempts to regulate their operations, such as restricting the number of *shebeens* in an area and preventing their location close to schools, have not always been successful. While there is concern about the secular drinking habits of South Africans,[11] beer continues to play an important role in traditional celebrations and rituals.

---

[6]The first novels produced for African audiences in colonial Rhodesia (now Zimbabwe) in the 1970 s, were penned by the educated Christian African elite, who used their writings to deliberate on moral issues in society.

[7]Alternative leisure pastimes for workers living in hostels in town were singing, making music, and dancing as individuals or in groups. Traditional Zulu dance teams among the stevedores working on the Durban docks were sponsored by their employers, who provided the traditional outfits the men wore at events when dance groups competed against each other. Today, traditional dancers are most likely to entertain tourists.

[8]For further information on the so-called Cato Manor riots in Durban in 1959, and South African boycotts of municipal beer halls, see https://www.sahistory.org.za/article/women%E2%80%99s-revolts-natal-1959-nicholas-reed and https://en.wikipedia.org/wiki/Beer_Hall_Boycott (Accessed 13 May 2019).

[9]South Africa's shebeen culture as social meeting place is thought to have emerged as defiance reaction to the ban on access to alcohol for black South Africans during the apartheid era.

[10]Focus group discussants in the Eastern Cape of South Africa spontaneously identified the *shebeen* and the church as social institutions that compete for township dwellers' needs for fellowship and support, when discussing risk factors for the spread of HIV/AIDS (Møller et al. 2010).

[11]During South Africa's strict Covid-19 lockdown, which commenced on 27 March 2020, the sale of alcohol (and tobacco) were banned to reduce the impact of alcohol-related trauma admissions to hospitals, which might have overwhelmed the country's public health system. When the alcohol ban was lifted to allow the economy to gradually recover, the number of alcohol-related traffic accidents, injuries, and trauma cases surged. The ban was reinstated, which gave rise to heated debate across society on the pros and cons of prohibition of alcohol. President Ramaphosa announced the country was fighting the twin pandemics of the coronavirus and gender-based violence resulting from alcohol abuse.

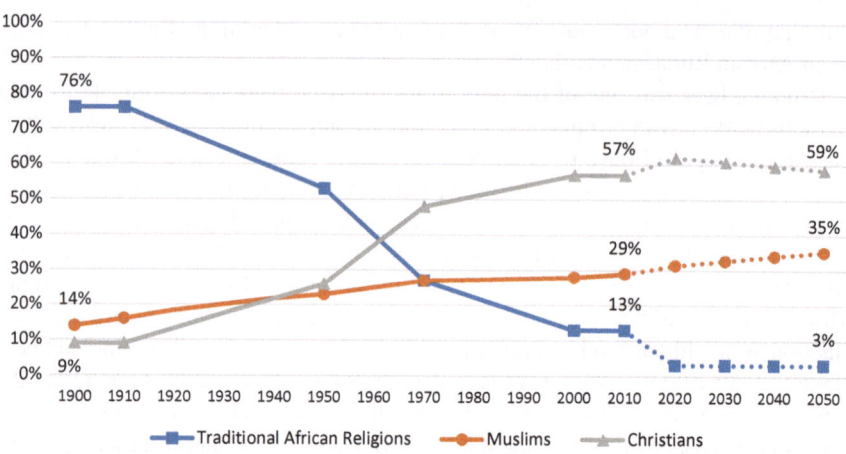

Fig. 11.3 Growth of Islam and Christianity in sub-Saharan Africa since 1900. Data covering 1990 to 2010 are from the Pew Forum on Religion and Public Life (2010) publication 'Tolerance and Tension'; while the 2010 to 2050 projections are based on the Pew Research Center (2015) publication 'The Future of World Religions: Population Growth Projections, 2010–2050'. The religious unaffiliated, Hindus, Buddhists, Jews and other religions are not displayed. The latter accounted for less than 4% in 2010

11.2.2   The Spirit Level: Mainstream Religion and Well-Being

An overwhelming majority of people living in sub-Saharan Africa express a robust commitment to the beliefs and practices associated with either Christianity or Islam. A 2010 report by the Pew Forum on Religion and Public Life found that at least 90% of all respondents across 19 countries surveyed[12] in the region indicated they belonged to one of these two religions, with slightly more than a tenth (13%) affiliated with a traditional African religion, and only a nominal share religiously unaffiliated (Fig. 11.3). This picture altered markedly over the last century, with Muslims and Christians accounting for barely more than a fifth of the population in 1900, while two thirds at that time followed a traditional African religion.

The rising dominance of Christianity and Islam does not, however, mean that traditional beliefs and practices have fallen away. In fact, a quarter of all respondents (including 20% of Christians, 26% of Muslims) also exhibited high levels of traditional beliefs.[13] Therefore, in contemporary societies in the region, the commitment

---

[12]More than 25,000 face-to-face interviews were conducted across Botswana, Cameroon, Chad, Djibouti, DR Congo, Ethiopia, Ghana, Guinea Bissau, Kenya, Liberia, Mali, Mozambique, Nigeria, Rwanda, Senegal, South Africa, Tanzania, Uganda, and Zambia. Collectively, these countries account for about three quarters of the region's population.

[13]These scores were obtained by means of an index created from 11 indicators: These included belief in (i) the protective power of certain spiritual people; (ii) the power of juju and other sacred objects; (iii) the evil eye; (iv) witchcraft; (v) evil spirits; (vi) the protective power of sacrificial offerings to ancestors; and (vii) reincarnation. Traditional religious practices were captured by four items asking about (viii) visiting traditional healers; (ix) owning sacred objects; (x) participating in

to Islam or Christianity tends to coexist with involvement in traditional African religions. The distribution of religions exhibits a distinct geographic pattern: Northern Africa is predominantly Muslim, southern Africa is heavily Christian, and a more even affiliation is evident in countries between these poles, stretching in a horizontal band across the continent from Senegal to Somalia, more or less coinciding with the Sahel region.

A further examination of the Pew data reveals that sub-Saharan Africa unquestionably remains one of the most religious regions of the world. In most of the African countries surveyed, around 90% of people stated that religion is an important part of their lives. Even in middle income countries such as Botswana and Namibia, where the importance attached to religion is slightly lower (69% and 74% respectively), more people reported that religion was an important part of their lives than in the industrialised countries such as the United States (57%).

Despite prevailing stereotypes, a clear majority of citizens across the region expressed the view that people of other faiths had widespread freedom to practise their religion (ranging from a low of 65% in Djibouti to a high of 93% in Senegal) and considered this as a positive attribute of their country. These findings, however, do not imply that the region is uniformly a place of religious harmony. On average, 28% of those interviewed reported that conflict between religious groups was a significant problem in their countries, with more than half the population voicing such a concern in Nigeria, Rwanda, and Djibouti.

People across the region also displayed a fair amount of uneasiness about religious extremism, with at least half of respondents in 11 of the 19 countries saying they were very or somewhat worried about this phenomenon. A sizable majority, however, expressed the view that the perpetration of violence against civilians in order to defend one's religion is rarely or never justifiable. Notable minorities do regard such violence as justified, ranging from 20% on average, to a high of more than 50% in countries such as Guinea-Bissau and Djibouti.

A recent event in post al-Bashir's Sudan highlights the importance of defending one's religion for strong believers. In 2020, pro-Sharia Muslims protested government reforms to lift strict Islamic laws introduced in the 1980s. The reforms allow non-Muslims to drink alcohol in private, scrap the apostasy law, and outlaw public flogging. Under the new laws, women no longer need permission from a male relative to travel with their children. The reforms come after al-Bashir was ousted last year following massive street protests[14] (BBC World Service Africa 2020).

---

ceremonies to honour ancestors; and (xi) participating in traditional puberty rituals. Those saying they believed or practised any six of these things were classified by Pew as having high levels of traditional beliefs and practices.

[14]The imposition of strict Islamist laws in the 1980s was a key factor in Sudan's long-running civil war which eventually led to independence for South Sudan, where the majority of people are Christian or follow traditional religions (BBC World Service Africa 2020).

11.3   African Optimism

> Optimism is important because it's a form of seeing what's possible and making it a reality.
> Melinda Gates (Gates and Gates 2018, p. 7)

Optimism that 'many things' will change for the better, to paraphrase the Gallup-Kettering question put to African respondents in its 1970s global survey, is a further coping skill perfected by African people. The Gallup-Kettering study asked respondents if they thought they would be happier if things could be changed about their lives. The desire for change was greatest by far in sub-Saharan Africa. Some 90% of African respondents wished for change in their lives, and the vast majority in this group wanted not a 'few' but 'many' things to change to improve their lives.[15] When disappointed that these changes have not occurred, optimism has still prevailed regardless. People living on the continent have developed this skill over time, to make daily hassles and hardships tolerable.[16] For example, a series of studies of democracy and happiness in the authoritarian states of Chad and Zimbabwe, and in South Africa's new democracy, suggest that even when the demand for democracy in Africa is not matched by satisfaction with living conditions, discontent is tempered by optimism for the future.

Helga Dickow's study conducted in Zimbabwe in 2005 classified 45% of respondents as very democratic and a further 36% as democratic. While only 11% of Zimbabweans were satisfied with life at present, twice as many (22%) thought they would feel satisfied with life in ten years' time (Dickow 2007, pp. 111, 121–2).

In Chad, a country Dickow has visited over many years, her survey conducted in four of the country's main cities in 2004 found that 60% of respondents supported democratic principles. Only 14 percent were very happy with their life at present, but more than twice as many (35%) thought they would be very happy with life in future (Dickow 2005, pp. 112, 128–9).

An earlier study, conducted in South Africa in 2002, reported that 51% of black and 74% of white South Africans supported democratic values and were classified as either 'very democratic' or 'democratic'. Although the black respondents reported the lowest levels of current life satisfaction (37%) and happiness (38%), a larger proportion (45%) projected their life satisfaction to increase in future (Møller and Hanf 2007, p. 99ff.).

---

[15]Of the 90% in the sub-Saharan sample who wished for change in their lives, 67% wanted 'many things' to change, 22% 'just a few' things. The question on the 'extent of change necessary for a happier life' read: 'Thinking about how your life is going now, do you think you would be happier if things could be changed about your life? (If yes) Would you like many things about your life changed or just a few things? See Table VI in the Gallup-Kettering Global Survey (1976) summary volume's reprint of: Human Needs and Satisfactions, Mankind: The Global Survey and the Third World, Blue Supplement to the "Monthly Public Opinion Surveys" of the Indian Institute of Public Opinion, Vol. XXI, Nos. 9 and 10. http://worlddatabaseofhappiness.eur.nl/hap_bib/freetexts/~Gallup_Kettering_1976k.pdf.

[16]Renowned happiness scholar Veenhoven (2005) reports that happiness in hardship is possible if people rise to the challenge of coping with difficulties in life.

11.3.1 Jobless Happiness?

Empirical studies of human well-being tend to focus on the present. Studies that include both present and future evaluations of life usually assume that appreciation of the present will influence future ratings. A recent study overturns this assumption. Piper's (2019) study employing data from the German socio-economic panel study, SOEP, floats the idea that projections of future happiness may also exert a positive influence on present evaluations of life. He singles out the case of unemployed respondents for special mention. He found that unemployed SOEP respondents who gave higher future ratings were also less dissatisfied with their present lives. A substantial proportion of those whose outlook on future prospects in life were positive, rated their current life situation higher than those who were not as positive. Piper believes this finding may call for a revision of our existing models of happiness research.

Piper's SOEP panel study findings are from a very different social context. Nonetheless, they may provide pointers for African happiness, as joblessness is one of the greatest problems for people living south of the Sahara. Readers will recall that, according to Afrobarometer studies, unemployment is rated as the region's top priority problem, which citizens want their governments to address urgently. We know from the literature that unemployment depresses well-being, not only in Africa but throughout the world. So we might want to assume that Piper's research, which suggests optimism may make you feel better even if you are without paid work, may apply no matter if you are living in Europe or Africa. If unemployed people in Africa share the high levels of optimism found across the continent, their chances of feeling better about their lives in spite of being jobless, may also be exceptional.

11.3.2 Africa's Exceptional Future Happiness Ratings

Africa lags behind most other countries in the world in its evaluation of subjective well-being in the present time. This is not the case for average future ratings. The majority of African countries rate life at present below the mid-point of the Cantril ladder scale in the Gallup World Poll, but rate their future lives higher than present on the ladder.

Gallup asks respondents to rate where they presently stand on a ladder whose rungs are marked with 0, the worst possible situation, to 10, the best possible situation. Respondents are also asked to rate where they think they will stand in five years' time.

Projected future ladder ratings are uniformly higher than present evaluations across all countries on the continent. In fact, the percentage increase in future expectations of life is often higher among some of the least contented nations.

Nigeria's track record of such positive expectations for the future is well documented. Cantril's classic 1960s study already reported a difference of 2.6 points

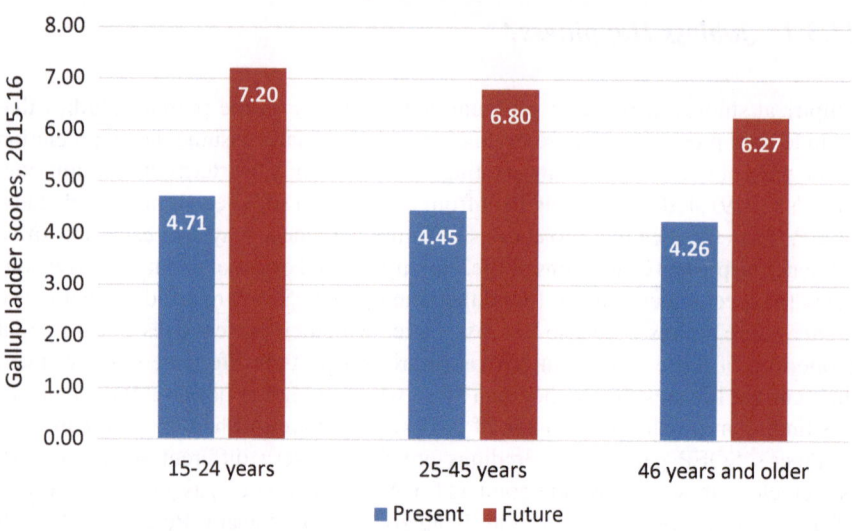

Fig. 11.4 Average Cantril present and future ladder evaluations by age group, 37 African countries, 2015–16. Average contentment for select sub-Saharan African countries, by age group. Life today and Life in 5 years are measured using the Cantril ladder questions with respondents asked to choose a rung on a 0-10 ladder. Ladder-of-life data from the Gallup World Poll

between the country's average present (4.8) and future (7.4) ladder ratings (Cantril 1965, p. 78).

Similarly, in 2016, there is a difference of 2.9 points between Nigeria's present (5.3) and future (8.2) ratings in the Gallup World Poll. An international study of comparative ladder ratings in ten countries with large populations, including China, India and the United States, found Nigeria's 2.6 point difference between present and future ratings to be by far the largest (See Gulyas 2015).

Nigeria's spirit of optimism may be exceptional by world standards, but not in Africa. On average in African countries, future life evaluations are much higher than present ones. Optimism, the gap between present and future ladder ratings, is greatest for Africa's youth and decreases somewhat with age (see Fig. 11.4). In almost all African countries, youthful optimism is above the national average (see Fig. 11.5).

It is likely that this belief that things may change for the better helps African people to manage their lives in difficult circumstances. African children may grow up with such a sense of optimism, as suggested by the findings of the Children's World study[17] that included three African countries.[18] Children in Algeria, Ethiopia

---

[17]The Children's World Study is the largest comparative research on children's own views of their lives and well-being (Rees and Main 2015; Savahl et al. 2015; Tiliouine 2015, www.isciweb.org).

[18]The 2013–14 Round of the Children's World Study tracked just over 53,000 children aged about 8, 10, and 12 years in 15 countries, including Algeria, Ethiopia and South Africa. Although present life evaluations differed for the three African countries, their future ratings of 8.7 out of 10 were the highest among the 15 countries, apart from Romania's score of 9 (see technical box on 'African children's well-being in an international context' in Møller et al. 2017, pp. 104–5).

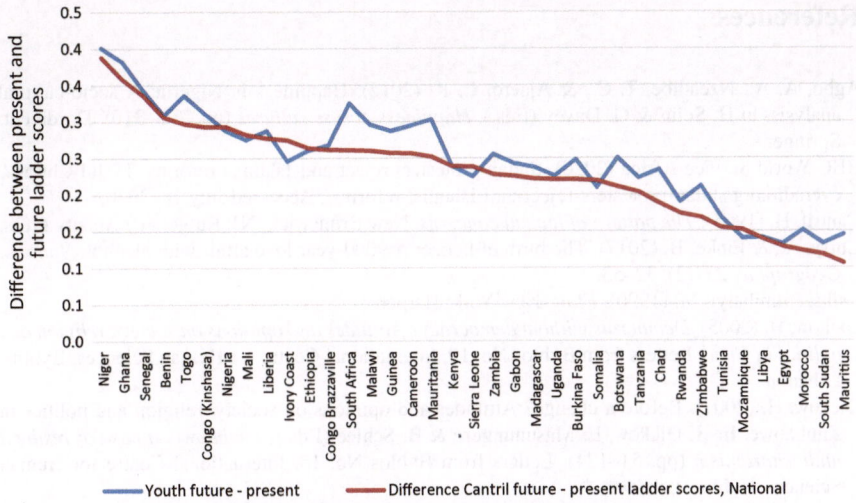

Fig. 11.5 Comparison of differences between the future and present ladder scores between youth (15–24 years) and the national average, 37 African countries, 2015–16. Differences between future and present contentment scores for youth and all adults in select sub-Saharan African countries. Data are ranked from highest to lowest difference in ladder scores based on national averages. Ladder-of-life data are from the Gallup World Poll

and South Africa were more optimistic about the future than children in the other non-African countries surveyed (Møller et al. 2017, pp. 104–105).

11.4 Summary

In this chapter we have highlighted the important role of resilience, religiosity and positivity in assisting people living in sub-Saharan Africa to survive, endure hardship, retain their identity, and find solace. As was the case with Africa's acceptance of innovations, developing resilience to cope is likely a strength born of necessity. However, it has contributed to sustaining hope for the future. It is also significant that people in sub-Saharan Africa express genuine joy when celebrating the rituals and religious ceremonies related to their different persuasions and customs. Given the diversity of ethnicities and religious persuasions across the region, there is a healthy support for religious tolerance and harmony as contributor to peace and political stability. While African countries have yet to attain the happiness scores found in countries elsewhere in the world, their outlook on the future is remarkably positive. Positivity among the youth, who have their lives ahead of them, is particularly high.

References

Agbo, A. A., Nzeadibe, T. C., & Ajaero, C. K. (2012). Happiness in Nigeria: A socio-cultural analysis. In H. Selin & G. Davey (Eds.), *Happiness across cultures* (pp. 293–310). Dordrecht: Springer.

BBC World Service Africa (2020). Sudan protesters reject anti-Islamist reforms, 17 July. https://eyeradio.org/sudan-protesters-reject-anti-islamist-reforms/. Accessed July 18, 2020.

Cantril, H. (1965). *The pattern of human concerns.* New Brunswick, NJ: Rutgers University Press.

Curry, A., & Finke, B. (2017). The birth of booze: A 9000-year love affair with alcohol. *National Geographic, 231*(2), 32–53.

Csikszentmihalyi, M. (1990). *Flow.* New York: Harper.

Dickow, H. (2005). *Democrats without democracy? Attitudes and opinions on society, religion and politics in Chad.* Letters from Byblos No. 10, International Centre for Human Sciences, Byblos, Lebanon.

Dickow, H. (2007). Before a change? Attitudes and opinions on society, religion and politics in Zimbabwe. In H. Dickow, E. Masunungure & B. Schlee (Eds.), *Zimbabwe, a case of resilient authoritarianism* (pp. 51–124). Letters from Byblos No. 15, International Centre for Human Sciences, Byblos, Lebanon.

Dickow, H. (2012). *Religion and attitudes towards life in South Africa: Pentecostals, charismatics and reborns.* Baden-Baden: Nomos.

Dzokoto, V. A. A. (2012). Ghanaian happiness: Global, cultural, and phenomenological perspectives. In H. Selin & G. Davey (Eds.), *Happiness across cultures* (pp. 311–327). Dordrecht: Springer.

Fischer, (2018). *Der neue Fischer Weltalmanach 2019: Zahlen, Daten, Fakten, Schwerpunkt Arbeit.* Frankfurt am Main, Germany: Fischer Verlag.

Gallup-Kettering Global Survey (1976). Human needs and satisfactions in sub-Saharan Africa, summary volume. http://worlddatabaseofhappiness.eur.nl/hap_bib/freetexts/~Gallup_Kettering_1976k.pdf.

Gates, B., & Gates, M. (2018). Keeping goals in sight. *National Geographic, 7–11.*

Gulyas, J. (2015). Hopes and fears—Future views of quality of life. In W. Glatzer, V. Møller, L. Camfield, & M. Rojas (Eds.), *The global handbook of wellbeing and quality of life* (pp. 869–894). Dordrecht: Springer.

LaMothe, K. L. (2019). Dancing on earth: The healing dance of Kalahari Bushmen and the Native American ghost dance religion. In K. Bond (Ed.), *Social indicators research series, Vol 73. Dance and the quality of life* (pp. 117–133). Cham: Springer.

Mayer, P. (1963). *Townsmen or Tribesmen: Conservatism and the process of urbanization in a South African city.* Cape Town: Oxford Press.

Møller, V., Erstad, I., & Zani, D. (2010). Drinking, smoking and morality: Do 'drinkers and smokers' constitute a stigmatised stereotype or a real TB risk factor in the time of HIV/AIDS? *Social Indicators Research, 98*(2), 217–238. https://doi.org/10.1007/s11205-009-9546-2.

Møller, V., & Hanf, Th. (2007). *South Africa's new democrats: A 2002 profile of democracy in the making.* Lettres de Byblos/Letters from Byblos No. 21, Centre International des Sciences de l'Homme/International Centre for Human Sciences, Byblos, Lebanon. http://hdl.handle.net/10962/d1010768.

Møller, V., & Roberts, B. (2017). New beginnings in an ancient region: Well-being in Sub-Saharan Africa. In R. J. Estes & M. J. Sirgy (Eds.), *The pursuit of well-being: The untold global history* (pp. 161–215), International Handbooks of Quality-of-Life Research. Springer International Publishing Switzerland.

Møller, V., Roberts, B. J., Tiliouine, H., & Loschky, J. (2017). 'Waiting for happiness' in Africa. In J. Helliwell, R. Layard & J. Sachs (Eds.), *World happiness report 2017* (Chapter 4, pp. 84–120). New York: Sustainable Development Solutions Network http://worldhappiness.report/ed/2017/, http://worldhappiness.report/wp-content/uploads/sites/2/2017/03/HR17-Ch4_w-oAppendix.pdf. ISBN 978-0-9968513-5-0.

Norris, P., & Inglehart, R. (2011). *Sacred and secular: Religion and politics worldwide.* Cambridge: Cambridge University Press.

Pew Forum on Religion & Public Life. (2010). *Tolerance and tension: Islam and Christianity in sub-Saharan Africa.* Pew Forum on Religion & Public Life, Washington, DC, Pew Research Center. https://www.pewforum.org/2010/04/15/executive-summary-islam-and-christianity-in-sub-saharan-africa/.

Pew Research Center (2015). *The future of world religions: Population growth projections, 2010–2050,* April 2. https://www.pewforum.org/2015/04/02/religious-projections-2010-2050/.

Pew Research Center (2018). *The age gap in religion around the world,* 13 June. https://www.pewforum.org/2018/06/13/the-age-gap-in-religion-around-the-world/.

Pew Research Center (2020). *The global God divide,* 20 July. https://www.pewresearch.org/global/2020/07/20/the-global-god-divide/.

Piper, A. (2019). Optimism, pessimism and life satisfaction: An empirical investigation. *SOEP papers on Multidisciplinary Panel Data Research 1027,* (The German Socio-Economic Panel Study at DIW Berlin), pp. 1–44. http://www.diw.de/soeppapers.

Pokimica, J., Addai, I., & Takyi, B. K. (2012). Religion and subjective well-being in Ghana. *Social Indicators Research, 106,* 61–79.

Rees, G., & Main, G. (Eds.) (2015). *Children's views on their lives and well-being in 15 countries: An initial report on the children's worlds survey, 2013–14.* York, UK: Children's Worlds Project. www.isciweb.org.

Savahl, S., Adams, S., Isaacs, S., Hendricks, G., Matzdorff, A., Wagenaar, C., et al. (2015). *Children's worlds national report: South Africa.* Children's Worlds Project www.isciweb.org.

Tiliouine, H. (2015). *Children's worlds national report: Algeria.* Children's Worlds Project (ISCWeB).

Van Wyk, I. (2014). *A church of strangers: The Universal Church of the Kingdom of God in South Africa.* Cambridge: Cambridge University Press.

Veenhoven, R. (2005). Happiness in hardship. In L. Bruni & P. L. Porta (Eds.), *Economics and happiness: Framing the analysis* (pp. 243–266). Oxford: Oxford University Press.

Chapter 12
Imagining Future Sub-Saharan Well-Being

Abstract In this final chapter, we reflect on progress made in achieving basic needs and better living conditions in sub-Saharan Africa since independence and the prospects for future well-being for the people living there. We speculate on possible development trajectories and on how citizens and their leaders can advance happiness for all south of the Sahara. The region has plentiful valuable assets, in the form of its material resources and human capital, on which to build its future well-being. The health and economic crisis created by the Covid-19 pandemic should be used as an opportunity to respond to the call for action to realise the region's potential.

Keywords Sub-Saharan Africa · Well-being · Sustainable development · Resource management · Good governance · Social progress · Youth dividend · Optimism

12.1 Sub-Saharan Africa's Glass is Half Full

12.1.1 Progress in Achieving Sustainable Development Goals and Happiness

Worldwide, there have been remarkable advances in human well-being since the mid-1960s. African advances in well-being are no exception (see Estes 2019; Estes and Sirgy 2018). Our report on social indicators for sub-Saharan Africa tell a promising story. On balance, the gains in life expectancy, literacy, and standards of living suggest that people in the region are better off since independence. A number of countries met their Millennium Development Goals by the target date of 2015; others will have reset their aims to achieve the new Sustainable Development Goals. According to the Weighted Index of Social Progress (WISP) measure discussed in an earlier chapter, a majority of sub-Saharan countries have experienced progress.

Levels of happiness have also increased between 2005 and 2019. A slightly higher number of sub-Saharan countries experienced rising rather than falling levels of happiness during that period according to the latest 2019 and 2020 *World Happiness*

© Springer Nature Switzerland AG 2021   183
V. Møller and B. J. Roberts, *Quality of Life and Human Well-Being in Sub-Saharan Africa*,
Human Well-Being Research and Policy Making,
https://doi.org/10.1007/978-3-030-65788-8_12

Reports. Indeed, between five and six sub-Saharan countries[1] feature among the top 20 countries worldwide that have experienced the greatest gains in happiness over that period, albeit from a low base (Helliwell et al. 2019, 2020).

Until 2016, sub-Saharan happiness levels have consistently been lower than any other region in the world. Its level has remained fairly stable though with some decrease in 2013 and then a recovery. Now, for the first time ever, the most recent 2020 *World Happiness Report* shows sub-Saharan Africa's happiness level has surpassed that of South Asia, a region whose life evaluations have worsened dramatically since 2017 (see Helliwell et al. 2020, pp. 24–25).

12.1.2 Good Governance and Happiness

Since gaining independence in the 1960s, citizens of sub-Saharan Africa expect democracy to provide more than basic freedoms. Democracy is associated with decent living standards and opportunities for personal and community advancement. Governments play an important role in meeting such expectations.

Africa's lower levels of happiness compared to other countries in the world might be attributed to disappointment with different aspects of development under democracy. Although most citizens still believe that democracy is the best political system, they are critical of good governance in their countries. While there has been significant improvement in meeting basic needs according to the Afrobarometer index of 'lived poverty', population pressure may have stymied infrastructure and youth development.

World Happiness Report editor Helliwell and colleagues (2019, Chap. 2, p. 4) note that governments set the institutional and policy framework in which individuals, businesses and governments themselves operate. 'The links between the government and happiness operate in both directions: what governments do affects happiness …, and in turn, the happiness of citizens in most countries determines what kind of governments they support … It is sometimes possible to trace these linkages in both directions.'

People in sub-Saharan Africa look to democracy and its institutions to fulfil their dreams of a 'better life'. They expect better performances from their governments, which need to address issues ranging from corruption to fixing infrastructure that has suffered from years of 'maintenance-free abuse', to cite Mills (2014, p. 267). Sub-Saharan wealth has benefited mainly a small elite. In past decades, the elite in a number of sub-Saharan countries have enriched themselves with oil and mineral wealth at the expense of the poor. The emergence of a middle class has not contributed

---

[1]Benin, Togo, Guinea, Congo (Brazzaville), Côte d'Ivoire, and Senegal are among the 20 top countries gaining happiness from 2008–2012 to 2017–2019 (Helliwell et al. 2020, p. 27) The 2019 *World Happiness Report* listed five sub-Saharan countries among the 20 top gaining happiness from 2005–2008 to 2016–2018: Benin, Togo, Congo (Brazzaville), Côte d'Ivoire, Sierra Leone, and Cameroon (Helliwell et al. 2019, p. 34).

to levelling of economic differences in society, and rapid urbanisation has often created slums of despair rather than hope.

Democracy in Africa is a work in progress. We have outlined the ebbs and flows of democracies in Africa since independence and presented some evidence that democracy goes hand in hand with prosperity. However, there is still a mismatch between the supply of democracy and citizen demand for democracy in the sub-Saharan region. Citizens may be excused for being attracted to authoritarian leadership styles—which may pose a threat to their basic freedoms—in the hope that a strong leader will satisfy their aspirations now rather than in a distant future.

Therefore, an urgent task in the twenty-first century will be to grasp the opportunities in the Africa Rising narrative and to take a long view on how best to increase the life chances and happiness of a greater number of people in the region. The Covid-19 pandemic has brought into sharp relief, what needs to be done. Africa watchers, whose call for action we have referred to earlier, are confident the region can realise its resources and youth potential (Mills et al. 2020; Soko 2020). The prospects are promising.

12.2 Reinventing Sub-Saharan Society

12.2.1 From 'Basket Case' to the World's Food Basket

For millennia Africa has struggled to produce enough food to feed its people. Consequently, it only reached its full population growth potential in the middle of the twentieth century. In the twenty-first century, sub-Saharan Africa has the highest fertility rates in the world, and it is estimated that by mid-century, a quarter of the world will be African, with the continent's population likely to rise from 1.2 billion today to 2.5 billion in 2050.

One of the new challenges for Africa's decision makers will be to provide food security for a rapidly growing population. Meeting this goal will require good governance and prudent resource management. The green revolution that accompanied rapid population growth in Asia in the twentieth century bypassed Africa, and climate change may pose a greater threat to Africa's food production than elsewhere. Many sub-Saharan countries currently import food. However, agricultural experts are of the opinion that Africa could become the world's food basket if it realises its potential for combining subsistence agriculture with agribusiness (Bourne 2014). African leaders are exploring such opportunities.

Whereas earlier explorers, colonial powers, and post-independence investors were interested in exploiting Africa's gold, mineral, and oil and gas reserves, it is now agricultural land that is up for grabs. Between 2006 and 2009, an estimated 15 to 20 million hectares of land—roughly the combined area of Denmark, the Netherlands, Switzerland, and Macedonia—were the subject of negotiation for foreign investment by African governments (Robertson and Pinstrup-Andersen 2010). As has been the case with oil and gas reserves in sub-Saharan Africa, agricultural reserves could become a burden rather than a blessing for the people of the region. The land grab has already displaced thousands of subsistence farmers who can no longer feed their families and have effectively joined the refugee population of sub-Saharan Africa. It will therefore be important that the neo-colonial scramble for Africa's agricultural land not jeopardize food security but enhance quality of life in the region. In an earlier chapter, we noted that Kenya's Nobel laureate Wangari Maathai had championed this cause to conserve Africa's natural environment and its agricultural potential.

There are promising signs that African leaders are becoming more careful when managing agricultural and wildlife resources and more circumspect when partnering with international investors to ensure that returns stay in the country and benefit their people. In metropolitan areas, there are initiatives to plant sustainable vegetable gardens to provide greater food security for urban dwellers living in Africa's 'smart' cities of the future (Houessou et al. 2019). Earlier chapters have drawn attention to new technological advancements, such as digital farming, that may make agriculture a more attractive career option for youth (Daum 2019) and may contribute to stemming rural-urban and overseas migration.

12.2.2   Turning the Youth Bulge into a Youth Dividend

In previous chapters we have reported examples of both leaders, African start-ups and ordinary citizens, taking initiatives to advance life chances for both rural and city dwellers. We have noted that innovations in Africa tend to address 'lived reality' and may therefore assist people living in sub-Saharan Africa to cope better with everyday hassles and problems than elsewhere. There is growing recognition that Africa's youth are its future. African youth have an important role to play in reinventing African society to meet their aspirations. The late French philosopher Serres (2012, 2015; Howles 2015) envisages a new generation of digitally savvy and connected young people worldwide, the 'Petites Pousettes' or Thumbelinas,[2] who have no inhibitions in challenging their elders. His Pousettes are poised to reinvent a society that meets the demands of the twenty-first century. Africa's cell-phone generation may well typify the Pousettes of Serres' utopia who are intent on reshaping the continent's societal order.

Indeed, we have reported on how youth across the region are a force for change and innovation. They are intent on holding their governments accountable to meet the needs of the people. Their growing self-confidence and agency represent the new drivers of positive change in Africa.

We have argued that Africa's presidents for life, the 'Big Men' who cling to power, may be out of touch with the aspirations of the youth in their countries. In recent years, youth have tended to vote with their feet by protesting when leaders hold on

---

[2] 'Thumbelina' is the affectionate nickname Serres gives to the young digital generation, who use their thumbs to type on their mobile phones. He observes young women are the most nimble!

to power beyond term limits. They are setting the stage for a more inclusive model of caring governments in the sub-Saharan region.

In turn, many African leaders are fast becoming aware that if sub-Saharan youth lack avenues for social mobility and a political voice, they may resort to staging protests at home or seek to fulfil their dreams beyond African shores. An additional concern is that disillusioned, frustrated youth may become easy recruits for extremist groups intent on destabilising society. Sub-Saharan leaders are increasingly taking such threats seriously.

To date, most African economies have not been able to absorb new entrants to the labour market. Afrobarometer findings suggest that youth would be eager to grasp local opportunities on the continent if they were on offer. While porous borders do not prevent epidemics from moving to neighbouring countries, Afrobarometer reports that workseekers find it difficult to cross borders. The Covid-19 pandemic brought into sharp relief the importance of African supply chains, free trade areas, cross-border investment in infrastructure, and less reliance on the extraction of raw materials in favour of developing local industry and manufacturing (see Gnimassoun and Tapsoba 2020; Ismail 2020; Russon 2020). The region needs to update its health, food, and social protection systems to face future health and socio-economic crises (Arndt et al. 2020; Eccleston et al. 2020; Hane 2020; Mausch et al. 2020). A new task for African governments will be to work together to stem Africa's brain drain[3] and reliance on remittances to ensure that African skills and creativity resources remain in Africa to develop the regional economy.

Africa is a youthful continent; its youth represent a development potential. Thanks to its youthfulness, sub-Saharan Africa was thought to be less vulnerable than other regions during the Covid-19 pandemic. It is common knowledge that this youth potential can only be tapped if sub-Saharan youth are afforded opportunities to access quality education and acquire the types of skills that will enable them to contribute to a modern economy. There are signs that governments across the region recognise the importance of skilling the next cohorts of youth to develop local economies. In our review, we have provided a few examples of new initiatives to drive maths and science and technology education and training. Another encouraging development is that Africa is starting to experiment with training young people to become self-employed as entrepreneurs and is making attempts to include the youth in shaping their own economic opportunities. Digitally savvy urban youth are in the forefront of such developments to reimagine sub-Saharan African society. The coronavirus pandemic which took the world and the sub-Saharan region by surprise in 2020, may accelerate what is already in motion to create the more equal and inclusive society of the future.

---

[3] Habib and Valodia (2020) promote the idea of replacing Africa's brain drain with brain 'circulation', that is, the exchange between African and international institutions.

12.2.3   Optimism as Social Capital

Most countries in the world project that life circumstances will improve in future (Cantril 1965; Gulyas 2015). In the midst of the Covid-19 pandemic, there has been much speculation on how the world order will look like in the post-corona pandemic future. The World Economic Forum launched the idea of a 'great reset', an initiative to build a more fair, sustainable and resilient future that addresses the underlying structural and institutional inequities that were laid bare during the Covid-19 pandemic (Mehra 2020). Positive predictions of a 'reset' envisage greater global co-operation to deal with climate change, the crisis of democracy, and greater equality and social justice in world society (Carr 2020). There can be no doubt that people living in sub-Saharan Africa would hope for this type of outcome.[4]

Africa's optimistic outlook on life may be exceptional. African people demonstrate ingenuity that makes life bearable even under less than perfect circumstances. Coping with adversity and setbacks in life as well as everyday hassles due to poor infrastructure, are examples of the remarkable resilience that African people have perfected. Time and again, sub-Saharan societies have responded to and adapted to overcome crises, such as the recent coronavirus, and have emerged stronger to cope with new challenges. African people are essentially optimistic, most of all the youth who have their lives ahead of them. This optimism might serve as a self-fulfilling prophecy for the continent.

What if sub-Saharan Africa looks to its youth to realise the continent's dreams of prosperity with the 'great reset' after Covid-19? What if the African youth's confidence in their future and their entrepreneurial spirit were to be matched by substantial investment in their development? Then, no doubt, African countries may be poised to join the ranks of the world's prosperous and happy nations.

12.3   Summary

Sub-Saharan Africa has experienced dramatic changes in the past 60 years. Substantial improvements that have occurred in living standards and human development are reflected in rising levels of well-being. Nonetheless, the people of the region are still among the least happy in the world, which belies the impression of cheerful, smiling Africans who love to sing and dance at every occasion. It is this positive outlook on life that has kept Africa going for centuries; the history of well-being in Africa south of the Sahara is one of resilience combined with hope of better times to come. Sub-Saharan Africa's greatest asset is its youthful drive and creativity. If this energy

---

[4]South African historian Maylam (2020) provides an excellent overview of the optimist and pessimistic scenarios for a post-corona future. Although it is impossible to foresee the outcome, he notes that a key factor will be the length of time needed to bring Covid-19 under control and the economic devastation caused by the pandemic.

is put to work (see Mills et al. 2019), the dream of a happy 'African Century' may yet become a reality for the generations to come.

References

Arndt, C., Robinson, S., & Gabriel, S. (2020). Who has been hit hardest by South Africa's lockdown? We found some answers. *The Conversation*, 11 June. https://theconversation.com/who-has-been-hit-hardest-by-south-africas-lockdown-we-found-some-answers-138481.

Bourne, J. K., Jr. (2014). The next breadbasket. *National Geographic, 226*(1), 46–77.

Cantril, H. (1965). *The pattern of human concerns*. New Brunswick, NJ: Rutgers University Press.

Carr, P. R. (2020). Returning to 'normal' post-coronavirus would be inhumane. *The Conversation*, 13 May. https://theconversation.com/returning-to-normal-post-coronavirus-would-be-inh umane-136558.

Daum, T. (2019). What young Zambians have to say about making farming more attractive. *The Conversation*, 22 April. https://theconversation.com/what-young-zambians-have-to-say-about-making-farming-more-attractive-115395.

Eccleston, Keogh, & Fisher (2020). Coronavirus has forced us to embrace digital healthcare—it could transform how we look after patients. *The Conversation*, 11 June. https://theconversation.com/coronavirus-has-forced-us-to-embrace-digital-healthcare-it-could-transform-how-we-look-after-patients-138557.

Estes, R. J. (2019). The social progress of nations revisited. *Social Indicators Research, 144*(2), 539–574. https://doi.org/10.1007/s11205-018-02058-9.

Estes, R. J., & Sirgy, M. J. (2018). *Advances in human well-being*. London: Rowman & Littlefield Ltd.

Gnimassoun, B., & Tapsoba, S. J. (2020). La pandémie de Covid-19, une occasion historique de réinventer le développement de l'Afrique. *The Conversation*, 7 June. https://theconversation.com/la-pandemie-de-covid-19-une-occasion-historique-de-reinve nter-le-developpement-de-lafrique-139697.

Gulyas, J. (2015). Hopes and fears—Future views of quality of life. In W. Glatzer, V. Møller, L. Camfield, & M. Rojas (Eds.), *The global handbook of wellbeing and quality of life* (pp. 869–894). Dordrecht: Springer.

Habib, A., & Valodia, I. (2020). How universities can play a role in shaping a new post-crisis world, *Business Day*, 24 May. https://www.businesslive.co.za/bd/opinion/2020-05-24-how-universities-can-play-a-role-in-shaping-a-new-post-crisis-world/.

Hane, F. (2020). Les «invisibles» du système de santé au Sénégal, *The Conversation*, 7 June. https://theconversation.com/les-invisibles-du-systeme-de-sante-au-senegal-137456.

Helliwell, J. F., Huang, H., & Wang, S. (2019). Changing world happiness. In J. Helliwell, R. Layard, & J. Sachs (Eds.), *World happiness report 2019 (chapter 2* (pp. 11–45). New York: Sustainable Development Solutions Network.

Helliwell, J. F., Huang, H., Wang, S., & Norton, M. (2020). Social environments for world happiness. In J. F. Helliwell, R. Layard, J. Sachs, & J.-E. De Neve (Eds.), *World happiness report 2020 (chapter 2* (pp. 12–45). New York: Sustainable Development Solutions Network.

Houessou, D., Thoto, F., Sonneveld, B., Aoudji, A., Dossou, S., & Agbandou, B. (2019). *Urban agriculture in Benin: How can policy support gardeners?* Faculty of Agricultural Sciences/University of Abomey-Calavi, Benin. https://doi.org/10.13140/rg.2.2.11319.57766, https://www.researchgate.net/publication/333059073_Urban_agriculture_in_Benin_How_can_policy_support_gardeners. Accessed July 6, 2019.

Howles, T. (2015). Thumbelina: The culture and technology of millennials (Review). *Critical Research on Religion, 3*, 326–329.

Ismail, F. (2020). How a post-COVID-19 revival could kickstart Africa's free trade area. *The Conversation*, 26 May. https://theconversation.com/how-a-post-covid-19-revival-could-kickst art-africas-free-trade-area-138223.

Mausch, K., Hauser, M., Rosenstock, T., & Gichohi-Wainaina (2020). COVID-19 recovery is a chance to improve the African food system. *The Conversation*, 10 June. https://theconversation. com/covid-19-recovery-is-a-chance-to-improve-the-african-food-system-139134.

Maylam, P. (2020). A post-pandemic world is unlikely to focus on meeting need over human greed. *The Conversation*, 30 June. https://theconversation.com/a-post-pandemic-world-is-unlikely-to-focus-on-meeting-need-over-human-greed-141228.

Mehra, A. (2020). *The great reset after COVID-19 must put people first*. World Economic Forum, 23 June. https://www.weforum.org/agenda/2020/06/covid19-reset-people-first-inequa lity/. Accessed July 20, 2020.

Mills, G. (2014). *Why states recover: Changing walking societies into winning nations, from Afghanistan to Zimbabwe*. Johannesburg: Picador Africa.

Mills, G., Obasanjo, O., Herbst, J., & Biti, T. (2019). *Democracy works: Rewiring politics to Africa's advantage*. Johannesburg, South Africa: Picador Africa.

Mills, G., Obasanjo, O., Desalegn, H., & van der Merwe, E. (2020). *The Asian aspiration—Why and how Africa should emulate Asia*. Johannesburg, South Africa: PanMacmillan.

Robertson, B., & Pinstrup-Andersen, P. (2010). Global land acquisition: Neo-colonialism or development? *Food Security, 2*, 271–283.

Russon, M.-A. (2020). Coronavirus: How Africa's supply chains are evolving. *BBC News*, 25 June. https://www.bbc.com/news/business-53100287. Accessed June 25, 2020.

Serres, M. (2012). *Petite Poucette: De vivre ensemble, des institutions, une manière d'être and de connaitre*. Paris: Editions Le Pommier.

Serres, M. (2015). *Thumbelina: The culture and technology of millennials* (D. W. Smith, Trans.). Lanham, MD: Rowman & Littlefield.

Soko, M. (2020). What drove Asia's economic success stories, and what should Africa emulate? *The Conversation*, 24 July. https://theconversation.com/what-drove-asias-economic-success-sto ries-and-what-should-africa-emulate-143361.